LAST DAD

LOOKING FOR ANSWERS WHEN THE DAD PIECE IS MISSING

To Rebekah

Zephaniah 3:17

Louie Kaupp

LOUIE KAUPP

TABLE OF CONTENTS

Act III: The Last Dad

HOW TO GET THE MOST
OUT OF THIS BOOK:

E ACH CHAPTER OF *THE LAST Dad* begins with a story about Mildred, a single mom, and her son Louie. The first dad abandoned them when Mildred was 7 ½ months pregnant. The second dad enforced his rules with a bullwhip. Mother and son spent years looking for the next dad. Finally, they discovered the best dad was there all of the time. He was the last dad they would ever need. They hope you will find the parallels between your story and theirs.

At the end of each chapter the grown-up Louie added Reflections, looking back at life lessons they learned. They are practical and scriptural. His deepest hope is that you will become better acquainted with the Last Dad and that you will find a few simple, life-changing truths.

After Reflections he added Questions to Consider, hoping the questions would provoke you to thought, dialogue, prayer, and then, discovery.

Finally, as you discover God's plan for your life, please tell your story, too.

With a joyful heart,
Louie

AN EXPRESSION OF GRATITUDE

IRST, A SINCERE THANK YOU to all the people who encouraged me to write a book. It has been a marvelous voyage of discovery for me. The Lord has reminded me of His daily involvement in my life for more than 70 years.

Beverly and our three sons have been very supportive during the five years of shaping my writing skills and searching for the stories within the larger story.

Richard McAfee taught me to ask better questions; Charles Simpson, Larry Crabb, Jr. and Philip Yancey challenged me to think deeply and to change radically; the Christian Writers' Guild encouraged me to show, not tell; Gloria Gomez, Mark Colaw, Steve Babinsky, Greg Kaupp, and Lori Rhodes invested in the project; David and Jonathan Kaupp offered absolutely essential computer help whenever I needed it; Beverly, Glenna Gates, Andrea Kaupp, and Jonathan were marvelous and constructive critics; Kevin and Tara Bove' offered perspective at critical moments; and dozens of you promised to buy the book and prayed for me, so, I couldn't stop writing. Finally, Athena Dean has been a wonderful publishing coach.

Mother prayed, persevered, loved deeply, demonstrated great loyalty, endured pain from neck to feet, offered wonderful hospitality, kept her sense of humor, and maintained her faith. This is her story, too, and I am deeply honored that I was her son.

ACT I: THE MISSING DAD

CHAPTER ONE

IT'S MY FAULT

*W*HY HADN'T DAD COME BACK*? I didn't get it. Did he leave because of me?*

Mother used a do-it-yourself photo booth at the grocery store to shoot a bunch of pictures of me because we didn't have a camera. I wore my Sunday clothes and it was hot in there. Finally, Mother said she had the perfect picture. Everywhere she went, she showed people.

"Isn't he the cutest kid?"

That couldn't be true. Dad didn't come back. Apparently, I was deep down ugly and Dad knew it.

I felt really sad, like the time I got a magnifying glass for my birthday. I took it to preschool for Show and Tell and somebody stole it. Dad leaving was like that, only worse.

I was small for my age, but for a five-year-old, I had a big memory. The last time I saw Dad was like a movie that kept playing. His tired words and the look on his face stuck in my head.

I was sitting on the brown stool Dad gave me, trying to figure it out. This was the first store-bought gift he gave me when he returned from the war. I thought he would notice me there, but he never even looked my way.

He took his coat off the hook. It was an army jacket with the stripes removed. I noticed the hole in the sleeve.

Mother said, "Where are you going?"

She brushed the hair out of her eyes. I couldn't tell whether she was mad or sad or scared. I wanted to ask what was wrong but I felt invisible.

Mother had fixed hamburgers with melted cheese and her best-ever fries. The house had a happy smell. How could she be sad after eating cheeseburgers?

Dad did not look at her.

"I am going to the Rainbow Bread Company. I hear they are hiring."

She began crying.

"When will you be home?"

"If I get the job, I will be late."

He put on his Santa Fe cap. I rode on the Santa Fe Railroad once, all the way to Dodge City. It was my favorite train. I liked that cap.

He headed for the door.

Please say, "Goodbye."

Without another word he turned and walked out of the house.

The voice in my head did not let up.

Run to him and hug him.

My arms weighed a thousand pounds. My feet were stuck to the floor. I wanted to fly after him but I didn't have wings.

The house was quiet except for Mother crying.

Mother put me to bed early. I thought she was going to forget our Bible story but she didn't. She let me read. I only missed a few words. She said my reading made her forget everything else. Before she tucked me in, we sang, "Jesus loves me."

The next morning Dad wasn't there. I ran outside to see if he was in the car. He usually went there to smoke. Mother would not let him do it in the house. She called it "a bad habit left over from the War."

I ran around the outside of the house but I could not find him anywhere. It was hot and sticky so I gave up and walked back inside.

"I didn't hear you leave. Were you looking for your dad?"

Without me asking, Mother answered my question, "He didn't come home last night."

"Why?" Sometimes at night Dad went to the library to study so the lights wouldn't keep me awake. He always came back before breakfast.

"I don't know."

She sounded very tired.

She left me with the next-door neighbor for most of the morning. I did not waste a second.

"What is Mother doing? When will she be back? Do you know where my daddy is? Did your daddy ever leave and not come back?"

The neighbor patted me on the shoulder.

"Maybe we could do something besides questions and answers. Would you like to play a game?"

We played but I asked more questions. She didn't answer. She just smiled. Then she fed me a snack—not as good as Mother's but I was too hungry to care.

Mother told me the Bible college would let us stay in the duplex for a week. They, also, bought two train tickets for us to go to Kansas. That confused me. Mother tried to explain.

"Louie, we are going home to Grandpa and Grandma's."

She looked out the window for a long time.

"I don't think your dad is coming back."

I had a huge, empty feeling in my heart. It felt like someone placed a vacuum sweeper hose on my chest and sucked everything out.

Many students from the Bible college came by our house and prayed for us. They all said, "Everything is going to be all right." But it wasn't.

I said to Mother, "Please don't answer the door anymore. They make me sad."

She didn't look at me but she nodded. She washed the same dish three times.

Dad called four days later. Mother didn't seem surprised. She was frying chicken. The smell was wonderful. Except for the sounds of cooking, the house was very quiet. I stood close to Mother so I could hear Dad.

"Mildred, I didn't get the job."

"That was four days ago."

There was a long silence before he answered.

"I was really discouraged. I didn't know what to do. I started driving. I ended up in Denver at my folk's house."

Neither of them spoke for a long time. Finally, he said, "Can you and Louie get on the train and come to Denver?"

Mother sat down on a kitchen chair. She ran her fingers through her hair.

"This is the seventh time you have done this."

"You have been counting?"

"Numbers are important to me."

Dad groaned and then, Mother continued.

"I thought you learned your lesson when the army busted you from sergeant to private for letting that prisoner go."

He said a bad word—one I can't repeat.

For a while no one spoke. I could barely hear Dad's next words.

"I thought you forgave me."

"I did. I borrowed the money from the neighbors and took the train from Georgia to San Francisco. Have you forgotten? When I got there, you were on your way back to the brig at Fort Benning. Another two and a half days on the train with a two-year-old was a lot of forgiveness."

"You were my wife. Remember? For better or for worse!"

She brushed the hair out of her eyes. Her face looked like storm clouds.

"I haven't seen much for better."

Another long silence followed.

"Clay, I cannot chase after you this time. I am seven and a half months pregnant. I thought I was going to lose my mind the last four days. You left me with a small child and no money. We cannot stay in student housing." She paused. "I don't have any tears left. I am going home to Kansas."

She hung up. I was really scared. I cried hard for a long time and she held me close. My shoulders hurt. It felt like I was carrying a bag of rocks. Dad was gone because I was ugly and now I could not keep Mother from being sad either.

Finally, the mother from the family in the other half of the duplex knocked softly on our door.

"We heard crying and wondered if you were okay?"

We were not okay but Mother said we were.

She tucked me in.

"Tomorrow will be a new day."

Reflections

For forty years I blamed myself for Dad abandoning us. I thought I drove him away. If only I had not asked so many questions. If I had thanked him more often for the small stool he bought me. If I had not distracted him when he was studying. There was something wrong with me. That is why he left and never came back.

When someone complimented me, I thought, "They wouldn't say that if they really knew me." If they criticized me, I knew they saw the flaws that drove Dad away. I didn't ask anyone if this was true. Dad was gone. That was all the evidence I needed and I accepted it.

Why did I and many other children accept the blame? One possible answer: parenting by accusation may have opened the door for false guilt. For instance, if the mother says: "Janie, I cannot find my scissors. Were you playing with them?" Or, the baby brother cries and the dad says, "Cody, what did you do this time?" The assumptions are judgmental even though they may be accurate. As a result, the child may think, If anything bad happens, *it must be my fault.*

Teach teamwork. Mother to Janie: "I cannot find my scissors. Would you help me find them?" Dad to Cody: "Your brother is crying. Let's see if you and I can figure out what's wrong."

Teach personal responsibility. When you as the parent are judgmental, admit your own sinful mistake. Use James 1:14 (NLV) as the standard, "A man is tempted to do wrong when he lets himself be led by what his bad thoughts tell him to do."

"Son, when I automatically blame you, I am wrong. Please forgive me. You do not cause me to say the wrong thing."

Questions to Consider

1.
- During your childhood did you receive a) more judgment or b) more grace?

- Were your parents more likely a) to blame you or b) to ask thoughtful questions until they (and you) knew what happened (or was said)?

- Did you, as a child blame yourself for anything that happened between your parents: a) yes or b) no?

If you answered a) to one or more of the questions, please examine the differences between false guilt—accepting the blame for someone else's sinful words, deeds, or thoughts—and God-prompted conviction of your own sin.

2.   As a parent are you the sheriff? The keeper of the rules? The judge? Are you more likely

   a. to jump to conclusions, handing out swift justice, or

   b. to withhold judgment and wait on the Lord to bring clarity.

3.   Are you, the parent,

   a. a taste of grace,

   b. the one who listens carefully to God and to others, and

   c. a person who loves well?

4.   What if one child is at another extreme? Not struggling with false guilt? Seemingly oblivious? Unresponsive? Disconnected?

   • Ask simple questions: What made you sad today? Happy? Was anybody funny? Mean? Hurtful? Friendly?

   • Will the child talk more freely if you are at the park? At McDonald's? On the bed, side by side? Late at night? Early in the morning?

   • Are you the problem? Ask these questions: "Who's really easy to talk to? What makes it hard to talk?"

   • When the child does not talk, do you take it as a personal insult? Do you push? Manipulate? Is your goal to help them open up, however and whenever?

   • Ask God for direction. "Lord, how do I love this child well? "Lord, who should I agree with in prayer for this child?" "Who would give me good counsel?

CHAPTER TWO

WHEN DAD COMES HOME

I WAS TWO WHEN THE ARMY sent Dad to India. He only wrote once a month but we kept the letters in a special cigar box. Mother taped a picture of Dad to the lid. He had on his sergeant's uniform, a rifle on one shoulder, and an American flag draped over the other. I found a long branch for a rifle and a red towel for my flag. Mother would always salute and stand at attention.

"Hey, soldier, going my way?"

Mother read all of his letters to me more than once. My favorite stories were about the mess hall.

"The supply ship did not make it this month. Torpedoed, I guess. Because of that, they served us ready-to-eat meals. I think they found a dead cow by the road and ran over it with a big truck so it would be flat. Then, they cut it into squares, added salt, and sent it to us. Figured we were so bored, sitting here in India with nothing to do, we would eat anything."

"Don't worry. It wasn't really road kill—just C rations. They call it Meat Hash! Somebody Stateside who failed cooking school mixed together beef and pork, put in salt, awful (he crossed out a bad word but we could still make it out) spices, and chopped onions. We can eat it or go hungry."

I did not understand why the army would keep Dad in India eating bad food. I could not wait to have him come back.

Three years later the war ended. Mother read that news to me from the front of *The Denver Post*. Dad would be coming home.

The Army discharged him at Fort Benning, Georgia. They gave him a ticket to Denver. When he got off the train after two days of travel, he hugged and kissed Mother and then patted me on the head. He had a gift for her.

"I bought this in Calcutta."

He gave Mother a plain brown bag. She unwrapped a carved ivory tiger. I wished he had given it to me. Then, he handed me a pack of Juicy Fruit gum—five sticks just for me. I was happy; Mother was not.

"That's the gift for your son?"

"What is wrong with gum?"

Mother just stared at him.

"After three years?"

He picked up his duffel bag and started walking out of the train station. I knew they were angry but this was supposed to be a happy day.

"Please don't fight."

Dad's voice was calm but firm.

"Stay out of this. This is between your mother and me."

"He is upset, Clay. Can't you see what you are doing to him?"

"He is just a kid. He needs to mind his own business."

That was not their last argument. Their fights made me sad. I lost count of how many times I prayed. "Thank you for bringing Dad back. Please make Mother and Dad happy."

I kept trying to get close to Dad.

"Dad, will you have time after dinner to play checkers or throw a ball outside?"

The answer was always the same.

"Kid, I don't have time. Quit bugging me."

Maybe he will tell me a story.

"What did you do in the war?"

"I was not in the war. I sat on my butt in India for three years. Bad food. Sacred cows we could not eat. Stupid people. Now you have heard about the war in India."

Mother always said to me, "Be patient; good things take a little longer."

I could tell Dad was worried. The day after he got home, he began looking for a job.

"Every soldier in the army is looking for work in this town. I think half the vets in the whole army moved to Denver."

No one hired him. Then, two weeks before school started, he contacted Southwestern Bible College in Waxahachie, Texas. Mother said it was a miracle that the college accepted his late application.

To make room for the huge numbers of new students and their families, the school moved converted World War II barracks to the campus. We lived in one of the duplexes they fixed up.

Dad sounded like a record that was stuck. "I cannot believe I am still in a barracks. I feel like I am back in the army."

"You are in school, Clay. You should be grateful."

"It is a barracks, Mildred. I try to serve God and I end up in army housing all over again."

Our duplex was one room with a kitchen on one end and a bed and a desk at the other. I slept on a mat on the floor. The bathroom tucked in the corner was tiny but at least it was my size.

Mother said our one-room home was a miracle.

Dad said, "Open your eyes. This is a mosquito-sized dump. No wonder they accepted my late application. They had to find somebody to live in these shoeboxes."

Dad doesn't seem to be happy about anything. What would make him smile?

Mother said, "He is that way because of the war."

I did not know what that meant. Now he was gone. I couldn't get "Why?" out of my head.

Am I too small? Do I talk too much? Did I pray the wrong prayer? Is God mad at me, too?

Normally, I would have asked Mother but she wasn't happy either.

This time there were no monthly letters from Dad.

Reflections

Kids want connection and they will pursue it even if they are pushed away. For instance, a child scribbles on a paper and then says, "Look, Daddy, I drew a picture of you." If the father has no clear internal picture of himself, if he does not see himself the way God sees him, the child's unskilled drawing may seem insulting or simply foolish. The dad may react negatively because of his own lack of wellbeing and pass the disconnection on to an impressionable young artist and perhaps to another generation.

When my dad returned from World War II, confusion followed him like a dark cloud. He hadn't seen his wife and son for three and a half years and they were strangers. He couldn't get a job. The housing at the Bible college was a former army barracks. He felt neglected, abandoned, and cheated. So, by default he neglected and abandoned his family. When Rainbow Bread didn't hire him, he began driving and didn't stop until he reached Denver, his hometown, a day and a half from us.

What could have happened if he had known the truth that sets men free? In my mid-forties I heard the truth. It has been like a slow-release capsule, freeing and healing me since the day I first heard it.

Questions to Consider

1. What kind of connection did you have with your parents when you were growing up? How did you feel? Chosen? Created as an example of God's best work? A person of destiny? Or did you feel neglected? Abandoned? Unimportant?

2. Did either parent tell you what the Bible says about you? Here are five life-giving truths:

   • *God Made You!*

      "So God created human beings in his own image …. Then God looked over all he had made, and he saw that it was very good!" (Genesis 1:27, 31, NLT).

- *God has a plan!*

   "For I know the plans I have for you," says the Lord. "They are plans for good and not for disaster, to give you a future and a hope" (Jeremiah 29:11-14, NLT).

- *God delights in you!*

   "For the Lord your God is living among you. He is a mighty savior. He will take delight in you with gladness. With his love, he will calm all your fears. He will rejoice over you with joyful songs" (Zephaniah 3:17, NLT).

- *You have gifts (what you are capable of) and His grace (how He will empower you)!*

   "Yet grace (God's unmerited favor) was given to each of us individually [not indiscriminately, but in different ways] in proportion to the measure of Christ's [rich and bounteous] gift" (Ephesians 4:7, Amplified Bible).

- *Don't miss the party in your honor!*

   Remember the story of the prodigal son (Luke 15:11 – 32).

3.   Here are the five truths in easy-to-remember phrases.

   - God did good work when He made me.

   - God has a plan for my life!

   - God sings (insert your name) songs!

   - I am capable. God will help me.

   - When I return to God, He throws a party for me.

4.   How can you and your children take the five truths to heart?

   - Memorize them.

   - Print them and put them on the refrigerator.

   - Pray them over yourself and your children each day.

CHAPTER THREE

THE CANDIDATE

I HELPED MOTHER PACK FOR THE trip to Kansas. It didn't take long. I put my red fire truck, three storybooks, the checkerboard, and some crayons on the kitchen table. Mother gave me a small box with a ribbon on it to carry my treasures. She did not want me to feel bad because I didn't have a suitcase.

"We will tell people it's your birthday box."

We rode the first train all the way to Kansas City. Mother let me sit by the window. It was dark outside when we left but I didn't mind. The clickety-clack of the train on the track was music. I slept so long I missed the sunrise. Walking from one end of the train car to the other was an adventure, too. I almost forgot Dad wasn't there. I ate an orange for breakfast. I was too excited to think about eating anything else.

Mother's watch said 12 o'clock when the conductor came to the car. All of a sudden, I was starved.

"Lunch is served. The dining car is straight ahead."

He sounded like a storybook character when he said it. He was old enough to be my grandpa and he was nice to us. *Why couldn't Dad be like that?*

We talked about food before we got on the train. Mother had warned me.

"Their food is so expensive you can't even enjoy it." I would have been willing to put the dining car food to the test, but she had that please-don't-ask-me look. She pulled box lunches down from the luggage rack. The backs of the seats had pull-down trays to eat on. I put that on my Christmas list: special trays just my size.

The neighbors from the Bible college had fixed bologna sandwiches. Mother told them to put extra mayonnaise on for me. It was so good. They also sent Oreo cookies, my favorites. "The dining car couldn't compete with this," Mother said. I had to agree.

Union Station in Kansas City was like a castle. We had to wait there several hours but the time raced by. There were more places to eat and to buy treasures than I could ever imagine. Mother told me we had to save our money but we could look all we wanted to. The noise of the trains coming and going was like living in a dream. I decided to be a train engineer when I grew up. The people moved around us like we were on an island in the middle of the ocean. I wanted to talk to them but Mother warned me, "Not everyone is safe." I tried to obey her but I was so curious. Finally, I could not be quiet anymore. I started to talk to two people. She squeezed my knee really hard.

"I thought they looked safe."

She gave me her look.

Finally, we got on the Missouri Pacific passenger train and headed west. The scenery after Kansas City looked a lot like the countryside before we got there.

"I'm bored."

Mother took the checkerboard out of my birthday present box and we played. She won three times in a row. I was glad to have time with Mother but I was tired of losing.

"I can't win."

"Think how happy you will be when you finally beat me."

I thought I would enjoy winning now but I knew I wasn't supposed to argue.

"Can we go to the lounge car? Let's explore! Besides, it will be more fun to play checkers on a table."

"It's hard for a pregnant lady to walk on a moving train. I don't know if I can make it but I'll try."

The lady across the aisle offered to help but getting there was only half the problem. Because of the size of her tummy Mother could not sit straight at the table. Our new friend went back to our seats and got pillows. With those behind Mother's back she could sit sideways with her back to the wall. She did not look comfortable but she said she was okay.

I set up the game. Seeing the checkerboard, a soldier in uniform stopped at our table.

"I'll bet you beat your mom every time."

He was nice so I didn't tell him she wanted to be called Mother. I had heard her tell her sister Verleen, "Mom wasn't always a mother to me. None of my kids are calling me Mom."

Instead, I paused when I answered, hoping he would get it.

"No, Mother ... says it builds character when I lose."

People at several tables nearby began laughing. I could tell from the look on Mother's face she did not enjoy their laughter.

The name on the soldier's shirt was Newsome. He said, "Son, would you like a little help?"

"Sure!"

He hesitated and looked at Mother. She looked uncomfortable but nodded okay.

While we played, Sergeant Newsome told us his story.

"For the last four years I have been in France. Haven't been home since '41. I am on my way to Colorado. Our farm is straight east of Denver. Today I am going to see my parents. Don't know what I will do next. Maybe I will just help out on the farm."

He smiled when he said that.

While we talked, he gave me tips about checkers. We won the first game and Mother agreed to play again. We won a second time.

"Mother, you were right. Beating you makes me very happy. I guess my character is growing."

For some reason everyone around us laughed again.

"Sergeant Newsome, have you ever thought of being a dad? My dad left and he isn't coming back. You would make a really good dad!"

Mother groaned. "Louie! Sir, I apologize."

"No need to apologize, Ma'am. That is the nicest thing anyone has said to me in a really long time."

He turned to me.

"I can't take you up on your offer but I have really enjoyed playing checkers with you."

He put his hand on my head and messed up my hair. With a big smile he got up.

"Thank you, Ma'am, for letting me play. Son, you are really good at checkers."

He pulled the door open and left the lounge. I guess his seat was in a different car because we didn't see him again.

Mother was upset. She whispered, "What were you thinking? You can't just ask someone to be your dad."

"Well, you said my dad has run away seven times. You said he is not coming back."

"It's not that simple! Help me back to my seat. I am worn out."

I didn't know why but people smiled and patted me on the back as we went by.

Back at our seats, the clickety-clack of the wheels on the track was music for my ears. We were going to see Grandpa and Grandma. That was enough to make the trip seem even shorter.

Reflections

For all of my growing-up years, I carried too much responsibility. Dad was gone and Mother leaned on me. Years later I realized I didn't have a childhood—I had a premature adulthood. As a result, I learned too much too soon about adult crises, conflict, and confusion. I, also, learned "adult language." I could fake understanding when adults talked to me because I had heard the language and listened to their stories. It gave me a false sense of being grown up.

When I had children, I invited them to be a part of my life. We ran errands. They went with me when I worked on my To Do List. They got in on a number of quick visits with other people. Clearly, those were my choices.

I learned to enjoy their choices as well. They wanted father-son time but they needed the freedom to dream, create, and invent. One day the Lord prompted me to ask Greg what he would really like to do. It would be his choice and I would do it with him.

He hesitated, smiled a huge smile, and said, "Let's play Bullets."

"How do we do that, Son?"

Someone had given him one hundred empty .22-caliber shell casings. He wanted to stand them on end—all of them—and arrange them in rows. It was mind-numbingly boring but he was so pleased to have me play his game. In the days that followed, he not only invented games, he asked dozens of imaginative questions.

Here are my responses:

1. I asked questions to be sure I understood what he was (asking, or telling) me.

2. I protected his childhood. If I answered one of his questions, I first considered whether the answer would be too heavy for him to bear.

3. I asked about his day, making sure that his questions didn't mask something more serious. One approach was to talk about the unfolding story of that day: "Greg, if I had a news camera and I followed you around, what would I have seen today? Is there any bad news to report?"

It was vital that my son had a safe place to ask his questions and that he received answers which reflected God's heart and mind.

Questions to Consider

1.   What should a parent do when a child seems "old for his years"?

- Put him in his place: "You are not old enough to ask those questions."
- Send him to someone else: "Go ask your father."
- Use a funny remark. Help him lighten up and act like a child again.
- Pray! Ask God why your child is smarter than you.

I hope you are smiling and that none of the four responses describes your parenting style.

2.   Good questions are very important.

- You might ask, "How do you feel? Please help me understand." or "What do you want to know?" Help the child discover what question(s) he really wants the answer(s) to.
- Ask gentle, thoughtful questions about his questions until you know what he is really asking.
- To connect with his world, you could ask, "What was the best thing that happened today? The scariest? Was anybody funny? Sad?" What disappointed you? Did the teacher speak kindly? Could you understand the class stuff today?
- To offer safety, ask him, "Did someone tell you not to tell me...?"
- When you are sure you know what the child is really asking, give age-appropriate answers.
- Perhaps you can identify with this mother: five-year-old Billy asked her where he came from. She had wondered when he would ask about "the birds and bees." She

stalled for time. Finally, she began a thirty-minute talk about sex, pregnancy, and birth. Billy said, "Wow, Mom, Allen said he came from Philadelphia!"

3. What resources are available? Focus on the Family's website has good age-appropriate material.

4. Who offers reliable counsel? Call a counselor or psychiatrist you trust to find out what small groups, classes, or material they recommend.

CHAPTER FOUR

A YELLOW FLAG NIGHT

V ISITING GRANDPA WAS ALWAYS EXCITING. He was a mailman for the tiny town of Arnold, Kansas. Every night he waited for the 11 p.m. Missouri Pacific passenger train. If there was outgoing mail, he hung the mailbag on the hook by the tracks. The mail car on the Denver-bound train had a long metal arm that reached out and snagged Grandpa's mailbag. The train kept on rolling. On special nights he raised a yellow metal flag, indicating a passenger was waiting to get on or off of the train. This would be a yellow flag night because we were coming. I knew all this because he took me with him at Christmas time.

We only stayed in Arnold a few days. Grandpa's house wasn't much bigger than the Bible college duplex. Mother slept with Aunt Judy in Grandpa and Grandma's room. I shared a bed with Uncle Jerry. He was just two years older. Having a big brother would have been fun but the bed was really small. I fell out of bed twice the first night.

I quickly realized our Bible college home had something Grandpa did not have—an indoor toilet. Instead, there was what he called a *slop jar* under his bed. I could tell from the smell that's how he avoided going to the outhouse in the middle of the night.

Every morning I woke up while it was dark outside and went to the bathroom. To do that at Grandpa's house, I had to go out the kitchen door, down the sidewalk, past the garage to the two-holer, an outhouse with space for two people to do their business at the same time.

The best part of our stay at Grandpa and Grandma's was chocolate chip cookies and her stories. Almost every day she baked cookies.

"Don't you kids get into those cookies!" She said that every time. As soon as she left the room, we raced to the cookie jar and grabbed a still warm chocolate chip cookie.

When she came back in, she would say, "What am I going to do? You boys always eat the cookies. I guess I will just have to live in the kitchen to guard the cookie jar."

She always gave us a big hug. Then, she would smile.

"Did I ever tell you about the time the cat fell in the well and Grandpa fished him out?"

We didn't care whether we had heard the story before or not. "No, Grandma, we have never heard that story."

Being with Grandma was like Christmas all over again.

Grandpa was another story. I watched to see what kind of dad he was. He didn't say much and when he spoke, no one seemed to pay attention.

One morning he told Jerry, "Take the trash out to the bin when you go to the barn."

Jerry did not move until Grandpa said in a loud voice, "Jerry, trash."

He said, "Okay, you don't have to yell."

That surprised me! I thought everyone knew they were supposed to obey their parents.

That evening Mother and I went for a short walk.

"Mother, I think Grandma is more the dad in this family than Grandpa."

Mother had a long coughing fit and then she began laughing.

"How did you figure this out in three days?"

"Was that funny?"

"I am sorry I laughed. Tell me how Grandma is more like a dad."

"She pays attention to us. She does stuff for us, like baking cookies. When she is not joking, we do what she says."

"What about Grandpa?"

"I tried to tell him two times about the train ride. Once he started talking about the weather in the middle of my story. The other time, about milking the cows."

"Is there more?"

"Am I going to be in trouble for telling you this?"

"I am a safe person. You can tell me."

"When he tells Jerry to do something, Jerry ignores him unless he shouts. Am I right?"

She stopped walking and drew a circle on the ground with her toe. "Yes, you are."

"What are we going to do about that?" I asked.

"We need wisdom. If God shows you something, you need to ask Him what to do or say."

We stepped off of the trail and prayed for everyone in Grandpa and Grandma's house. Then, Mother prayed a special prayer for me.

"Lord, thank you for giving Louie the gift of sight. Now, please help him know what to do with what he sees. Give him patience so he will trust your timing. Fill his heart with love for broken people. Amen."

I wanted to ask questions about broken people but Mother took my hand and started walking. I knew that was a signal to have a quiet heart.

She was a good mother.

Reflections

One afternoon our boys came home from the other grandpa's house. He told them pastors like me could not afford Buicks; we should drive Chevys. They were caught in the middle.

Looking back, I understand my father-in-law's concern. He knew I flew to Chicago and picked up a brand-new, fully loaded, yellow Buick station wagon. I did not tell him that a pastor in Chicago arranged the deal with a car dealer friend. I did not have to pay to have the car transported, and the dealer sold it to me at his cost.

Back then I didn't know men who talked openly with one another about anything involving money. If I could go back to that moment, I would talk to him as soon as possible, tell him enough about my finances and car purchases to reassure him—"Your daughter and your grandsons are in a safe place!" Then, I'd apologize for not telling him sooner.

I did have that openness with the boys. I assured them they could ask me any questions about our car purchases. They were concerned. "Are we running out of money?" I assured them we were not. In fact, the Buick station wagon was paid for. Also, they wanted to know what to say when they felt like they were caught between their Grandpa and me.

"Boys, it is okay to tell me or Grandpa what makes you uncomfortable." We role-played, using personal boundaries statements. They stated what they could or would do or say and what they couldn't or wouldn't do or say.

We talked about how to follow Ephesians 6: 2-3 (NLT), "'Honor your father and mother.' This is the first commandment with a promise: If you honor your father and mother, 'things will go well for you, and you will have a long life on the earth.'"

Finally, we prayed.

Questions to Consider

1. Do your children honor you? Do they interrupt you when you are talking or do they wait until you acknowledge them? When they want or need something, what tone do they use? Do they cry and manipulate? Do they ask and then trust your answer? Are they grateful, affectionate, and obedient?

2. When your entire family visits your parents, do you teach your children how to honor their grandparents?

    - Are there questions they should ask? Topics they should avoid?

    - Are there ways they can honor them? A gift? A handwritten note? Sitting beside them, quietly listening?

    - What physical limitations do the grandparents have?

    - How should they respond if the grandparents are funny or cruel, permissive or controlling, honoring you or telling stories that discredit you? Do your children know how to state their boundaries without dishonoring the grandparents? Can you help them learn boundary statements that fit their age and verbal skills?

Here are some examples:

"Grandpa, I don't want to hear stories about Dad. Please tell me stories about you."

"Grandma, if Dad has questions about what you're telling us, is it okay for him to call you?"

"Please, work that out with Dad. He asked me not to get in the middle when the two of you have a disagreement."

CHAPTER FIVE

THE CHINA CABINET

MOTHER GOT A JOB IN Ransom, six miles away. Arnold, Grandpa's town, had less than two hundred people. Grandpa said that included cats and dogs. He was funny. Ransom was much larger—twice as many people. I wasn't sure whether that included pets. It, also, had a twelve-bed hospital.

The nurse in charge offered Mother a job planning all the meals, purchasing the food, preparing it, and serving it. The bonus was a small, one-room apartment in the basement of the hospital. We both slept on the pullout couch. I liked being close to Mother except when she cried at night.

Mother arranged all her treasures in the china cabinet. Grandpa had stored it for her in his garage. It stood next to her only other piece of furniture, a dresser. She said, "You have to turn sideways and think small thoughts to get past it."

I was glad for the very tiny indoor toilet. When I used it, I did not have to share with anyone.

Mother left me alone in the basement room while she worked. I had books to read and I played checkers all by myself.

I decided to explore Mother's treasures. I could not reach the top shelf of the china cabinet, so I stood on the bottom shelf and reached up. It tipped over and crashed to the floor. I jumped out of the way so it didn't hit me.

Mother always said, "I don't have much but at least it's safe in the china cabinet." The fall changed that.

I raced upstairs and told her I had accidentally tipped the cabinet over. She had said many times, "If anything bad happens and you tell me immediately, I will not punish you."

She hurried downstairs, slumped to the floor, and cried. I did not know what to do so I cried with her. She said she forgave me and I believed her, but she was sad for a long time.

Grandpa fixed the door to the cabinet. He said it was a miracle none of the glass broke. I could tell he thought tipping the cabinet over was really bad, but he didn't say anything. He just looked at me and rolled his eyes.

For the next several days we tried to save the stuff that fell out of the cabinet. The carved ivory tiger Dad brought home from India was not damaged. The wedding pictures survived, too. But, Mother's special wedding china was in a million pieces. We were able to glue together one teacup. Mother put the rest of the broken china in a plastic container. She did not throw the pieces away for several days. We tried to glue back the hummingbird's beak. It didn't work. We gave up and laid the tiny beak beside the bird. Mother saved some of her coffee cups from Colorado. Some were in one piece; some we glued together; others, we saved the biggest piece. I knew the storm was over when Mother started laughing.

"Now that I think about it, those years in Colorado weren't all that great. I guess broken pieces were all I had anyway." She patted me on the head. "We are a good team, aren't we?"

The next morning I was alone in the basement again. The ivory tiger fascinated me. Mother placed it on the top shelf because it was the most interesting piece that survived. I knew now not to climb on the shelves of the cabinet to see the tiger.

What if I stood on a chair and reached the top shelf?

I got a chair from the hospital dining room, placed it next to the cabinet, opened the door, and reached for the tiger. Because I was standing on the edge of the chair, it tipped forward, crashed into the glass panes, broke three of them, and knocked the door off of the cabinet.

I didn't quite reach the tiger. When dad's gift fell to the floor this time, the wooden base broke free from the ivory.

I headed for the stairs to tell Mother. At the top of the stairs I stopped and sat down. I shook like a leaf in the wind. Finally, I went into the busy kitchen.

"Something bad happened in the basement."

Without a word Mother flew down the steps. When she saw the cabinet, she didn't cry. She just began hitting me softly, over and over, on the shoulders and chest. The blows didn't hurt me half as much as disappointing her did.

"How could you do this? How could you do this? You should know better!"

One of the nurses heard Mother crying. She ran down the hall and looked in the room.

"Are you an idiot, Louie? How could you do this a second time? You need a dad to pound some sense into you."

She went to the kitchen, got a broom and a dustpan, and began cleaning up broken glass. Suddenly, she stopped.

"Mildred, I thought your husband brought this ivory tiger home from India. This label says Atlanta's Best Curios."

I had never heard Mother use a bad word before but she did that day. Normally, I would have asked her questions about that. This time I stood in the corner without saying a word.

Forty-three days after we moved to the hospital, we had a bigger event than the falling china cabinet. My brother Phil was born. I stayed with Gladys, one of the nurses. Mother spent two days in bed and then went back to work, running the hospital kitchen. Now she had a baby. Part of the day Phil was in a crib next to the kitchen cabinets. That was free time for me. However, it was summertime and I was out of school. So, the rest of the day I was the designated babysitter in our basement apartment. My instructions were simple.

"If he cries, rock the crib. If that does not work, give him his bottle. If he still cries, run upstairs and get me."

Mother would fly down the stairs, change a diaper, fix a new bottle, sing a song, say a prayer, and give me new instructions. Sometimes, one of the nurses would watch Phil while I went out behind the hospital and played in the sand pile.

Mother worried about me. I heard her telling the other nurses, "He's a handful." I had no idea what that meant.

The nurses said I needed to be in church on Sundays. Mother talked on the kitchen phone to the pastor of a church in Ness City, the biggest town in the county with 1,600 people, the court house, and two grocery stores. He arranged for a very old couple, Art and Betty Cofer, to pick me up every Sunday morning in their black, two-door Ford coupe.

For me it was a major adventure. I counted everything and I counted out loud. How many cows in each field? I added up the fence posts. I pointed out every jackrabbit running across the fields. I counted the cars on the road.

Mother always had me read the Sunday school lesson in advance. Each time I told Mr. and Mrs. Cofer what I learned, both on the way to the church and on the trip home. They nodded. When they answered, they never said more than one word at a time. But, I didn't mind—anything was better than staying in the basement with the china cabinet.

Reflections

Out of economic necessity in the 1950s, there were many latchkey kids. Mother's defense was, "I am doing the best I can do." Nevertheless, she should not have left my brother and me alone in the basement while she worked

Parenting styles then were more authoritarian. Parents often assumed that children would be well-mannered robots. If not, they would "get a good whipping." Mother rarely spanked us but she did think God would help us be good while she was working.

She talked to the pastor and arranged a ride to church. However, I needed more than transportation. It would have helped if we had talked about respecting this elderly couple, being quieter, thanking them often, and serving them whenever possible. For instance, I could have opened the car door for Sister Cofer or carried her casserole to the church basement for "dinner on the grounds."

We were young. We were boys. We were alone for hours at a time. One could safely predict that something would be broken. Hopefully, we would survive childhood.

Mother did teach one thing well. "If something bad happens, tell me immediately."

It happened. I pulled the china cabinet over. I ran to tell her. We did work together to clean up the mess. She was thoughtful and very sad but she was not bitter or judgmental.

Whatever she failed to do, she did what was most important. She prayed nonstop for my brother and me. And she modeled trusting God every day with every question she had. I will be forever grateful for that.

Questions to Consider

1. Are your children comfortable with quiet times? Can they read or play by themselves? Do they need people and noise? Have they learned to entertain themselves when they are bored?

2. What can they learn from you about handling boredom? Have you learned to be quiet, inside and out? You can't teach what you don't know.

3. How should you respond to big mistakes (i.e., disobedient acts that lead to damage or accidents that break, tear, and render useless)?
    What is most important? What questions do you ask first?

    - Was the child hurt?
    - Did your child lie or tell the truth?
    - Did your child tell you quickly?
    - Could or should the child have known that the activity was dangerous?
    - How can he learn from the incident?

CHAPTER SIX

A FIERCE WARRIOR

I KNEW FROM DAY ONE THAT Eugene was *trouble.* There were only ten students in the second grade but they could have counted Eugene twice. He had been held back two times so he was really the size of a fourth grader.

Compared to Eugene, my friend Delores was tiny. She, too, was a second grader. I stayed with her and her mother Gladys, the head nurse, when my brother Phil was born. I told Mother, "Delores always smells like soap. She must be the cleanest person in the whole world." Delores was quiet and shy. I thought I should look out for her.

The first day of school I said "Hi" to Delores. I knew boys didn't talk to girls but Delores wasn't just a girl; she was my friend. Eugene and some boys who followed him around began singing, "Louie and Delores, sitting in a tree. K-I-S-S-I-N-G."

I whispered to Delores, "Follow me." We ran to the other end of the playground to swing on the big swings. Thankfully, one of the teachers threw a basketball to Eugene. It distracted him and he began shooting hoops. We survived the first recess.

Since Mother was working, I rode my tricycle seven blocks from the hospital to the grade school. Mother mapped out a very specific route. She did not know that the highlighted path ran in front of Eugene's house, which was across the street from the school.

I wondered all day if Eugene had forgotten me. Unfortunately, he hadn't! When the end-of-the-day bell rang, I waited until Eugene passed the evergreen trees at the edge of the school grounds. Then, I headed home. When I got to the school crossing near his house, he was waiting for me. He yelled. "Get off the trike."

I did and he pedaled down the street. I was desperate. Mother would be worried.

"Stop! I have to get home!"

He laughed and then rode straight towards me. I jumped out of the way, dropping my book bag. It popped open and the wind blew my class work all over the intersection.

I have to get my papers or I'll have nothing to show Mother and the nurses!

I chased papers while Eugene rode up and down the sidewalk. After what seemed like forever, he got off and pushed the tricycle towards me.

"Go home, Baby!"

Calling me "Baby" made me really mad. I totally surprised him. I ran toward him, knocked him to the ground, and punched him in the stomach. He yelled in surprise and pain. I needed more than tears from him.

"Promise me you will never touch my trike again."

"I promise. I promise."

"Promise you will never sing that stupid kissing song to me again."

He agreed as tears ran down his face.

I jumped on my tricycle and rode home in triumph. This moment was as good as the Bible stories we read each night. Dad might think I was ugly but I was a fierce warrior.

During the first recess the next day Mrs. Rogers, the second grade teacher, asked me to stay in the classroom and talk to her. I stood beside her desk.

"Eugene's mother said you beat him up yesterday. Louie, I am surprised. That does not sound like you."

"He took my trike."

"Why didn't you tell me?"

I couldn't imagine Mrs. Rogers pounding on Eugene. I was pretty sure nothing else would have made a difference. I just shrugged.

"Tell me you will not do that again. Tell me you will come to me the next time you have a problem with Eugene."

I could not promise that. Warriors do not ask women to solve their problems. And I could not believe she would ask me to. Did she want me to lie and say I would not defend myself against Eugene? I jumped back from her desk and ran into the boys' bathroom. That was the one place she could not get me. To my total surprise she marched into the bathroom, grabbed me by the arm, and dragged me back to her desk. That embarrassed me so much I wanted to run away and never come back.

"I will be calling your mother. I will tell her that you were fighting and that you ran away while I was talking to you. I do not think she will be pleased by your behavior."

My greatest victory had turned into a nightmare.

I told Mother the whole story. She laughed until tears ran down her face. Then she hugged her fierce warrior for a long time. Finally, she called the teacher.

"Mrs. Rogers, thank you for your concern. I had a very serious talk with Louie. He understands what he did."

She hung up and turned to me.

"If you decide to pound on Eugene again, you will have another talk with Mrs. Rogers. Understand?"

She hugged me and patted me on the head. I felt totally understood. That day Mother was better than a really good dad.

Reflections

When my son Greg was in the eighth grade, another student knocked his books out of his hands and ran. Greg said he tried to think what I would want him to do: chase the kid and pound on him or pick up his books and papers and let the kid get away. He picked up his stuff and the other boy escaped. Greg wanted to know what I thought.

I said, "If you know where the kid lives, should you and I go over there, call out him and his dad and beat them up?"

"Are you serious?"

"Greg, there is no such thing as a good war. A few wars are necessary but none are good. Should we go to war against this family?"

"Can I have some time to think about it?"

The next morning he was calm and clear. "That kid is not worth a war."

When I first heard his story about the other boy's attack, I offered empathy. All of our options were open, but we were going to face the problem together. To do that, we needed to hear what would please God. (No, we were not going to fight another family, but we were going to think about all the possible responses.)

As a family we had already prayed about angry reactions especially when we were not at fault. James 1:19 – 20, 26 (NLT) was the template for an appropriate response:

> Understand this, my dear brothers and sisters: You must all be quick to listen, slow to speak, and slow to get angry. Human anger does not produce the righteousness God desires … If you claim to be religious but don't control your tongue, you are fooling yourself, and your religion is worthless.

What the kid did to Greg was wrong. Would that excuse Greg (and me) being wrong? We took time to think and pray about a righteous response. There were two possibilities:

• Speak the truth in love. See Ephesians 4:15.

- Overlook the offense because that's what the Lord told us to do. Jesus said He only did what the Father told Him to do. If God is silent, why are you (or I) talking?

Questions to Consider

1. When a member of your family is angry, whatever the catalyst is, what would be a life-giving and redemptive (i.e., God is at work) response? James 1:19 – 20 suggests three steps:

   - "Slow to get angry."
     James puts this after listening and talking. I moved this step from third to first. When I am really hot, I do not hear well. First, I have to shut up, back off, and calm down. For years I went to the bathroom or stood outside the sliding glass door—my safe places. I was not running away; I was calming down. I was praying, "God, help me!"

   - "Quick to listen."
     Don't just hear but listen until the other person says, "You have heard me." Hear more than words; hear their heart. Hear more than words; hear their meaning. After you have heard the other person, be sure you hear God.

   - "Slow to speak."
     Has the Holy Spirit prompted you to say anything since you listened? Wait until He does.

2. Is there conflict in your home? Between you, the parents? Child to child? Between parent(s) and children? How can you and they live out James 1:19 – 20?

   - Get quiet & Calm down (I had to Be Silent)
   - Love well by listening well.
   - Only say what encourages & builds up.

3. If another child mistreats your child and provokes him to anger, does he know how to respond?

   - Don't hit unless you are protecting yourself.

- Don't hurt people with your words.
- Go to a safe person or a safe place. (Identify safe people your child can turn to when someone mistreats them or threatens to do so.)
- If you are angry, admit it. Then, don't sin against yourself or others.

CHAPTER SEVEN

WHITE LIES

I LIED. I DIDN'T THINK OF it as lying. I was telling Mother a version of the story that would not make her sad.

I don't know how she always knew what really happened but she did. One of Mother's favorite sayings was, "You might as well tell me the truth every time because God will tell me if you don't."

Her Bible was open to Luke 12:2-3 [Phillips]:

> For there is nothing covered up which is not going to be exposed, nor anything private which is not going to be made public. Whatever you may say in the dark will be heard in daylight, and whatever you whisper within four walls will be shouted from the housetops."

I had to learn that lesson over and over.

I dropped a jar of apple butter in the nurses' dining area. Miriam, one of the nurses, scolded me. "Can't you do anything right?"

It seemed so unfair. Adults could say anything they wanted to but kids had to be quiet. I was angry. However, Mother taught me to speak with respect or say nothing.

Later that evening Miriam brewed a cup of hot tea. I sat quietly at the end of the table. I had no idea what I was waiting for. The phone rang. It was the nurses' station. A patient's call light went on. She quickly left the kitchen.

It was the perfect opportunity. I put a spoonful of coffee in her hot tea. When she returned, she took a long drink and spat it out.

"What in the world is wrong with this tea? It tastes like coffee."

I expected at any moment for her to turn and look at me. Apparently, it did not occur to her that I was guilty.

Later that evening Mother interrupted our Bible story.

"I have a story for you. Once upon a time in a land not so far away, a lady insulted a boy. Her words hurt him. That night she left the castle and the boy put coffee in her tea."

I sat up in bed.

"How did you know?"

"Gladys told me what Miriam said to you today. I am sorry she said that. When Miriam spat out her tea, I asked the Lord how the coffee got in that cup. Suddenly, I remembered. Miriam insulted you today. You had a chance to get even. So, what did you, my amazing son, do with this opportunity?"

"I can't get by with anything."

"We live in a hospital. Some people already think that is a bad idea. They are afraid you boys might catch some bug the patients have. Can you imagine how worried they would be if they thought you were going to put stuff in their food? I would lose my job and we would lose our apartment."

She motioned to me to move closer. She put her arm around my shoulders.

"Louie, I want you to learn two lessons. Life isn't always fair. What Miriam said today was wrong. She wants you to be a perfect kid who never drops anything. You think someday she will be a perfect adult who never says anything unkind? The two of you need to learn how to live side by side in this world.

"Please learn this as well. Funny stuff can cause great harm. What you did was funny but you were the only one laughing. You did not mean to hurt Miriam, but her cup of tea helps her be a good nurse during her eight hour shift. You took that from her."

Mother was not in the room when Miriam insulted me and she

was not there when I spooned coffee into the tea. I had a cold chill. God was taking a personal interest in what I did. That made me very nervous.

I didn't mean to but I gave Mother many chances to be wise. She did not disappoint. The coffee in the tea wasn't the only time I ignored what she taught me about honesty.

For Christmas I wanted a ranch set—$7.99 in the Sears' Christmas catalog. In the month before Christmas, Mother did not say a word about my present. That made me think she had already bought it. I looked in every storage space, cabinet, or hidden compartment on each of the hospital's three floors. I examined the kitchen last because it was such a busy place. She had not hidden it well. It was behind the cups on the top shelf in the kitchen cabinet. I played with it once and put it back on the shelf.

Mother had warned me.

"I am praying every day that you will not be a happy sinner."

When I found the hidden Christmas gift, God answered Mother's prayer. I felt far worse than unhappy. My stomach was tied in knots and there was pain behind my right eye.

To make it worse, there was no name on the package. What if it wasn't mine? Any of the nurses could have hidden it there.

After supper Mother said, "What do you have to be sad about?"

Her question startled me. I could not hide the truth anymore.

"I found the ranch set on the top shelf. I opened it and then put it back. I don't know if it is mine."

"Yes, I bought it for you."

Her long pauses were so painful. "Now I don't know if I should give it to you."

She always figured out what I did. I was very sad each time, and at the end of the story I had to tell the truth. *I feel so much better when I confess. I feel clean again. Why don't I remember that before I mess up?* Once again, she forgave me and the package under the Christmas tree had my name on it. But I never did enjoy the ranch set as much as I thought I would.

A year later I stole a fifty-cent toy car. While Mother was grocery shopping, I had extra time in the Ben Franklin "Five and Dime."

After three trips back to the corner store, I put the car in my pocket. Mother discovered what I had done and drove me back to the Ben Franklin store right away. It was not a quiet ride to town.

"Louie, that car belongs to someone else. I know it is one-of-a-kind, but it is not your car."

What was I thinking? I always get caught.

"You lied, too."

I nodded. When she first asked me where I got the beautiful toy car, I said, "I found it outside the school." She questioned me until I told the truth.

"When you took that little Chevy, you took more than someone's stuff. Stealing makes it harder to trust people. It robs us of the peace God intended. Did you know it makes me doubt myself? How could I have failed you so badly as a parent? I hope you know it takes time to get peace and trust back."

We turned onto Highway 96.

"I am glad you finally told me the truth about the toy car. That's a first step."

By the time we parked in front of the store, I was ready to face the manager. I confessed and gave him two quarters. He thanked me and then repeated much of what Mother had said. I was sure I would never make that mistake again.

In the years that followed I was honest most of the time. However, when I was under stress, I went back to old habits.

After three years of teaching high school English, I received a promotion to Department Head for Secondary English. Ordering books for the English department was one of my responsibilities. I thought this was a great opportunity to showcase my skills. Then, I saw how many orders the teachers placed on my desk. Each teacher insisted I treat her order as my number one priority. My door of opportunity led to a torture chamber.

I did not keep up with the orders. The pressure mounted. I began telling white lies. For instance, when Mrs. Railsback asked me about her order, I said, "I've sent it already." As soon as she left my office, I filled out the order and turned it in. *It's just a white lie. She'll never know.* From my point of view this was necessary to maintain the peace.

The teachers never let up.

"Have you sent my order yet?"

"How long do you think it will take to receive my order?"

"Did we have enough money to cover my order?"

I had dreams about hundreds of teachers gathering outside my house and shouting, "My order! My order!"

I told them what I thought they wanted to hear.

One morning during my daily devotions I had a thought that I was sure came from the Lord.

You are lying to the other English teachers.

"Lord, I can't stand the constant barrage of questions and demands. I don't have a choice. Besides, they are only white lies. I am just leaving out a few facts so they won't get upset."

You are lying and it grieves Me.

Why hadn't I remembered the Lord? I asked for forgiveness and never lied to the teachers again. In fact, I told them I had lied. Then, I gave them new guidelines: Submit the order. Write out any questions. I would put a note in their office mailbox, answering their questions and letting them know when I placed the order.

I immediately felt a fresh sense of peace. Memories from childhood flooded back. I remembered Mother's warnings. I realized the Lord was unrelenting and kind. All my life He had stressed the need for honesty.

Lies were lies. White lies were simply lies with a coat of white paint. No matter what the color, they didn't work and they were a mess to clean up.

Reflections

The enemy has a standing order for all his troops:

1. Assault integrity. Make honesty seem like an impossible goal.

2. Help people make excuses.
   - "Nobody knows the trouble I seen!"
   - "I deserve a break."
   - "Other people don't understand."
   - "God's laws are old fashioned."

3. Encourage them to blame others.
   - "My husband is controlling."
   - "My wife is moody."
   - "My kids are demanding."
   - "My boss is confusing, irrational, and clueless."

4. Tell them selfishness makes sense.

Questions to Consider

1. When you are dishonest, what excuses do you make? Lying is deeply selfish. Calling it a white lie or a small lie is just a cover-up.

2. Do you talk about honesty during family meetings? In your family devotions? At mealtimes? Do you have a strategy to train your children in integrity?

3. After reading the scriptures that follow, what would you say is the Bible's standard for honesty? What has diluted that standard in our work place, sports teams, and even in our homes?

- Romans 12:17 (KJV), "Recompense to no man evil for evil. Provide things honest in the sight of all men."

- Deuteronomy 25:13-16 (MSG), "Don't carry around with you two weights, one heavy and the other light, and don't keep two measures at hand, one large and the other small. Use only one weight, a true and honest weight, and one measure, a true and honest measure, so that you will live a long time on the land that God, your God, is giving you. Dishonest weights and measures are an abomination to God, your God—all this corruption in business deals!"

- 2 Corinthians 8:21 (AMP), "For we take thought beforehand *and* aim to be honest *and* absolutely above suspicion, not only in the sight of the Lord but also in the sight of men."

CHAPTER EIGHT

THE TRIP TO ROME

I HAD NEVER PAID ANY ATTENTION to Catherine Freese. She was in my third grade class but she was a girl. That changed when I heard the nurses talking at the dinner table.

"You know Mrs. Freese just missed her trip to Rome."

"What trip to Rome?"

"Well, I heard the Catholic Church rewards any family that has twenty children. They get an all-expenses-paid trip to Rome and a private audience with the Pope."

"How many children did she have?"

"Nineteen. After nineteen babies in nineteen years, Dr. Miller told her if she had another baby, it could kill her."

"Nineteen—that's incredible. Are you sure that's true—I mean the free trip to Rome?"

"I am not Catholic but my neighbor is. She is the one who told my older sister."

I couldn't wait for school next day. I sat on the front steps until Catherine came.

"Hi, Catherine. How are you?"

"Fine." Then, she whispered, "Why are you talking to me?"

I knew that third grade boys didn't talk to girls but curiosity filled my head with questions. I had to find out about this Catholic family and the missing trip to Rome.

"How many brothers and sisters do you have?"

She looked at me for a long time.

"Eighteen."

Catherine answered my next question before I asked it. "Daniel, number seventeen, is in the fourth grade. I am number eighteen. Maurice, number nineteen, is in the second grade."

I wanted to tell her how sad I was that her mother missed her trip to see the Pope, but I didn't know how to say it.

For a girl she was very nice. The next several days during both recesses I asked her every question I could think of about a family of nineteen children.

"How big is your house?"

"How many bedrooms are there?"

"How many cars does your family have?"

"Do you like being in a large family?"

Catherine seemed to enjoy my interest. She told me the house was very big. There were five bedrooms for kids with no more than two kids in each room. That did not count the room over the garage. Two of the older boys slept there. Only eleven of the kids were still at home. To my amazement they only owned two cars, a Ford and a Buick. The littlest kids sat on their brothers' or sisters' laps when they traveled. And yes, she loved all her brothers and sisters very much.

Finally, she invited me to come home with her after school on Friday. She had not asked me to spend the night so I didn't have to pack a bag. Because of the excitement I barely slept the night before the trip to the farm.

After school her brother Richard, a high school senior, picked up Catherine, Maurice, Daniel, and me in a full-size, coal black Ford. I imagined we were riding in a limousine. They lived about four miles out in the country off a gravel road down a tree-lined lane.

It felt like a fairytale. The two-story, white house had a porch across the front and along the right side. The lawn was buffalo grass, the same as their pasture. Right beside the house three of the older girls were working in the huge garden, pulling the weeds and putting cucumbers in a large plastic tub.

Catherine introduced me to her parents, who were sitting in rocking chairs on the porch. Mrs. Freese was knitting and Mr. Freese was smoking a pipe. They welcomed me like I was a grown up, introducing themselves by name and shaking my hand.

Catherine invited me to help her bring the milk cow in from the pasture. It was easy. She hollered at the cow and the large black and white animal headed obediently to the barn. She attached the cow's halter to a stall inside the barn. Next, she sat down on a one-legged stool, placed the bucket on the ground, between her knees, and under the cow's udder. She took hold of one of the cow's teats and used a squeezing and stripping motion. Milk poured into the bucket. She asked if I would like to try. With a little practice I was able to get some milk to come. I felt a real sense of accomplishment.

We carried the milk bucket to the kitchen, poured it in one-gallon jars, and put them in the refrigerator.

So, this is life in a large family.

For dinner the thirteen members of the Freese family and I sat at a very long table. Papa Freese's place was at the head of the table. He looked like an ordinary farmer with his overalls and blue flannel shirt. When he bowed his head, everyone joined him. The whole family prayed the same prayer out loud.

The meal included my favorites: fried chicken, mashed potatoes and gravy, huge slices of homemade bread and butter, Mrs. Freese's for-real apricot jam, and tall glasses of the milk Catherine and I brought to the house. During the meal, Mrs. Freese asked her children questions about school, work in the garden, and various chores involving the cow, the horse, and the chickens. Finally, she turned to me.

"We are honored to have you as our guest. I hope you have enjoyed your evening."

"Thank you, Ma'am. It has been great. The food is very good, too."

"Catherine tells me you have lots of questions. I wonder if you have any you have not yet asked?"

This looked like my golden opportunity. "Ma'am, if you adopted another child, would you get your free trip to Rome?"

The whole room froze in place. Mrs. Freese broke the silence.

"Son, what trip are you talking about?"

"We have heard that the Catholic Church gives a free trip to Rome to any family that has twenty children. Oh yes, they get a private audience with the Pope, too!"

I have never heard such laughter. Several of the kids choked on their food. Mr. and Mrs. Freese simply smiled. Finally, the laughter died down and the conversation continued.

"Louie, that is the happiest thought I have heard in years. Let me see if I understand you. You would be willing for this family to adopt you so my husband and I could have a free trip to Rome and a private audience with His Holiness?"

The laughter had puzzled and embarrassed me. I wasn't sure whether I had said something wonderful or totally stupid. Mrs. Freese's kind response brought calm to everyone.

"Yes, Ma'am, I have always wanted more brothers and sisters, and I felt sad ever since I heard you missed your trip."

"I will tell our priest, Father John, on Sunday about your wonderful idea—a trip to Rome for Papa and me. Perhaps the church will reconsider and let us go with just nineteen children."

She took a long drink from her cup of coffee.

"To be honest I have never heard of such a trip, but it is still the best idea anyone has shared at this table in a long time. Papa, you and I may be the first to take a free trip to Rome from Ransom, Kansas."

No one was laughing now. We waited while she drank more coffee.

"Now, what about adopting you? We didn't have number twenty because of my health and our belief that God had given us all the children He intended. If we were going to adopt anyone, you would be a wonderful choice. I think your mother would be very sad if you moved here to the farm. It is probably best that we stick with nineteen and think of you as a very special guest."

She motioned to everyone that the meal was over. They could begin clearing off the table.

"Richard, why don't you and Catherine give our guest a ride home so his mother won't worry."

She pushed her chair back, walked around the table, and gave me a big hug. Mr. Freese shook my hand and patted me on the back.

Richard turned on the radio during the ride back to town. That was okay. I had no more questions anyway.

When I got home, Mother asked me to tell her the whole story. I didn't leave out any details, including my thoughts about Mr. Freese.

"He didn't do anything. He just sat at the table and gave orders. I don't know what kind of dad he would be."

Usually, Mother had thoughts about my search for a dad. Today, she wiped tears from her eyes.

"You asked them to adopt you? I wish you had told me that was your plan."

For some odd reason I had never thought about hurting her feelings. I simply wanted a dad and a family. I knew the Freeses would like the idea because of the trip and a visit with the Pope.

Mother washed her face and then went upstairs to the kitchen to call Mrs. Freese. She did not realize I was listening in the stairwell. It was late. The kitchen was quiet and I could hear every word.

"Mrs. Freese, this is Mildred, Louie's mother."

"Please call me Marie."

"Marie, thank you so much for inviting Louie to dinner. He had a wonderful time. He told me about his ideas."

Mrs. Freese laughed. "He has a huge imagination and a bigger heart."

"Well, I called to apologize for his questions."

"Oh, no, please don't apologize. No one else has ever thought I deserved a trip to Rome for having all those children. I couldn't wait till Sunday to tell our priest, Father John. In fact, we just talked a few minutes ago. At first he laughed and then he agreed with me. Perhaps the congregation should take up an offering and send us to Rome. He plans to submit an article to *Catholic Digest*, telling about the amazing boy who offered to change families so the Church could honor a mother. Don't worry, Father John will not use your son's name. He plans to tell the congregation on Sunday about the thoughtfulness of an eight-year-old boy. Again, no names. So please, please, don't apologize. You are raising an amazing son."

Mother simply said, "Thank you, Marie," and hung up. When she came downstairs, she said, "Louie, I have one simple request. Please tell me the next time you have an amazing plan." While she held me close, she laughed and cried at the same time.

Reflections

While I was growing up, I focused most of the time on what I didn't have or couldn't get. Being small, having acne, living in a tiny apartment, and longing for a dad were a few of my causes for distress. Because of that focus on the negative, I was rarely content. I didn't know how to trust God fully as my source.

Parenting three sons gave me a second chance to discover what I missed the first time.

While he was still in high school, our oldest son Greg said, "Dad, when you are old, I am going to take care of you."

Caught off guard, I laughed.

"Dad, I am serious. It is part of my life's purpose."

"I am sorry I laughed. If that's a God idea, I will look forward to that chapter."

Years later I called him after a painful day at work. He was a college graduate, married, and living in California.

"Greg, I think I may get fired. The senior pastor rarely gives me any feedback unless it's negative. I almost never know what he expects."

"Was he negative today?"

"I asked him what scripture he would like on the back of a brochure. That pressed some hot button. For the next thirty minutes he told me why he had the right to fire me. I think he described every termination this church has ever had. That gave me time to regain my equilibrium so I could think of an intelligent and respectful question."

"What did you ask?"

"In the future what would be a better way to handle questions about a brochure?"

The senior pastor calmed down.

"First, call my ministry friends, the ones I trust. Get ideas from them. Narrow the list to two or three possibilities for the brochure. Offer me choices. It will take me about two seconds to figure out which one I like."

"Dad, if you do that and he still fires you, come and live with us."

That offer from my oldest son to live with his family for a while warmed my heart.

The revised brochure worked. Thankfully, I wasn't fired. More importantly, I was content, knowing God had a place for me, no matter what.

Questions to Consider

1. What do you say when a child who is eight or twelve or seventeen complains, "I want to be older"? My response was, "Oh please, be eight for a whole year. Don't miss one surprise or one lesson or one opportunity because you are looking forward to next year."

2. Are your children content with the toys they have? The room they sleep in? The clothes they wear? Have you taught them to be grateful for what they have and to express their gratitude?

3. For five years I kept a gratitude journal, writing down what I had to be grateful for each day, no matter how small. That daily discipline made me keenly aware of how much I took for granted and how often I focused on the negative. It was life changing.

4. Train your children to express insightful gratitude. In other words, they don't deserve most of what they receive. They are not entitled to it so they should not demand it. (That's insight.)

   They are the recipients of God's grace and favor. They should be grateful for everything God sends. That's insightful gratitude.

   Ask them to consider whom they should thank. Encourage them to express that gratitude. Then, you and they can address their felt needs.

CHAPTER NINE

THE MINIMUM REQUIREMENT

MOTHER'S ALL-TIME, NUMBER ONE CONCERN was that she would fail as a parent, and as a result, I would waste my life.

"Louie, you are in high school now. Break the old patterns. Live on purpose."

Mother found practical examples every day. She would question me.

"You picked on Phil until he cried. What was your purpose?"

"He would not leave my stuff alone."

"So, your purpose was to protect your stuff?"

"I guess so."

"Let me ask you again. How did being mean to Phil fulfill your life's purpose?"

I must have looked miserable.

"Louie, is this helpful or should I stop talking and begin peeling the potatoes for supper?"

"I don't know what would help. How do I glorify God when Phil grabs my model airplanes? I am afraid he will break them."

"You haven't answered my question. Is this helpful?"

I didn't want to give her an honest answer. She waited until I did.

"It is really hard work to think about purpose all day long. Sometimes I just want to be an ordinary kid and not think about the rest of my life. Larry's parents told him they will buy him a new car when he graduates from high school. They never talk about purpose. Linda has one subject—Andy. Being with him is her only purpose. When I see the way she looks at him, I think I would like an identical purpose. Coach Nichols, my English teacher Mrs. Floyd, and you encourage me almost every day to be all I can be, the best Louie possible. I know that's good but it is still hard."

She hugged me and then pointed to the verse taped to the refrigerator door: "So whether you eat or drink or whatever you do, do it all for the glory of God" (I Corinthians 10:31, NIV).

"Louie, you will always hear two voices. The Enemy will usually speak first: *If you are not happy, no one else should be happy either. Make Phil as miserable as you are.*

"Mother, the only voice I hear right now is yours. Are you saying, 'Don't worry about what happens to the airplane models.'"?

"No, I am not saying, 'Let Phil break your models.' I am asking God to show you a creative way to love your brother and to save the airplanes at the same time."

Aunt Verleen and my cousin Doug were staying for a few days at Grandpa's house in Arnold six miles away. They came into the hospital basement apartment while Mother and I were talking.

Verleen had a very different idea.

"Mildred, he is just a kid. He ought to be outside climbing a tree or throwing a ball or riding that bike the hospital auxiliary gave him."

It was hard to believe the two were sisters.

Mother remained calm.

"He can go outside whenever he wants to."

"Why are you teaching him to trust God? That didn't work for either of us. My ex, Eddie, abandoned Doug and me. Then, Clay drove off and left you in Texas."

"I am not teaching him to trust men. I am teaching him to trust God."

Verleen grabbed her cigarettes and headed outside to smoke.

"Sis, I am going back to Arnold unless we change the subject."

Mother quietly set the table where the nurses ate. She fought back tears.

"When you come back in, we will eat."

I realized I should never complain about Mother pushing me to trust God and live with purpose. I could have had Verleen as my mother.

Verleen's visit discouraged Mother. That worried me.

A few days later I came home from school and entered the hospital kitchen. Mother was unusually cheerful.

"I found the answer to my big questions today."

"Where?"

"In the Bible, 1 Corinthians 7:14. It's on the table. Read it out loud so I can hear it again." She had several translations of the verse with the Amplified Bible on top.

> For the unbelieving husband is set apart...by union with his consecrated (set-apart) wife, and the unbelieving wife is set apart ...through union with her consecrated husband. Otherwise your children would be unclean (unblessed heathen, outside the Christian covenant), but as it is they are prepared for God [pure and clean].

Mother had notes in the margins: J.B. Phillips New Testament says, "the children are consecrated to God." The King James Version translates the end of the verse, "now are they holy."

She couldn't stay in her seat.

"This is what the verse says to me. 'If a man holds onto his faith, his wife is set apart for God's purpose. The wife's faith does the same thing for her husband. God honors the faith of a believing mother and her children are set apart for God's purposes."

Mother was preaching to the two of us.

"One believing parent is enough. I meet the minimum requirement."

She had a the-devil-can't-stop-us-now look in her eyes. She looked at her notes.

"You are set apart—prepared for God, consecrated to Him, holy. All these years, I thought a child had to have two faith-filled parents to get the job done right. God says He and I are enough."

She said it with such confidence I believed it

"Mother, do you think that is why you haven't found a dad for me yet?'

"Louie, I am going to answer your question with a question. What do you think would happen if you honestly believed you are set apart for God's purpose?"

"Are you saying a dad would show up?"

"I am saying you would find God's purpose for your life no matter who does or does not show up."

The next evening Nurse Miriam tried to continue an old conversation about me.

"Mildred, I know you said someone you know is too much for you."

All the nurses looked at me and laughed.

"Have you found a tall, dark, and handsome stranger who can help with that?"

Mother's answer silenced Miriam.

"Yes, I have. It's me. I'm enough!"

Then, she told them about her new verse in 1 Corinthians.

"As long as I walk in faith, I meet the minimum requirements and God makes up the difference."

Miriam never asked that question again.

Reflections

On my 71st birthday I asked the Lord, "Can I be extraordinary in my 70s?"

He immediately reminded me of Romans 8:26 – 28 (NLT):

> And the Holy Spirit helps us in our weakness. For example, we don't know what God wants us to pray for. But the Holy Spirit prays for us with groanings that cannot be expressed in words. And the Father who knows all hearts knows what the Spirit is saying, for the Spirit pleads for us believers in harmony with God's own will. And we know that God causes everything to work together for the good of those who love God and are called according to his purpose for them.

I made an outline of these verses:

- We are groaning as though we are in childbirth (vs. 22-23). The Holy Spirit groans with us (vs. 26). That's empathy. He comes alongside us in our struggle.

- We don't know what to pray for (vs. 26). The Holy Spirit "knows the mind of God." The Holy Spirit intercedes for us "in accordance with God's will" (vs. 27).

- We are weak (vs. 26). The Holy Spirit helps us in our weakness (vs. 26).

- When we line up with God's will "all things work together for good" (vs. 28)

Please examine these Scriptures again carefully. Invite the Holy Spirit to come each day. Then, simply be quiet. The Holy Spirit will intercede for you, lining you up with God's purpose.

A Question to Consider

I began asking almost two years ago, "Can I be extraordinary in my 70s?" I have discovered a better question, "Will I welcome the Holy Spirit every morning, line up with God's will, and see Him do extraordinary things through me as often as He chooses?"

ACT II: THE NEXT DAD

CHAPTER TEN

CHICKEN DINNER FOR TWO

G LADYS, THE HEAD NURSE, WAS more than Mother's boss—she was a good friend. They had heart-to-heart talks nearly every night.

Mother and I ended each day with a Bible story. Then we sang our song, "I was born to be God's dwelling place..." We called ourselves the Norman Tab 'N Apple Choir. That was always funny. She tucked me in and went upstairs for her evening talk.

I pretended to go to sleep quickly. As soon as she left, I quietly raced up the stairs. I entertained myself by sitting around the corner and listening in. One evening I was the topic of their conversation.

"Mildred, I heard you. The Bible says you and God are enough, but I still think that boy needs a dad. He needs someone strong enough to handle him and smart enough to answer his non-stop questions."

"Is there someone in one of those hospital beds I don't know about?"

"Well, there's Mr. Whitney in Room #103."

"I want someone who's conscious."

They laughed and then there was a long silence while they drank their coffee. It was really hard for me to stay quiet.

"Oh, Mildred, what about that farmer from Ness City?"

"You mean Fred. He'd marry me in a heartbeat if I said, 'Yes.'"

"You have two reasons to say, 'Yes.' Your son is the first one. And this job is the other. It's making you old and tired. You need a break."

So that explains why she's been asking me what I think about Fred Keller.

Every other Sunday for the past two months he had invited us to his farm for Sunday dinner.

Mother joked about the first invitation. "Fred invited us to chicken dinner if we bring the chicken."

"What does that mean?"

"I was trying to be funny. I am frying chicken for dinner and we are eating it at his farm."

We attended the same church in Ness City as Brother Fred. That's what everybody else called him. I wondered why Mother called him Fred? Just Fred!

"What do you think of Fred?"

"What don't you call him Brother Fred?"

"He is not like a brother to me. Please don't ask me to explain that."

She didn't ask again. I was glad. I did not know what to think.

I noticed one Sunday—without Mother knowing it—that she only had five pieces of chicken in her basket. Not enough for four people. I didn't understand why until Pastor Stuart and his wife invited Phil and me to the city park for lunch. Lunch was sandwiches in the park. If he had invited us to dinner, it would have been fried chicken with all the trimmings, served around the big table. Until now our family always had dinner after church!

Lunch with the pastor and his wife puzzled Phil and me. They had never seemed interested in either of us.

For a month we ate at the city park on Sundays. All of the adults at the church knew about the lunches. They acted like bologna sandwiches were a wonderful surprise.

"You boys are so blessed—lunch with the pastor and his wife."

We had no idea what to say so we were quiet. We got in the back seat of the car and waited for the Sunday schedule to unfold.

They let us choose the picnic table in the park. When we finished the bologna sandwiches, they asked what we would like to do next. We didn't know what our options were so we just shrugged our shoulders.

"Would you like to go for a drive?"

We nodded, "Yes."

They drove forty miles north to Wakeeney. On the way there they asked a hundred questions about school and church and youth camp and life in the hospital basement. Phil and I had no idea what was going on.

In Wakeeney the pastor's wife said we could have whatever we wanted at the Dairy Queen. I ordered a tall chocolate shake, a double cheeseburger with fries, and an order of onion rings. Before Phil could say what he wanted, the pastor and his wife asked us to wait while they had a private talk. Finally, they returned to the table and included us in the mystery.

"Please forgive us. We forgot how much boys eat. Phil, would you mind sharing what Louie ordered?"

We said we wouldn't mind. Our family never ate out so we had no idea how much things cost at the Dairy Queen. When the food was ready, the pastor prayed a blessing. Then the two of them asked if we would object if they filled the car with gas while we ate. That's when I realized they couldn't afford to buy anything for themselves. We felt really bad but we didn't know how to solve the problem. We enjoyed the very tasty Dairy Queen food.

The final shock that day was their request on the way back to our town.

"Would you mind not telling your mother we didn't bring enough cash? It was just poor planning on our part."

Mother warned us many times. "If anyone ever tells you to keep a secret from me, tell me immediately."

When she asked about our day, we told her about the poor planning and the request for secrecy. Her response was totally out of character.

"Oh, that's nice."

Phil and I dropped the subject. Something strange was going on. The most unusual part was Mother's silence. For five years she had told us everything—as far as we knew. But this whole Fred topic was a huge secret.

Our second and third and fourth Sunday lunches with the pastor were the same, brief stops for sandwiches at the park picnic tables, followed by a short ride to the parsonage. The pastor played a game of checkers with me. Phil and I had the rest of the afternoon to read books or play games their children had left behind. No more long drives in the country. No more trips to the Dairy Queen. No more poor planning.

Each Sunday we had lunch but Phil and I had no one to talk to about Mother and Fred. The pastor never mentioned them. We didn't know the people in the church. We knew every funny thing they did on Sundays, thanks to Mother's humor, but we had not had an important talk with any of them. Almost all of the adults were married or much older so they had never invited our single mother and her two boys to their homes. Another wall: they lived in Ness City, eight miles from the town of Ransom. That meant we didn't go to school with their kids.

The biggest headache: we didn't really know Fred Keller. Now, he and Mother were having chicken dinners and Phil and I weren't invited anymore. I could not ask Mother. I had overheard Gladys and Mother talk and I couldn't let her know I had listened from the steps.

Once again, I felt abandoned. Five years earlier our first dad drove away. He didn't even say, "Good bye." This time the chicken dinners were only for two. A whole church full of people were wrong. They thought we were blessed.

Later on, I pieced together more of the story. Two weeks after I heard Gladys, talking to Mother, she said, "Yes," to Fred. We would get a dad and she would get away from the hospital. Even Gladys was surprised by how much Mother's job description included. The hospital had to hire two full-time employees and one half-time person to replace her.

Mother married our new dad when she was thirty and he was sixty. On her wedding day she took my face in her hands.

"Louie, I have prayed about it and I believe this is God's provision for us. Finally, you will have a dad."

I was more surprised than happy but I knew she wanted me to be happy so I was.

Fred Keller was full of smiles, too. His first wife had died after a prolonged battle with tuberculosis. He was alone and times were hard. Western Kansas was in a prolonged drought—no rain for 150 days. Food and fuel were scarce. There were jars of canned food in his basement but very little money for a trip to the grocery store. In the midst of all that he married for the second time.

Our new family numbered four or more, depending on who was counting. Mother brought just-turned-eleven-year-old me and my five-year-old brother Phil to the farm. Fred Keller had raised two girls. They were both married and lived on farms with their husbands and children. The marriage completely surprised them. Their frustration was an eleven on a ten-point scale. They came to the wedding but they were very cold to us boys. I was sure they did not count Mother or us as family.

Surely there was a better way to get a new dad.

Reflections

Mother thought she needed a clear head to decide about marrying for a second time. She thought I was too eager to have a dad, so she didn't include me in any discussions. However, neither she nor Fred listened to his married daughters because both of them were totally opposed.

What she overlooked was that we boys were part of the decision, like it or not. We, too, moved to the farm and lived in Fred Keller's house. We didn't need to make her decision, but we did need to understand what would be expected of us and how we would fit with Fred Keller.

She assumed that any Godly man would be a great disciplinarian. He assumed that there was one right way to discipline kids. I assumed that his approach to discipline would be a lot like Mother's.

She thought that any man who loved her would also love her boys the way she did and as much as she did. He thought that his greatest kindness would be to save us from being stoned at the city gates. I thought that Mother heard from God one hundred percent of the time. Given that, we would find a great dad in the Promised Land.

It didn't take long for us to discover the danger of assumptions. However, even though they were dangerous, we did not give them up quickly. Was there any other choice? We only saw two alternatives: the tiny apartment in Ransom or the elegant farmhouse. We thought God wanted us to have the dream-come-true farmhouse but it belonged to Fred and his whip.

I felt like God offered me two options: I could accept the hole in my heart because there was no dad or live with a dad who was on duty all the time, looking for reasons to use the whip. I couldn't say "Yes" to either choice.

Mother and I thought so much about our disappointment, we almost missed what God was doing. It was a painful lesson to understand that God still had a plan even though it did not line up with our assumptions.

Mother and her sister Verleen had similar stories. Verleen's alcoholic husband Eddie abandoned her and her three children.

Unlike Mother, Verleen turned her back on her faith and chose a career as a waitress in Los Angeles. The *Los Angeles Times* singled her out as the best waitress in that West Coast city.. Despite being featured in the press, her story did not have a good ending. She drank heavily and died of cirrhosis of the liver at age forty-three. Her children did not do well. One became an alcoholic. Another was homeless at the time of his death. The third has had severe health problems for many years. The best news: he has a gracious wife and he is recovering in their mountain home.

Mother did not become bitter and she did not turn away from God. He met her needs and ours even in the most difficult times. We were better off on the farm with Dad than we would have been with Verleen in LA.

What if we had stayed in Ransom, Kansas? A couple of years after we left, the kids who were my age in Ransom vandalized the high school. Before they were adults, they had criminal records. I could have been on the same path.

The youth group at the small church in Ness City included three kids: Gary, a high school senior; me, a high school freshman; and Beverly, a fifth grader. Mother and Beverly became close friends. They talked on the phone an average of two times each week. Mother said to me, "Be nice to Beverly. Someday she'll look very good to you."

I protested, "Mother, she's just a little kid who talks too much."

Nine years later I graduated from college and married Beverly. Mother was right.

Much of our attitude towards Fred Keller changed drastically when we asked God for His point of view. His Word described not only Fred but each of us as sinners. In so many ways, we all had missed the mark—angry comments, frustrated silence, criticism and judgment, fearful decisions, impatience, and a lack of trust. God was still present even when we didn't see His hand at work. One by one we gave up our assumptions and began trusting God.

Questions to Consider

1. Can you think of a time when God redeemed your circumstances and you realized your assumptions had been wrong?

2. Are you in the middle of a difficult time now? This is the message God gave Jeremiah for the Israelites when they were in serious trouble:

   "You sent me to the Lord, the God of Israel, with your request, and this is his reply: 'Stay here in this land. If you do, I will build you up and not tear you down; I will plant you and not uproot you. For I am sorry about all the punishment I have had to bring upon you. Do not fear the king of Babylon anymore,' says the Lord. 'For I am with you and will save you and rescue you from his power. I will be merciful to you by making him kind, so he will let you stay here in your land'" (Jeremiah 42: 9–12, NLT).

3. Why would God say, "Your (or their or my) fears are for nothing"? Does 2 Timothy 1:7 (NLV) answer the question? "For God did not give us a spirit of fear. He gave us a spirit of power and of love and of a good mind."

CHAPTER ELEVEN

THIS OLD HOUSE

Y ELEVENTH BIRTHDAY WOULD BE in a real home with a real dad. We had lived for five years in a tiny, one-and-one-half-room apartment in the basement of the hospital. The half room, Mother's bedroom, was a converted walk-in closet. In sharp contrast, Fred Keller offered us more than an amazing house. We would be a family. Phil and I called Fred Keller "Dad" the day we moved to the farm.

The two-story farmhouse was a showplace, built in 1926, twenty-five years earlier. Curious people from Dodge City and Wichita drove long distances to see this home. It featured five large bedrooms; a drawing room with dark wood paneling, a wood-fired heating stove, and an upright piano; a dining room with very tall windows all along two sides and a chandelier. There was no electricity but the beautiful light fixture added a distinctly elegant touch. There was a spacious pantry and a dream-come-true kitchen. Anyone with a camera or a sketchpad loved the home.

It did have drawbacks. The indoor plumbing offered cold water only. Hot water came from a teakettle, continuously heating on the four-burner kitchen stove. Dad did not connect to the recently developed Rural Electric Association's power lines so propane-fueled Coleman lamps provided light. One room, the kitchen, had a recently developed, propane-powered heater for use during the winter. Mother and Dad's bedroom was over the kitchen. A one-foot square vent on the floor of their bedroom provided some warmth. That was the only bedroom with heat.

The window frames were not a tight fit and there was only one pane of glass in each. When the bedroom doors were open, we could feel an icy draft. The first night we slept in the house the temperature inside was a painfully cold 28 degrees F., just 10 degrees warmer than outside. Eleven covers, piled one on top of the other, shielded Phil and me from the cold. It was November in western Kansas.

Before we moved, Mother and Fred Keller were married on another very cold night in November. During the reception Dad's son-in-law Nolen painted "Just Married" in permanent, bright yellow paint on the trunk of the blue 1950 Buick. It was his idea of humor. He had tortured other honeymooners with similar jokes. Many couples had elaborate plans for him if he ever remarried.

If the paint set, it would never come off. The newlyweds drove to the farm and spent most of their first night applying various paint removers. Just before dawn they decided they had done all they could do. There were faint traces of yellow remaining on the trunk. When Phil and I joined our parents later that day, they were tired and very quiet.

Our first morning as a family started slowly. We woke up late, took our time coming down the stairs, and enjoyed an all-you-could-eat breakfast. Then, we crossed the road and entered the milking shed. Mother helped us milk the eight cows.

The milking shorthorns produced small quantities of milk, but Dad said he liked their reddish-brown color. Choosing milk cows for their color made no sense to me. Beyond that, we were the only farm on Star Route that did not have electricity. Consequently, we milked the cows by hand, morning and evening.

The second morning was totally different. I did not hear him coming. All of a sudden the covers flew back, exposing me to the below-freezing temperature. I was sleeping on my stomach. Dad started hitting me with his bullwhip. I flew out of the bed, grabbing my overalls and all-purpose black shoes. Trying to dodge the bullwhip, I ran down the stairs to the freezing-cold kitchen. My brother and I huddled around the propane stove and shivered. The heater had not had enough time to warm the room. My back was on fire. Welts covered my shoulders but I wasn't bleeding. I carefully pulled my shirt on, groaning with pain. This was a nightmare. So much for my storybook ideas about life on the farm.

Phil whispered, "Didn't you hear him the first time?"

I just shrugged. Dad had opened both of our doors and said, "Boys!" That was a seriously shortened form of, "It is 5:30, time to get up, or I will be back with the whip."

Yes, I had heard him but it was like Antarctica in the upstairs bedrooms and it was still dark outside. I thought Dad was giving us a friendly wake-up call.

Phil was quick. He heard Dad whipping me and raced down the stairs before he got the same treatment.

We waited quietly by the stove. I looked at Mother but she did not say a word. She simply put a tall glass of orange juice, three eggs over easy, a huge bowl of Cheerios, four strips of bacon, and two slices of toast on the table for Phil and an identical feast for me. Dad broke the silence with a long prayer. When he finished, we all began to eat with urgency—there were chores to do before the school bus came.

Mornings became a nightmare. I never slept through his one-word wake-up call again but there were other reasons to receive a whipping. One day he awakened us and then noticed that Phil had wet the bed. He yanked him to his feet. His tone was flat.

"I will teach you not to pee in your bed."

I jerked with each blow to Phil. I tried to count how many times he hit him with the bullwhip but it was way too many. Phil continued to wet the bed until Mother began taking him to the bathroom in the middle of the night.

The next whipping I received was punishment for reading late at night. Mother told me to turn out the kerosene lamp and go to sleep. The pull of my books drowned out her instructions. I read long hours every night. I had to know how Danny Orliss, Nancy Drew, and the Hardy Boys solved their dilemmas.

One night Dad came with his bullwhip. I lay across the bed without any protest and took the blows. When he was done with me, he blew out the lamp and closed the door. He did not say a single word. I might have listened to words but the whip did not move me to obey.

Those stories were my safe place, my new home. I could not imagine life without them. I reached under my bed, found the big flashlight with the size D batteries, pulled the covers over my head, and finished the last forty-three pages. I was a stubborn kid.

The next morning Mother asked me, "Did you turn out the lights when Dad came in?"

I was so angry my head throbbed.

"You can freeze me and beat me but I will not stop reading. I have to read or I can't stand it here. Dad gave us a house but this is not a home."

Reflections

The five-bedroom farmhouse blinded us. We had no doubt life would be grand in a home with a large kitchen, a wraparound porch, and a chandelier. Mother had worked eighty hours a week at the hospital. I was stuck in the hospital basement for five years. When we moved to the farm, we expected good times. And there were good times.

Dad had an old but reliable, two and one-half gallon, hand-crank ice-cream freezer. Mother would fix peach ice cream, invite people from town to help us with the hand crank, and then we would all enjoy the ice cream. Since we didn't have electricity, we hung Coleman lanterns from the trees.

Years later, one of our guests who obviously didn't know our limitations, said, "You guys always had amazing parties. You turned out the electric lights, hung lanterns in the trees, and stuffed us with the best ice cream ever."

During pheasant-hunting season we would have as many as fourteen hunters walking through our fields of milo maize. At the end of their hunt they all competed to tell the biggest story of the bird that got away or the miracle shot that killed two birds or the hunting dog that set a prize-winning point and retrieved their bird from a wicked hiding place. Those were not-to-be-forgotten good times with hunters who came back each year.

The bad times were like dark clouds, blocking out the good times. What were we missing? Even God must prefer peach ice cream and roast pheasant.

Dad was reading in Hebrews one morning for our family devotions. After three verses I spoke up. "Would you mind reading those verses again?"

He read Hebrews 12:1-3 (NIV):

> Therefore, since we are surrounded by such a great cloud of witnesses, let us throw off everything that hinders and the sin that so easily entangles. And let us run with perseverance the race marked out for us, fixing our eyes on Jesus, the

pioneer and perfecter of faith. For the joy set before him he endured the cross, scorning its shame, and sat down at the right hand of the throne of God. Consider him who endured such opposition from sinners, so that you will not grow weary and lose heart.

I was excited. "That's our answer. We haven't waited long enough."

Mother didn't take time to explain to Dad why we were suddenly fully awake at 5:30 in the morning. She closed her eyes and prayed.

"Lord, we have not run the entire race. Please forgive us. We have not kept our eyes on You. We need forgiveness for that, too. We have grown weary and lost heart. We are sorry. This morning Your Word has given us fresh hope!"

In the days that followed we found many verses about delays. Most of them did not explain why the delays occurred. One fact was clear: those who waited on the Lord always received an answer but it came on God's timetable.

Questions to Consider

1. Have you struggled with delays? Did life seem hopeless in that season? Where do you turn when you feel hopeless? God's Word? A trusted friend? Or do you just rage?

2. Find a verse that encourages you deeply about delays. One suggestion is James 1:2-4 (NCV):

   My brothers and sisters, when you have many kinds of troubles, you should be full of joy, because you know that these troubles test your faith, and this will give you patience. Let your patience show itself perfectly in what you do. Then you will be perfect and complete and will have everything you need.

3. Prayerfully think about why you are in a hurry. May you (and I) learn to live at His pace.

CHAPTER TWELVE

SPARE THE ROD

FRED, OUR NEW STEPDAD, MADE it very clear. The gold standard for disciplining kids was Proverbs 13:24, "He who spares his rod [of discipline] hates his son, but he who loves him disciplines diligently and punishes him early" (AMP). Dad underscored *diligently* and *punish early* in his Bible.

The second evening on the farm Mother and Dad discussed the whipping that started the day. I couldn't tell whether we boys were invisible or it was a before-bedtime classroom.

Mother pled our case.

"Fred, please talk to the boys about obedience. Having a dad is new to them."

I had already discovered that Dad rarely joined in discussions. When he did, his answers were short. He, also, left no doubt his words were the last words on the subject.

"Mildred, I discipline the way my dad raised me. The Bible says to be diligent. That means firm parenting from first light to bedtime. Proverbs, also, says to 'punish early' so I will not hesitate."

"Can you at least tell them you love them?"

"The Bible says hate them or spank them. So, I spank them."

Dad shifted the focus.

"Mildred, is their cup half full or half empty?"

89

"What does that mean?"

"Are they looking at what they have or what they don't have?"

"What would you say they have?"

"Remind them of their blessings: God-fearing parents, a ride to worship every time the church doors are open, a roof over their heads, their own bedrooms, and three meals a day. Add discipline to that list. After all, it is straight out of God's Word."

"Speaking of discipline, why use a bullwhip?"

Dad opened his Bible. He had a bookmark, indicating the verses he needed.

"Deuteronomy 21: 18-21 says the father and mother should take a stubborn and rebellious son to the elders at the gates of his town. The men will stone him to death and purge the evil from among them. The entire nation will hear of it and be afraid to disobey. Teaching sons to obey is serious business. My father taught me to obey. I intend to pass the same principles on to your boys. I don't throw stones. I use a bullwhip. It gives the same message but with me they get another chance. Boys did not come back from the city gates."

For a while Mother said nothing. Her response was a short prayer.

"Lord, I asked for a home and a dad for the boys. What am I missing?"

I don't know how long we were silent. The wind-up clock's ticking was the only sound. Finally, Dad gave his version of the early morning whipping.

"This morning I called to the boys. They did not get up. I pulled the covers off of Louie. I applied discipline. I hit him six times. The whip left welts but I was careful to not draw blood."

He poured a cup of coffee for Mother before he continued.

"I will find out tomorrow morning if the boys learned their lesson. When they are grown up, they will be grateful."

Grateful? I kept hoping I would awaken from this bad dream.

Mother had tears in her eyes.

"What does the Bible say about giving a warning? Would it be wrong to talk to them first? Maybe, give them a couple of days to catch on before you use the whip."

"Mildred, that is permissiveness. I am serious about obedience. The boys are naturally rebellious. I have to drive that out. They will learn to obey the first time I call."

He opened his Bible again. He pointed at Proverbs 22:15 and handed the Bible to Mother.

"Please, read this out loud."

"Folly is bound up in the heart of a child, but the rod of discipline will drive it far away."

"Remember, this is God's Word."

He turned to the next marked passage, Proverbs 23:13 – 14 (KJV), and waited for her to read. "Withhold not correction from the child: for if thou beatest him with the rod, he shall not die. Thou shalt beat him with the rod, and shalt deliver his soul from hell. Do not withhold discipline from a child; if you punish them with the rod, they will not die."

Mother tried one last time.

"It does not say what the rod is."

"In my house it is a bullwhip."

Mother seemed lost in thought. She served a huge breakfast, all-we-could-eat waffles with Aunt Jemima's maple-flavored syrup. She, also, served orange juice, three eggs over easy, and bacon. The room was cold and quiet like the family cemetery just down the road.

Dad broke the silence with a long prayer. When he finished, Mother reached for Phil's toast and then mine, putting generous amounts of real butter and homemade peach jam on the bread.

That annoyed Dad. It had upset him the day before, too.

"Mildred, those boys do not need two spreads, both butter and jam. It will make them soft."

This was an every-morning drama.

"Oh, I am sorry. I forgot."

Mother loved to play innocent. My brother and I wanted to laugh. Instead, we quickly ate the "loaded" toast. We had to hurry—there were chores to do before the school bus came.

I thought the butter and jam issue was dead. The next morning I buttered my toast and put on a generous helping of newly opened plum jam. Before I could take a bite, Dad spoke.

"Louie, get the whip off the peg."

He hit me a half dozen times. His message was completely clear. Mother didn't have to obey him but I did.

I felt like I was walking in a deep fog. There was no point asking Mother because she was in the fog, too. I thought about praying but I was too confused to know what to ask.

Several days later I overheard Mr. Franklin, the principal, talking to Mr. Ross, one of the teachers.

"I know you think I should paddle Ralph. The coach did that last week and it didn't seem to make any difference."

Mr. Ross hesitated.

"Sir, with respect, do you believe in paddling?"

"Will you report me if I give you an honest answer?"

They obviously had forgotten that I was reading in the back of the room.

"No, I will not report you and yes, I would like an honest answer."

"I am in an awkward position as the principal. The entire community believes in spankings. They see that as part of my job. I'm just not sure it works. Beyond that, I have read all that the Bible has to say on the subject. I don't think the parents have read all the verses."

"Do you have the Scripture references written down?"

Mr. Franklin opened his desk drawer and handed Mr. Ross a sheet of paper. The bell rang for the next class, ending the conversation.

I had to see that paper. Moments later, Mr. Ross returned to my classroom and announced that he would teach us math today. Our teacher had gone home with an upset stomach.

Mr. Ross looked in his briefcase, pulled out the notes about spankings, placed them on his desk, and said he would be right back.

Mr. Franklin's notes were lying on the teacher's desk. I walked to the front of the room and copied the Scripture references. Since I was a new student in the school, no one knew me well enough to ask what I was doing.

As soon as I got home, I finished the evening chores at top speed. Finally, I had a moment to look up Mr. Franklin's scriptures. His notes were the answer to a heartfelt prayer. "God, help me. Please tell me what you think about punishing children."

I wanted to talk to Mother as soon as possible so I made a deal. If she helped me milk the cows the next afternoon, I would clean the house with her on Saturday.

While we milked, Mother asked what I thought about Dad's sermon on discipline.

"Mother, what happened to a God of love?"

"Dad thinks he is loving you."

"No, he just said he wasn't hating us."

She began to cry softly.

"Mother, you are the one crying but I am the one getting the beatings."

"What do you want from me?"

"Find some other verses."

She stopped crying and started laughing.

"Okay, Son, I am sure that's the answer."

I was quiet. I knew her curiosity would make her ask what verses I found. She finished milking Three Spot and turned to me.

"Okay, what are the other verses?"

I pulled a paper out of my overall pocket.

"Hebrews 12:6 says, 'God disciplines us because he loves us.' That's the biggie. But Hebrews 12:9 says, 'We have all had human fathers who disciplined us and we respected them for it.' I do not respect Dad for beating me."

Mother stood up and hung her milk bucket on a peg.

"You said you do not respect Dad. Help me understand, please."

"I have two reasons. He uses the Bible but he leaves out the verses that don't say to beat your kids."

"Okay, I hear you. What verse are you referring to?"

"He didn't mention Ephesians 6:4, 'Fathers, do not irritate and provoke your children to anger [do not exasperate them to resentment], but rear them [tenderly] in the training and discipline and the counsel and admonition of the Lord.' That's from the Amplified Bible."

Mother nodded.

"Did you hear Dad talk about raising us tenderly?"

"No, I didn't."

She sat down on her one-legged milk school and milked Brownie. I knew she was thinking. Then she said, "Okay, you have two reasons. What is your other one?"

"He thinks I am a liar."

"What are you talking about?"

"Do you remember the broken milk thermometer? When I told him I did not break it, he said I was lying and beat me anyway. The bullwhip was in the house. He was in a hurry so he hit me with a stick. When the stick broke, he went outside, cut and trimmed a green branch, and finished the job.

"I told him, 'I know you need to get this out of your system. Feel free to beat me till you feel better.'"

"You egged him on?"

"I had to let him know he cannot get to me. He can hit me but he cannot make me confess to something I did not do." I was so upset my whole body shook. "Mother, he really, really hurt me. But the biggest hurt was calling me a liar."

"Well, he did not break the thermometer and I certainly didn't."

"You have got to be kidding. So you think I lied, too."

"What were we to think?"

"I get it. If you two can't figure it out, Louie did it. You are the one who taught me not to judge others."

This was worse than the beatings.

Mother cried again.

"I am truly sorry. We were wrong to judge you."

I do not know whether she talked to Dad about this but he never apologized. It was like a knife in my heart.

For the next seven days Mother fasted and prayed. It was a water-only fast. I came in the house several times that week and heard her crying and praying. "Lord, do not let Louie be bitter. Quiet his heart. Do not let him miss his purpose in life."

For a while all I heard were deep sobs. Then, muffled words. "Forgive me, Lord, for everything."

I did not want to go without food for a week so I did not talk to her about fasting. The longer she prayed, the harder it was to carry a grudge. The house was calm and everyone was kind for that entire week. I felt betrayed to the deepest part of me, but as she prayed, I let go of the bitterness, especially my deep frustration with her.

When the week ended, she got out the Monopoly board. I knew that was her way of moving on. However, there would be no mercy after the game began. Mother almost always won. She made Monopoly real estate deals that would have made a banker proud.

Mother believed we boys should earn our victories. In time we learned to say "No" to lopsided board game offers. We learned math and probabilities and how to make a good deal and recognize a bad one. She taught us that winning was not as important as learning how to win. We earned our victories but the anticipation of beating her was the reason we played again and again.

I could tell Mother was continuing the apology when she helped us milk the cows without complaining about the barn. She did not like the milk shed with its dirt floors and a million flies. When she did help, she was gentle with the cows. They relaxed and let their milk down. Because of that, she could milk the cows in half the time we could. But she did not like it. She did say, "I do not like this shed but I like you."

Negotiating with Mother to milk the cows became Monopoly in real life. We did not ask her for help very often because her offers were so lopsided. For instance, it took her thirty minutes to milk eight cows. Washing the dishes in the evening took the same amount of time. She would offer to milk once if we did the dishes twice. We had to be desperate to accept her offers. The advantage of making a deal was talk time away from Dad.

Her prayers and her apologies helped but I lived on edge. When would the next beating come?

I did not receive a whipping very often but the whippings were like hailstorms. Every farmer feared hail. They never knew when it would come. Some summers it hailed many times; other years, no hail at all. The fear of the terrible surprise was worse than the actual hailstorm. Dark clouds rolling in from the west were awful even if they contained rain and no hail. Most summers we lived from dark cloud to dark cloud.

Whippings affected me the same way. I never knew when they would come. Dad rarely told us ahead of time what was a whipping offense. Twice I did not properly latch the corral gate. I received a whipping for the first time, not the second.

If Dad stated his rules, they often contradicted what Mother said. For instance, she told us, "It is okay to throw a tennis ball over the roof of the creamery building."

Dad was furious when he saw the ball bounce over the roof. "Those shingles are old and you could break them." He got the bullwhip.

I said, "Mother gave us permission." The response was a truly memorable beating.

Mr. Franklin's verses changed everything. God's idea of discipline was different than Dad's. I stopped crying every morning on the way to the milk shed. At least I wasn't crazy.

Reflections

What is the goal of effective discipline? a) Changed behavior? b) An attitude that pleases God? c) Both? As a dad, I could stop or at least limit some activities. For instance, I did not allow the boys to scroll through the TV channels. They had to look in the *T.V. Guide,* pick one or two programs to watch, circle them, and only watch them. If they violated that house rule, I promised that we would throw the TV out into the backyard. That did affect their TV watching behavior.

What was their attitude? Did they secretly desire to watch programs they shouldn't? When they were home alone, did they scroll through the TV channels and then lie about it? If they had lied and I found out, the consequences would have been more severe. However, I knew that would not change their hearts. I could require a change of behavior but the important goal was a heart change. The evidence of that: doing what was right when no one was looking.

Looking back, I made a discovery about effective discipline for me. I longed for acceptance. If I received it, it completely changed my response. I wanted to obey.

I experienced that acceptance my freshman year in high school at the league track meet. It was sixty miles to Scott City. That was a long trip for me. To be invited to go felt like a huge gift from Coach Nichols. On the way there he announced that he had entered me in the mile run. I would be running with Roger, a Ness City high school senior, who was the league front-runner in the mile run.

I didn't have the slightest clue about how to run this race. When the starting gun fired, Roger and a group of three upperclassmen quickly broke away from the rest of the pack. I ran a comfortable pace and surprised everyone because I stayed with the second group of runners. In fact, I was sixth at three quarters of a mile, running behind my friend Neil Kinlund from Tribune High School. Sixth place was a problem because only five runners scored points. Out of the corner of my eye I saw Coach Nichols running across the infield and towards me.

"Run, Kaupp, run! Pass that kid ahead of you or I will break every bone in your spindly body."

I found a new gear and passed Neil, taking fifth place and gaining one point. Teammate Roger finished a disappointing second. Coach was counting on five points in the mile run—Roger taking the gold medal. Instead, Roger's four for second and my one point gave Ness City, and especially coach, the point total he was counting on for this event. That made him very happy. He suggested that the other seniors carry me off of the field on their shoulders. And, they did. That was acceptance!

Coach could have gotten in trouble for the words he used. Threatening me was also grounds for a reprimand. It never occurred to me to object, let alone file a complaint. He accepted me. I wanted to get that team point for the coach.

My attitude changed about track workouts. My work ethic was different. I no longer objected to wind sprints or extra exercises. In fact, I interpreted his demands on my time as care. He was pushing me to do my best.

The next spring, my sophomore track season, I placed third at the district meet and tied for fifth in the regional finals at Hays.

Dad never saw me run at a meet. When he asked about coming, I said, "No, you don't need to. It will take too much gasoline. Thanks for asking!" When he used the bullwhip on me, I felt deep rejection. His favorite put down, "You will never amount to a hill of beans," had the same effect. I did not want him to see me run and then steal any of my joy.

Kids ask two questions, "Am I loved?" and "Can I have my own way?" The correct answer to the first question is, "Yes, I always love you," and the answer to the second is, "No, you cannot have your own way."

Tell your son or daughter, "If your highest ambition is living life your own way, you are on a dead-end street. God created you to serve and glorify Him":

1 Corinthians 10:31 (AMP), "So then, whether you eat or drink,

or whatever you may do, do all for the honor and glory of God."

Matthew 5:16 (AMP), "Let your light so shine before men that they may see your moral excellence and your praiseworthy, noble, and good deeds and recognize and honor and praise and glorify your Father Who is in heaven."

Every child needs to hear more than "No, you cannot..." Far too often, we answer the second question first. Then, kids think "No" is the answer to the first question, "No, you are not loved."

That was my belief: Dad said "No" many times but he did not say first, "Yes, I love you" or "I'm proud of you" or "I believe in you." His "No" at significant moments confused and terrified me because I hadn't heard his "Yes."

Off and on for years, I struggled with feeling alone or left out. When I was grown up, my counselor friend Dave asked me, "Has God abandoned and rejected you?"

"There have been half a dozen really important times when it seemed like He was not there."

"What does God say about that?"

The phrase, "I will never leave you nor forsake you," went off like a trumpet in my head and heart. Dave and I looked up the scripture references: Deuteronomy 31:6 (NIV), "Be strong and courageous. Do not be afraid or terrified because of them, for the Lord your God goes with you; he will never leave you nor forsake you." Verse 8 repeats the promise. Then, Joshua 1:5 (NIV) adds a phrase, "No one will be able to stand against you all the days of your life. As I was with Moses, so I will be with you; I will never leave you nor forsake you."

The New Testament offers the same heart-warming assurance: Hebrews 13:5 (KJV)," ... be content with such things as ye have: for he hath said, I will never leave thee, nor forsake thee." The same verse in The Message says, "Don't be obsessed with getting more material things. Be relaxed with what you have. Since God assured us, 'I'll never let you down, never walk off and leave you,' we can boldly quote, God is there, ready to help; I'm fearless no matter what. Who or what can get to me?"

The Holy Spirit is a vital part of this lifelong connection. John 14:15-17 (AMP) says:

If you [really] love Me, you will keep (obey) My commands. And I will ask the Father, and He will give you another Comforter (Counselor, Helper, Intercessor, Advocate, Strengthener, and Standby), that He may remain with you forever—The Spirit of Truth, Whom the world cannot receive (welcome, take to its heart), because it does not see Him or know *and* recognize Him. But you know *and* recognize Him, for He lives with you [constantly] and will be in you.

The Holy Spirit living with us constantly—now that's acceptance.

Questions to Consider

1. One of the enemy's favorite strategies is alienation, cutting us off from family. Has that happened at your home? If anything has come between you and your children, answer the first question first, "Yes, you are loved and accepted." Say it until they hear it in their hearts.

2. Memorize at least one of the "never leave you; never forsake you" scriptures.

3. Do you have any evidence today—this week—in the recent past—that God is with you and that you are accepted? In Jeremiah 29:13 (NIV) God says, "You will seek me and find me when you seek me with all your heart."

   • "You will find me" is a "you-can-count-on-it" promise. Verse 14 is double assurance, "I will be found by you."

   • When the boys were very small, we played Hide-'N-Seek in the living room. I would blindfold them and then hide in plain sight. They would stumble around the room with their hands outstretched, trying to find me. When they tired of the game, I gave them clues. Sometimes they found me; other times I helped them, making sure I was found by them.

CHAPTER THIRTEEN

THE FIERY FURNACE

FOR A LONG TIME I had a stomach ache, wanting Dad to love me. After a while, I gave up. During our first four years on the farm, he never said, "I love you" to me and he only hugged Mother. He apparently wasn't going to figure out even beginner stuff when it came to love. I wanted to be more to him than a stubborn animal who had to be tamed.

I talked to God each day. "Is it wrong to want Dad to be my friend? Please give him ideas about stuff we can do together. If it's possible, Lord, show him my good points."

I was fourteen when he said, "I love you," for the first and only time. He and I were at the barn. I was milking the cows. He was pitching hay into the haymow. He stopped, leaned on this pitchfork, and spoke. I had waited four years for those words. It felt really good until he burst into tears. Three words and then he cried hard for a long time. Not one word more. Talk about a roller coaster ride. I could hardly wait to ask Mother for an explanation.

"What was that about?"

She seemed sad. "His father was incredibly demanding. He would return from town late at night, get Fred out of bed, demand that he feed and rub down the four carriage horses all by himself. Then, he would have to completely clean the buggy. If the roads were muddy, it took him most of the night. He could not remember his dad ever thanking him. And he never told him he loved him."

"Then, why did he say it to me?"

She had tears in her eyes.

"I probably made a mistake but I encouraged him to talk to you. To be honest, I pressured him. I thought he needed to say the words and you needed to hear them."

"Mother, that doesn't make any sense. His dad didn't hug him or tell him he loved him. You said that was a major heartache. And yet, for four years he has treated me the same way he was treated. He finally said he loved me and then he fell apart."

I felt sorry for him after that, but I still felt a deep sadness for me. This was a second, major dad failure. Even though I prayed about it, I could not shake the feeling that this was somehow my fault. What had I done that kept this dad from telling me he loved me—except for one time? Four years and I still could not make sense of it. I knew Mother had been desperate to provide a home for us boys but why marry Fred Keller?

After one particularly painful whipping, I asked Mother, "Was there no one else to choose from?"

She sat down, took her glasses off, and ran her fingers through her hair.

"He was the only one who asked."

"Mother, I don't get it. You said coming to the farm was a God idea. This house seems more like a fiery furnace than a home. Are we going to meet the Lord in the middle of it?"

"What do you mean?"

As we ate our ice cream, I told Mother what I learned in Sunday school. The lesson based on Daniel 3 was about the choices three young slaves made.

"King Nebuchadnezzar ordered everyone to worship a golden statue, made in his honor. Three young men from Israel, captured by the Babylonians, would not do it because they served Jehovah. So, the king heated the royal furnace seven times hotter than ever before and threw them in. Then, he looked into the flames and saw a fourth person, walking around with them." I don't know how he figured it out, but he realized it was God in the furnace. The king quickly let them out and promoted them. One of the best parts of the story is in verse 27. When they came out, they didn't smell like smoke."

She took a plate off the table and stared out the window. Then, she took one more dish off the table, slowly rinsed it, and put it in the sink. Finally, she spoke. "Well, I think we were both looking for a man to keep us out of all furnaces."

"Or, to get us out!"

"I agree. That kept us from looking for God in the fire. Actually, I don't think we thought He would be in there." She wasn't done. "I'm amazed. They didn't smell like smoke. After a really hard day, I do not act like I met the Lord in the furnace. I smell more like smoke than fresh cut flowers."

It was my turn to be honest. "Mother, you remind me at least once a week that I am stubborn. When I think of my dads, I resent what they have done. That's a lot of smoke. I wonder if God sees this big, old farmhouse as our furnace? Instead of being thankful God is with us, we have been burnt on the edges."

She ran a comb through her hair.

"Can you think of a time God met us in the furnace?"

"Mother, Phil is alive. Remember?"

He and I were riding on the back of the Dempster drill, pushing the last of the oats to the drop-down openings. Dad said we barely had enough seed to finish planting the field. We had done it so many times, we didn't think about the danger. That day, like every other time, Phil and I were standing on the metal framework of the drill. He stepped forward, his foot slipped, and he fell through the cast-iron frame to the ground. Dad was driving the caterpillar tractor, pulling the drill. It was a miracle that he looked back at the exact moment Phil fell. He slammed on the brakes. I saw what was happening or the sudden stop would have thrown me off. Phil was pinned to the ground. One of the huge, cast iron wheels straddled his leg, pressing against his crotch. If Dad had stopped one second later—the time it took to count one thousand and one—it would have cut him in half. We had a hard time pulling him out but he had no injuries except for scratches. We all wept out loud, knowing how close we came to losing Phil. Dad parked the drill and we never used it again.

"If He met us once in the furnace, will He do it again?" I asked.

We finished the ice cream. Then, Mother prayed.

"Lord, meet Louie and me in the furnace again. You said we don't have to be afraid when we go through the valley of the shadow of death [Psalms 23:4]. We should have known you are here."

My turn! "Lord, I am sorry I have been so stubborn and full of resentment—not exactly the smell of roses. How can I get rid of this smoky smell? Thanks, Lord!"

We both wiped tears from our eyes.

Reflections

I used a variety of approaches to teach high school seniors to write intelligent, well-organized themes. That was how God taught me life lessons. He showed me again and again the error of living by assumptions. Then, I had to learn to live by His timetable, not mine. The story of the three Hebrew youths and the fiery furnace exposed much of my tendency to not trust God. I thought it didn't make sense for Him to meet me in the furnace; instead, *just put out the fire.*

My junior year in high school I went to the first track meet of the season and came in last in the mile run. I felt terrible. The following Monday, Mother took me to the doctor's office. My case puzzled Dr. McLean. He admitted, "I don't know what is wrong with you. My best guess is rheumatic fever. I would like to hospitalize you, run more tests, and keep an eye on you."

On my sixth day in the hospital, the doctor stopped by for his morning checkup.

"I am going to send you home. Your symptoms don't add up to anything I recognize. However, I don't think you are contagious. Go back to school when you're strong enough. One more thing—I don't want you to run track. It could put too much stress on your heart."

That stunned me. The doctor left the room. Mother broke the silence.

"Okay, God. Please meet us in the middle of this furnace."

Mother's prayer kept me from bitterness and despair. As a result, I wasn't mean to Phil or the cattle. I didn't resist Dad just to prove I could. I quit running on the stairs at school—something my Latin teacher Mrs. Linn had reprimanded me for many times.

Mother talked to the Brooks family and they invited us to their home. Beverly played the piano. She, her dad Mr. Brooks, her sister Glenna, and I harmonized. I truly enjoyed God's presence, giving me a sense of calm and the most joy I had felt in a long time. After a while, losing the opportunity to run track didn't seem important. Enjoying God's presence more than made up for it.

Questions to Consider

1. What does it mean, "God is in the furnace"? If you have never sensed that He is present when your life is really difficult, ask Him to help you understand what that means. Then, ask for a real-life example of Him being present. He may give you great calm inside. The kindness of a friend. A slice of apple pie. A longed-for visit. Healing. Provision. The song of a bird. Insight.

2. Why doesn't God put the fire out? Are you more likely to seek Him when you are facing the furnace?

3. Have you heard stories of other people meeting God in the furnace? At least six New Testament books assure us God does not play favorites. In other words, if others can find Him in the middle of very difficult places, He is present for you, too.

CHAPTER FOURTEEN

DID YOU SAY "*WE?*"

I FELT OLD. MY CONVERSATIONS WITH Mother were almost always on an adult level. Even her clowning around led to a serious message. When we played games, she always played to win. She was great help with milking but it had to be done at high speed. Phil could hardly get the next cow in place before she was ready to milk it. When she drove the truck, we loaded ninety bales in record time. She could cut up fifty chickens in a day and we did that for six days straight. When she finished, her hands had too many cuts to count. For the most part life on the farm was serious adult activity carried out quickly with little regard for cuts and bruises. Of course, we had lighthearted moments but they were not often enough. Consequently, I didn't feel like I had a childhood.

I learned to ask adult questions, looking for deeper meaning. For instance, when we were talking about meeting God in the fiery furnace, Mother said, "I think we were both looking for a man to keep us out of all furnaces."

I added, "Or, to get us out!"

We both struggled with guilt. What had we missed?

Mother asked, "Was it my fault? Did I move too quickly? Did I ask God the wrong question? Perhaps I misunderstood Him?" Mother had a favorite question she added to the list.

"Did I make a mistake, bringing us to the farm?"

"Mother, I am not blaming you. I am definitely your son. I thought I caused all this mess. I was going to ask you how I drove one dad away and made the second one so angry."

I hugged her before I responded. "We are in this together."

"There! You said it again—we. I thought you were blaming me for all of this."

"I wanted to but you read all those Bible stories to me. Most of the Bible characters were people like us. They faced worse people than we know. Their hard times were harder. They didn't point the finger at anyone else. They just trusted God and did what needed to be done."

"David faced a giant. His brother Eliab criticized him openly for coming to the battleground. Joseph's brothers sold him as a slave. They were furious because he told his dreams. Jesus was praying in Gethsemane. Judas betrayed Him. And Mildred didn't quit when her husband ran away. She prayed, got a job, and raised her boys."

"Thanks for putting me on your list. I don't think I belong there but thanks. By the way, where did you come up with all of this?"

"In Sunday School, Arlene, our teacher, asked us to make a list of Bible heroes. I added you. I don't think Dad fits on that list. You want me to not blame him or shame him. You are right. I am not his judge. But, that's a different subject. Our list of heroes includes people who understood what was going on and who did what God wanted them to do. I don't think Dad knows when he is wrong, and I don't think he knows how to hear God and make things better."

Mother wanted to make a case for Dad. "Wouldn't you say he was heroic because he survived his Dad's coldness? He, also, cared for a wife dying of tuberculosis and raised their daughters. Then, at sixty years of age he offered a home to a lady and her two sons."

She told me his story one more time. "Fred did not enjoy farming but he came home to run the family farm when his dad asked him to. It was the duty of the oldest son and a matter of honor.

He was the only farmer we knew who had graduated from a business college. He left an accounting job in Kansas City, which he described as a perfect fit, to take over the farm. His wife Emily was very sick for a long time and then, she died of tuberculosis. We were his next big challenge."

"Mother, I know he is a survivor, but he hasn't figured out yet what to do when God sends a woman with two kids. I don't think he is a hero until he sees clearly, hears God, and makes things better."

I knew it was off the subject but I had to say it.

"You know he's glad you married him. I am the one who makes him crazy. Yesterday, he asked me, 'Do you have to run everywhere you go?' I had no idea what to say to him.

"Last week he warned me about Star. I put a halter on the stallion and rode bareback to Uncle Gus's house, a quarter-mile down the lane. I let him run wide open on the way back. When we roared into the corral, he brushed the post, trying to knock me off.

"Star didn't surprise me. In fact, he does that every time we ride through that gate. I lift my leg so his plan doesn't work. For me there is nothing quite like that wide-open run.

"Dad was really mad at me."

"That horse is going to kill you and it will be your fault. Don't complain to me when it happens."

I laughed, picturing the dead me, complaining to Dad.

Before he walked away, he said, "If you don't care, why should I?"

"Mother, I make him crazy."

Mother walked out of the room and came back with a new Bible. She had been reading J. B. Phillip's translation of James 1: 13-16, "A man must not say when he is tempted, 'God is tempting me.'" For God has no dealings with evil, and does not himself tempt anyone. No, a man's temptation is due to the pull of his own inward desires, which can be enormously attractive. His own desire takes hold of him, and that produces sin. And sin in the long run means death—make no mistake about that, brothers of mine!"

"Thanks, Mother. I get it. Dad's sin expresses his own desire. He makes choices because of stuff inside him. That answers my question, too. I have sinned but I am not the reason he does what he does."

This was more than an aha moment. I felt like the doors to the jail just opened. All I had to do was walk out.

"Mother, this takes a huge load off of me. I thought I destroyed one family for sure and maybe now two families. So, I am not to blame. Both dads are responsible for their own sinful choices."

This discovery called for a celebration. We had not eaten all of the peach ice cream, the perfect food for a joyful moment.

I interrupted the party with a playful question.

"Tell me the truth. Did you write that verse and add it to your Bible?"

"Nope, it has been there our whole lives. I never saw it or understood it until today."

"I am glad it didn't take us that long to discover peach ice cream."

Reflections

For much of my life I thought, "If I don't understand what God's plan is, He must not have one."

In our Sunday school class we studied about Philip, the evangelist (Acts 8:26-40, NCV). The Lord told him: " ... go south to the road that leads down to Gaza from Jerusalem—the desert road." *Most of the time that road was empty. So, what was he doing there?* "On the road he saw a man from Ethiopia, a eunuch. He was an important officer in the service of Candace, the queen of the Ethiopians; he was responsible for taking care of all her money. He had gone to Jerusalem to worship. Now, as he was on his way home, he was sitting in his chariot reading from the Book of Isaiah, the prophet ... Philip, starting with the same Scripture, told the man the Good News about Jesus."

The man responded very warmly. They passed by a watering hole and at the man's request, Philip baptized him. "When they came up out of the water, the Spirit of the Lord took Philip away; the officer never saw him again. And the officer continued on his way home, full of joy."

For me, this was a puzzling example of God having a plan and Philip doing what the Holy Spirit told him to do even though he did not have a clue about what the plan was.

I asked the Sunday school teacher, "How did he know what he heard was the Lord speaking. What if it was just imagination or even indigestion?"

He stared at me for a full minute.

"This is God's Word. You should receive it by faith and not question it."

That response made me wonder whether it was the Holy Spirit's idea for Brother Merle to teach this class.

When I got home, Mother answered my question.

"You have to learn what the Lord's voice sounds like."

"Let's say the Lord speaks and I hear it. Can you imagine Him saying, 'Go to the most deserted road near Ness City? On Sunday morning start walking.' I probably wouldn't do it because it doesn't make sense to me. I think if I asked you to take me there and dump me off, you would say 'No.'"

Mother nodded, "You are probably right. I would not take you."

"How about my other question? Did God say Brother Merle was the right person to teach our Sunday school class?"

"I think he did it because Brother Frank promised to give him deer sausage when he returned from his hunting trip."

"Wow! So I am supposed to learn how to hear God and follow His plan from a guy who is there to get sausage?"

We both groaned.

"I know who knows how to hear God. I will ask George Cook. He is always telling stories about God talking to him." I realized that I was more likely to learn how to hear God and carry out what I thought He said if someone who heard Him well taught me.

How much would I have learned if I had asked George Cook? Before I had a chance to find out, the hospital admitted him and he stayed a long time. After that, he was very weak and he didn't recover. Mother and Dad didn't want me to bother him. I was sad but I understood.

Years later the Lord sent men who heard Him well. Dr. Ward Williams said, "James 3:17 tells us what wisdom that comes down from Heaven sounds like. That wisdom is pure. It isn't hiding anything or trying to deceive anyone. It is peace-loving and gentle at all times. It is considerate and willing to yield, full of mercy and produces good fruit. It doesn't show favoritism. It doesn't take sides. It's not hypocritical."

He said, "I use that as my guideline. When I think I have heard the Lord, I act. If what I say or do produces bad fruit, I go back to God and ask Him to repeat what He said. Over time, I have learned more and more about the sound of His voice."

"What do you do when what you hear does not make sense?" I asked.

"I trust His voice more than I trust my understanding."

Some people imagine they have heard God's voice but it is an illusion. They try to hear something spectacular so they can call attention to themselves or get great personal benefit. What they say

God says denies His nature and contradicts James 3: 17.

Now that I am older, I have years of experience hearing God and obeying. I have learned that:

a. I have to hear God if I want to please Him. That compels me to

b. listen well. When I am not clear about what I'm hearing,

c. I seek counsel from people whose lives produce good fruit.

d. I ask them whether Scripture confirms what I think I am hearing.

e. I invite the Holy Spirit to come. I need the accompanying peace of Christ to affirm what I've heard?

f. To hear God I must "believe that He is"—that He is really God and He really does speak. Then,

g. I have to "earnestly seek Him" and "keep on looking for Him."

Hebrews 11:6 (NIV), "And without faith it is impossible to please God, because anyone who comes to him must believe that he exists and that he rewards those who earnestly seek him." Verse 6 (NLV) says, "A man cannot please God unless he has faith. Anyone who comes to God must believe that He is. That one must also know that God gives what is promised to the one who keeps on looking for Him."

Questions to Consider

1.   How do you hear God speak?

- Thoughts (rarely out loud) that are completely consistent with Scripture.

- Changes in circumstances (e.g., getting or losing a job, an increase or decrease in income, illness or death, a car accident—or a near miss) may offer clues about God's direction, but the inferences drawn from these events must line up with God's Word.

- Godly counsel from a trusted leader. Ideally, you would already have a Spirit-led connection.

- By having or not having internal peace.

2. Do you earnestly seek Him and keep on listening until you encounter Him—or whomever He sends?

3. Do you respond in faith and obedience? In other words, when you hear Him (and after the message is confirmed), do you act on what you have heard?

CHAPTER FIFTEEN

THE WORD GAME

D AD DIDN'T TRUST ME WITH the farm machinery. His dad didn't trust him either. If they had looked beyond their sons' mistakes, I might be a farmer.

Dad told Mother his story. He was helping his dad fix the tractor and somehow he broke a gear in the engine. His dad called him "stupid" and yelled at him over and over again. "Why weren't you more careful?" Then, he beat him with a willow branch.

My stepdad accepted his father's judgment. Then, he passed it on. I, too, was dangerous in the farm repair shed. It was easier for him to fix his own tractor, skills his uncle taught him, than to have me break something.

On rainy days he sent me to the house. Dad used that time to repair equipment. I wasn't sad. I knew Mother would think of something fun to do. There was one problem. It didn't rain very much in western Kansas. The geography teacher said the annual rainfall was about 22 inches, compared to the national average of 36.5 inches. On those rare and surprising days when it did rain, I was very happy.

At lunchtime Dad would complain about "wasting time." Mother would suggest he teach me to fix the tractor engine. Dad would stop talking and stomp out of the kitchen. It was so predictable, I could quote their lines in the rainy day one-act play.

Let the games begin! We didn't have electricity or hot running water but we could make ice cream and play the *word game*. First things first! I got out the two-and-a-half gallon ice cream freezer, brought out the rock salt, and took all of the ice out of the milk shed refrigerator. Mother cut up fresh peaches, the few she had not canned. She added the milk and other stuff—just the right amounts, stirred it together, and poured it into the silver canister. Then, we cranked and cranked the homemade ice cream handle. Finally, Mother said it was ready—all the ice cream we could eat. Mother rang and rang a big bell until Dad stopped the repairs and joined us. During that time there was no complaining and no sermons about how to study the ant. "See how hard he works and try to copy that."

Eating the ice cream was as far as Dad would bend. He would not play the word game. If Mother invited him to play, we could count on that sermon about the hard-working ant or the foolish virgins who came to a wedding feast with no oil in their lamp or several verses from Proverbs, warning us about laziness.

Dad took a short siesta before he returned to the machine shed.

Mother created The Word Game because she was sure I would be a pastor. She was determined to improve my vocabulary.

She and I warmed up by comparing pronunciations. She would ask, "Which is correct? *nuke-clee-er* or *nuke-yuh-lure*?"

"In Kansas we say *nuke-yuh-lure*. That's incorrect."

Mother gave me credit.

"Next word. Which is right, according to the dictionary? *kumpf-ter-uh-bull* or *come-fort-uh-bull*?" Mother's breakdown of the word was unlike the dictionary's but I understood the question. I had struggled with this word.

In Ness County the pronunciation was the first one, *kumpf-ter-uh-bull*, which the dictionary did not approve. There was another correct pronunciation, *kumpf-tah-bull*, which I had never heard. I got points both times because I knew which was correct and I could pronounce the words correctly.

Then, we switched to the more challenging part of the game. Mother would name a person and I would choose an adjective that best suited him or her.

"Fred, your stepdad."

"*Plodding*. He is the slowest person on the planet. Two days ago he told me, 'Slow down. If you aren't careful, you will finish all our to-do list today and there won't be anything to do tomorrow.'"

I should not have responded disrespectfully, but I ignored the still, small voice. "Dad, that is how the Stums [our neighbors] make it to the state fair. They get their work done so they can have the day off."

"Go live with them! Just don't come back, crying to me about what you don't like on the other side of the road."

Mother interrupted my story. "Your word describing Dad was only two syllables. I will give you half credit because you can do better than that."

"Okay! Dad? I will use the word *unmovable*. Four syllables. Yesterday, Phil and Toby [our English Sheperd] and I were running in circles around Dad while he walked to the hay barn. He hollered, 'I am not moving until you calm down.' Get it? Not moving. *Unmovable*."

"Yes, I understand *unmovable*. I don't know why that is funny."

"I guess you had to be there. Do I get full credit?"

"Hmmm. Full credit for *unmovable*?"

Mother hesitated. If I fooled her, I received triple credit.

"Now I get it. The laughter was a smoke screen. Are you sure that *unmovable* is a word?"

"I thought I pulled it off. No, it isn't. The correct word is *immovable*."

"Nice try, smart guy. You almost tricked me."

Mother named another name. "Mrs. Linn, your English and Latin teacher."

"Thanks, one of my favorites. *Calcified*. No, wait. Only three syllables. I have it. *Intransigent*."

"I challenge you. I don't think you know what that word means."

If she won the challenge, I received no points. I had an answer. "Here comes double points. 'Intransigent. Uncompromising. Bullheaded. Will not change her mind.' Mother, when I heard the forecast, I thought we might play today and I looked up new words. I am so R-E-A-D-Y."

"Okay, one more name. Your Mother."

"*Ethereal*"

"Come on; be serious."

"Okay. *Unstoppable.* When you make up your mind, no obstacle will keep you from the finish line. Best example? Dad and I butchered fifty chickens and took their feathers off. In one day you cut all of those birds into sixteen pieces and prepared them for the freezer in town."

I walked around the room, pretending to preach.

"Brothers and Sisters, she had cuts on almost every finger. Her back ached and her head throbbed but did she falter? I tell you she did not. Not until every chicken was in its refrigerated resting place. Then and only then did this model of persistence rest her weary bones. I tell you, she's unstoppable."

Mother laughed till she cried.

"Okay, okay, double credit. But we have to have the final round. This time you have to use the adjective the Lord would use for each person I name. Start with Dad."

"*Traumatized.* He treats me the way he does because his heart is not healed. I should have compassion, not resentment."

"Mrs. Linn?"

"What word would the Lord use? *Reliable* is the best I can do. Small towns have trouble getting teachers. She has been here every year for twenty-seven years."

"Me?"

"Same as before. *Unstoppable.* That is the word God uses to describe you."

Mother had tears in her eyes and a smile in her heart.

"I'm adding one name."

"Changing the rules, huh?"

"Yes, I am. The last name is Louie—you."

I asked for a five-minute recess. She gave me two.

"I'm ready. Three adjectives for me, not one. *Intransigent.* I admit I'm bullheaded. *Traumatized.* After two dads I have earned that word. *Unstoppable.* I finish what I start even if it gets me in trouble."

"Very clever. So, you know you are not better than anyone else.

You see your weaknesses in others but you know you have strengths, too. Good work! You are the winner. And, thanks for my word!"

Who needed electricity and hot running water on a rainy day? We had ice cream and The Word Game.

Reflections

Mother was convinced that I would be a pastor. She knew that her dad Clayton and my dad Clay both turned their backs on the call of God. She thought it was my mission to pick up the baton they had dropped.

She focused on Proverbs 22:6 (AMP), "Train up a child in the way he should go [and in keeping with his individual gift or bent], and when he is old he will not depart from it."

She believed speaking in public was one of my gifts. She had no doubt she was right, but to test her theory, she helped me preach once a week for two years at our church's youth group.

I entered Bible contests such as "Facts from Acts," which used a spelling bee format. Each contestant would approach the microphone, hear a question, and answer the fact-based question within sixty seconds. It accomplished two purposes: more public speaking practice and I learned much about the book of Acts.

The Word Game was her most creative application of Proverbs 22:6. It helped me expand my vocabulary while I was developing skill with the English language. Mother would not have objected to Dad teaching me to repair farm equipment. However, she did not think God planned for me to be a farmer. Words, not wrenches, were to be my tools.

Questions to Consider

1. Proverbs 22:6 (AMP) "Train up a child in the way he should go [and in keeping with his individual gift or bent], and when he is old he will not depart from it." Proverbs 22:6 has three parts:

    • Training: repeated instruction until the skill or insight is acquired

    • Direction: "the way he should go." = "in keeping with his individual gift or bent"

    • Long-term benefit: "he will not depart from it"

2.   Can parents with no training in these areas help their children?

- They can become life learners: classes, books, bookstores, and websites offer instruction about individual gifting and finding God's direction.

- Ask whether there are parents in your church who are living out Proverbs 22:6.

3.   What can you do?

- Ask your children questions. What are their interests? What tasks or jobs would they like to explore?

- Go to the bookstore. What topics interest them? Can you find books that explore those topics?

- Provide opportunities for them to shadow trustworthy adults in various professions.

CHAPTER SIXTEEN

THE RACCOON'S DIET

W HEN WE MOVED TO THE farm, Mother parked her dark blue 1939 Ford coupe under the black walnut trees near the house. Dad couldn't figure out how to get the Ford in reverse, so it sat there for years, surrounded by five acres of trees.

We boys didn't care. Our parents never locked the car so we explored every inch. We practiced driving—propping ourselves up on the front seat, making engine sounds, and working the gearshift lever.

One day we were weary of the '39 Ford. Eager for a new adventure, we discovered field mice in the now empty, thousand-bushel grain bins. Dad was plowing in the field four miles from our house. He would have objected to this waste of time but on this wonderful day, he was far, far away!

I had an inspiration.

"Phil, I know how we can catch the mice. Bang on the back of the first bin. I'll hold a jar at the opening in front."

I wedged the gallon jar in front of the metal chute. That's where the grain came out when the bin was full. This was better than pretending to drive Mother's Ford. Phil hammered on the thin metal wall and the mice ran into the jar. There were three grain bins. After each catch we unloaded the jar into a fifty-gallon barrel.

"I can't believe it! We caught sixteen."

Phil was totally impressed. He had a great idea. "Let's figure out what they eat."

The sixteen terrified mice didn't eat anything we placed in the barrel. However, their squeaking was great fun. When Mother called us into the house for supper, we tipped the barrel upside down. The mice ran into our three-foot-high cardboard box, which we squeezed into the front seat of the '39 Ford coupe.

Five-year-old Phil jumped up and down.

"Can we catch more tomorrow?"

I was the eleven-year-old expert.

"Sure, there will be more in the bins by morning."

We slept and we assumed our sixteen field mice were dreaming mice dreams in the Ford. We checked on them the next morning after we finished breakfast. To our absolute horror they had chewed their way through the bottom of the cardboard box and gnawed a gaping hole in the front seat of the Ford. They escaped through a small hole beside the brake pedal.

"Oh, No! No! No! No! We can't let Dad see this. He will kill us for sure!"

At top speed we cleaned up the cardboard, the upholstery, and the seat stuffing. We, then, awaited a certain death.

Two days later with us close behind, Dad decided to try that reverse shifter again. He opened the door and jumped back.

"What on earth!"

He stared in utter disbelief at the huge hole in the seat.

"That had to be the work of a really big raccoon. Why would a raccoon eat through the front seat?" He took off his cap and scratched his head. "How on earth did the coon get in the car in the first place?"

We knew not to lie but we didn't offer any unasked-for information either. It was a miracle he never did figure it out.

That night we had trouble going to sleep. I kept asking Phil, "How could I have known those mice would eat a hole in the seat? I am an idiot! When Dad figures it out, I am going to be a dead idiot."

Phil nodded and trembled. Tears ran down his face. He feared for his life, too. Hopefully, Dad wouldn't discover that raccoons don't eat car seats. And, he never did.

The field mice on the farm rejoiced, also.

Until that Ford sold at our farm liquidation sale, I regretted never telling the truth about the mice and the hole in the front seat. Fear said, "It was a foolish mistake but you don't want another beating." Integrity said, "It would remove a load from your shoulders if you confessed."

For a while I prayed, "Lord, have Mother or Dad ask me one more time."

They didn't ask. Fear won this round.

Reflections

I can't believe the number of clueless things I did as a kid. On second thought, that cluelessness continued into my late teens. How should I feel about that?

Are there any examples of cluelessness in the Bible? Oh my, there are so many stories.

Consider John 18: 10-11 (NIV). When the crowd led by Judas came to assault Jesus, " ... Simon Peter, who had a sword, drew it and struck the high priest's servant, cutting off his right ear ..."

Jesus' answer is a classic understatement to a clueless disciple. "Put your sword away! Shall I not drink the cup the Father has given me?" That sounds like, "What are you doing? Did you hear anything I said about my purpose?" Jesus picks up the ear Peter cut off and calmly puts it back on. Yes, the extreme tension set Peter off. But, he had been with Jesus for three years. Had Peter been watching how Jesus responded?

Another nominee for "Most Clueless" would be the mother of James and John.

She "... came with her two sons and knelt before Jesus with a request. 'What do you want?' Jesus asked. She said, 'Give your word that these two sons of mine will be awarded the highest places of honor in your kingdom, one at your right hand, one at your left hand'" (Matthew 20:20-28, MSG).

The other disciples had to be saying, "You had your mother ask about a promotion? How old are you guys? Eight? Ten?" Surely someone added, "A promotion? What makes you two so special?" There had to have been a collective growl, "Clueless!"

Does Jesus' answer to the mother of James and John sound like, "You don't have a clue"?

Jesus responded, "You have no idea what you're asking." And he said to James and John, "Are you capable of drinking the cup that I'm about to drink?"

They said, "Sure, why not?" That answer was not only clueless but casual.

When the ten others heard about this, they lost their tempers, thoroughly disgusted with the two brothers.

This story encourages me. These men are the twelve handpicked disciples. By comparison, my cluelessness is not unique or remarkable.

In Genesis 3 [NIV] we read about the serpent, who was "more crafty than any of the wild animals the Lord God had made." He implied that God had cheated them, "Did God really say, 'You must not eat from any tree in the Garden'"?

She should have said, "Whoa, God is our creator and friend. I am not having this talk with you." How could she allow any living creature to discredit God, who made them and fellowshipped with them each day?

"When the woman saw that the fruit of the tree was good for food and pleasing to the eye, and also desirable for gaining wisdom, she took some and ate it. She also gave some to her husband, who was with her, and he ate it."

Adam joined her in the tragically clueless snack. [I label it clueless because neither of them took a moment to consider what God had really said. No thoughtful dialogue. No prayer. She did not fulfill her role as a helpmate. He did not lead. And they ignored what they knew about the snake's nature.]

When God appeared later in the day, He asked a simple question.

" ... Who told you that you were naked? Have you eaten from the tree that I commanded you not to eat from?"

What made these two mortals think they could hide the truth from God?

"The man said, 'The woman you put here with me—she gave me some fruit from the tree, and I ate it.' Then the Lord God said to the woman, 'What is this you have done?' ' The woman said, 'The serpent deceived me, and I ate.'"

The ultimate clueless response! *Blame it on someone else.*

Rereading the story of the Garden, I see the tragedy and the ordinariness of it. I, too, have been deceived. I, like Eve, have invited others to join me eating the apple. More than once, I have tried to conceal it from the Lord.

Shame will not help me (and us) but humility and genuine repentance will.

Questions to Consider

1. Cluelessness is not unusual. How should we think about it? What would be an appropriate response when our unthinking words or actions are revealed?

2. By the time our third son was born, I realized that many things he did were disobedient but very funny. I said more than once, "Sit quietly on that chair. I am going to enjoy a good laugh and then give you your consequences." Why was or wasn't that appropriate?

3. After a clueless or hurtful act or comment by your children, would it be appropriate to train for awareness (do they grasp how they affect others?) and appropriate responses (how should they respond to others?)

   Suggested topics:

   - Take a close look at triggers or catalysts. Did the serpent say, "It's just one apple" or "You can blame Adam if this turns out badly" or "God's rules are unfair"?

   - How can they slow down? How can they deal with impulsive behavior?

   - Examine alternatives. What else could they have done? What were the other choices?

   - Whose help do you, as the adult, need to learn and grow? Despite the difficult circumstances and relationships, has God sent a safe person—one who will mentor you?

CHAPTER SEVENTEEN

BORN SHORT

C HRISTMAS CAME FOUR MONTHS EARLY my eighth grade year. On the first day of school the coaches weighed each boy in the physical education classes. Then, Coach Nichols explained.

"Okay, all you gym rats, we have enough guys for a midget basketball team. Any middle school boy can play if he is ninety-nine pounds or less just before each game. If he is over by one tenth of a pound at the weigh in, he will not play that Saturday.

I hollered at the coach, "Thanks, Santa!"

He laughed and motioned us out of the locker room.

That year eight middle schools in western Kansas added midget basketball teams for boys ninety-nine pounds and under. I was right at the limit. In fact, I had to weigh in before each game. Twice, I had to pee repeatedly until the scales said "99.0 pounds"!

Finally, a place for people my size. I was born short. But this day on this team only Roger and Charlie were taller. The thought of being third tallest brought tears to my eyes.

Height was only the first hurdle. Would Dad and Mother ever agree to let me play? Beyond that, I would need a ride to town each Saturday. I had to start with permission. I worried about their "No" for the rest of the day.

I milked the eight cows, ran the milk through the cream

separator, gathered the eggs from the hen house, double checked the gates for the horses, and fed Toby, our cattle dog. I had to make sure everything was done well so they wouldn't have an excuse to turn me down. My stomach ached.

When shall I bring it up? How can I convince them I will die right on the spot if they say, "No"?

I ate slowly, praying for some sign from God about the right time to ask.

After supper Mother gave me an unexpected pep talk.

"Have you ever read the story in the Bible about Zacchaeus, the guy who wanted to see Jesus but couldn't? He was short so he climbed a sycamore tree. He saw Jesus and Jesus saw him. In fact, Jesus went to Zac's house for dinner."

Mother had a light-up-the-room smile. "It changed his life." She paused. "So, Louie, where is your sycamore tree?"

I took a deep breath.

"Have you ever heard of a basketball tree?"

I told her about the newly formed midget basketball team. I said weighing ninety-nine pounds, right at but not over the maximum, seemed like a sign to me. I concluded, "I think it would change my life, too."

That comment pressed some button. Dad and Mother both laughed for a long time. Mother finally replied.

"Well, we can't miss a chance for your life to change. Dad, what do you think? Can I take him to the games on Saturday and do my grocery shopping while he plays?"

Dad turned his palms up and gave her an it's-not-worth-an-argument look.

I was light-headed. "Yes" had never been this easy.

Our team won four and lost four. I hit a shot from half court to win one game eight to six. Meanwhile, the junior-high varsity boys had zero wins and ten losses. Short was the new "tall." For the entire basketball season I didn't complain about acne, my next major concern.

I was a short guard on the midget basketball team until I had a growth spurt the summer before the ninth grade. I added four inches and thirty-five pounds. I was full of hope. Would this miracle of having a place and being seen continue?

My hope didn't last long. Coach Matta did not include me on the varsity squad. That wasn't really a surprise but I wasn't on the "B" team or the ninth grade basketball roster either.

The school bus ride home, normally fifteen minutes, seemed to last forever. When I entered the back door, Mother could tell something was wrong.

"Why the sad face?"

"I didn't make either basketball team. I thought being taller would make a difference."

Tears ran down my face.

"There's more. Cathy and Ann ignored me all day unless I pestered them. Then, in study hall the librarian told me seventh graders were not allowed in the library during fourth hour. I am in ninth grade. I am like that raccoon we caught in a bear trap. He couldn't get away no matter what he did."

"Whoa, what do the girls, the librarian, and the raccoon have to do with each other?"

"I am all the way back to step number one. No matter how much I grow, I am still short. There's nothing I can do about it."

"Wait a minute. You are four inches taller than you were last year. So, the problem isn't how tall you are."

That got my attention.

"Why does this bother me so much?"

"It sounds like you give everyone permission to make you feel short."

"What choice do I have?"

"You can't make everyone see you the way you want to be seen. You do not have enough inches to do that, but you are tall enough to fulfill God's purpose in your life."

"You don't know how it feels to be me."

A pot on the stove was boiling over. Mother had to take care of it. I had to work in the garden. The conversation had to wait.

I do not know how long she looked but Mother found a story just for me. She told me the story author Ron Mehl wrote in *Surprise*

Endings about playing golf with three of his friends during the hottest part of the summer. At last, they reached the final hole. When they saw the clubhouse, all they could think of was an ice-cold drink. Then, Ron saw a small boy selling Kool-Aid. He had four cups of warm cherry left. All of the ice had melted. He had a tear in each eye but also a look that said, "I am not quitting until I sell the last cup."

The author knelt down, eye to eye, beside the Kool-Aid stand and the short salesman. Instead of buying one cup for a dollar, he gave the boy five dollars and took all four cups of warm Kool-Aid.

The story didn't help me. I knew Mother thought God would send someone to get on my level and take the warm cherry Kool-Aid. I was still skeptical. Obviously, my size didn't bother her but mothers are supposed to love you, no matter what.

Dad and I found one solution for the problem of height. As soon as I could see over the steering wheel, Dad put a big cushion on the front seat of the truck and taught me how to drive. To shift gears, I slid off the cushion and stood on the clutch pedal. I slowed down the same way, grabbing the top of the steering wheel, pulling myself into a standing position, and stepping on the brake pedal. The old '39 Chevy truck had a throttle which I could pull out or push in instead of pressing the accelerator. Eleven years old and driving a truck! I might have been short but when I drove all by myself, I was "king of the mountain."

I was king until I told Dad how I felt about driving the truck. His response stomped out my joy.

"Don't say stupid stuff. You really aren't tall enough to drive but I can't afford to hire anyone else. Keep your mind on the road."

Why did I tell him? I must be stupid as well as short.

I complained to God, "Mother says I can fulfill your purpose. I don't get it! I can't make the basketball team and Dad doesn't really want me to drive the truck. I thought moving the truck from one field to another was important. What about driving it into place when the combine bin is full? Who else will climb into the truck bed to smooth out the grain? Nope, I am only here because Dad cannot afford to hire a real worker."

God was at work but I couldn't see it so I didn't believe it.

Wheat harvest was almost always in late June. Our whole family worked long hours for two weeks, cutting the wheat. No one could leave until the last truckload of wheat was weighed and then emptied at the Farmer's Co-op.

Dad farmed eight hundred acres. He called it "five quarters of farm ground." Gravel roads maintained by the county connected all but one of the quarters. For access to the northwest wheat field, we used a two-wheel path that followed the fence line. The combine was slow and the truck was old. It was a long, time-consuming process to move from one field to another. I was Dad's only helper. If we had to drive on the county roads, we left early in the morning or just before sunset to avoid the sheriff on patrol since I wasn't old enough to have a driver's license. All of our neighbors' boys drove trucks, too, before they had licenses. And everybody did it before they were adult size. It was dangerous and illegal. At our house we never talked about that.

John, my seatmate on the school bus, had four acres of his own. His dad gave them to him because he helped out in the harvest. He told me he was saving up to buy a car. Carlin's dad bought a motor scooter for him the day harvest ended. Everybody who rode the school bus knew how each dad on the bus route rewarded their son or sons for working at harvest time. I was the only one who received nothing.

I knew Dad couldn't cut the wheat without me. It made me sick in my stomach that he didn't know I was important. I just said, "I'm short."

I could drive the truck but I couldn't control the weather. Hailstorms were a common occurrence in mid-summer. As soon as the grain was ripe, we hurried to cut it, hoping we would beat the next storm. Rain was not damaging to the crop unless it soaked the wheat straw and it fell over. After each thunderstorm the straw and the ground had to dry out before we continued harvesting. If the wheat stalks fell down, we put a special attachment on the front of the wheat combine. Long wires slid under the straw, lifted it up, and the combine sorted out the grain. The yield was never the same for wheat that had been flat on the ground.

Each day Dad would pop open several heads of grain and bite into the kernels of wheat. When they were hard and dry, we began harvesting.

The sale of the wheat provided the majority of our income for the year. When the wheat crop failed, we lived well below the poverty level. Mother said we were not poor; we were just broke.

The worst thing a farm kid could say was, "I do not care what happens with the harvest. I want to go to summer camp for one week." I didn't just say it; I prayed it.

Finally, we had a wet summer. Every few days the rain fell. The wheat was beyond ripe and the wheat straw was lying flat on the ground.

Before I entered the kitchen, I heard Dad and Mother talking.

"Fred, I think we should let Louie go to camp this summer."

"Mildred, it is harvest time. There is work to do."

"How long will it take for the wheat to be ready to cut?"

"It could be dry within one week but the county agricultural agent is predicting at least two weeks and only then if there is no more rain."

"How soon will the ground be dry enough for you to drive on it?"

"Everything depends on when the sun shines."

Dad was not budging so Mother changed her tactics.

"What if Louie learns more about obedience and respect at camp?"

Okay, you have a point. But if you spoil him, he will not amount to a hill of beans."

Finally, after twenty minutes of back and forth, Dad relented. I was going to camp.

Mother drove the Buick station wagon to the campground east of Wichita. We arrived two hours early and I was the first one to check in. I located my cabin. There was my dream-come-true top bunk. I claimed it. I was still a little guy but there was a ladder at the end of the bunk bed. From my mountaintop landing station I immediately imagined all kinds of exciting adventures. Pity the poor kids who had to sleep on the bottom bunks.

In the middle of the first night I had a major problem. I needed to go to the bathroom.

How am I going to get off this top bunk without waking everyone? They will be really mad. I hope they don't send me back home for making too much noise.

I leaped off the top bunk and hit the floor with a loud thump. I froze in place. My heart was beating forty million beats a minute. No one stirred.

They didn't hear me.

The boys' restrooms were four buildings away and all the building lights on the campground were turned off. No problem! One of my farm chores was to close the chicken houses every night after dark. Moonlight was enough.

It never occurred to me to put on my jeans. *Nobody can see me.* I slipped out the back door in my underwear, raced from building to building, did my business, and sneaked back to my cabin.

That grass is really cold and wet. I should have put on my shoes. Thank you, God, no one saw me. I thanked God too soon. To my horror, the dorm monitor, the really big guy named Bob, heard me vault off of the top bunk. He watched in sheer disbelief as I slipped out the back door, wearing only my white jockeys. When I returned, he was waiting. For one moment he towered over me. Then he sat down on his bunk and motioned for me to sit beside him. He wasn't scary big when we were sitting there side by side.

"The next time you have to go to the bathroom at night, put on your long pants."

I nodded.

He didn't hit me or yell at me. He smiled and lifted me onto my upper bunk. He was on my level, as tall as the top bunk. Finally, God had sent someone who knew how short people feel.

I felt tall when Dad taught me to drive until he told me I was not his first choice. Boxer Bob's kindness touched my heart. I got my height back. I never forgot his response to my naïve moment. After he became a missionary to Russia, my wife and I sent him a monthly contribution for thirty-five years.

Reflections

The enemy constantly tries to diminish who we are. "You finished the job this time but you'll never be able to do it twice."

If that doesn't work, he exaggerates what we don't have and can't do. "You are too short" or "You are very old." He knows when we lack training and experience: "You have never used an electric drill and you are not good with tools. Sounds like another chance to fail."

If we listen to his lies, we are no longer clear about our identity, who God says we are and what we are capable of.

For most of my life I didn't know how to handle criticism or compliments. After preaching each Sunday, I was available to pray for people or receive their comments. Because I still struggled with rejection, I was vulnerable to what they said.

I stepped off the platform one Sunday and a lady was waiting for me. "I heard what you said and I do not agree."

I heard the Lord communicating to me through my thoughts. *Be careful.*

"Carrie, I am responsible for what comes out of my mouth. Unfortunately, I don't remember saying what you heard. Would you mind if we prayed right now, asking the Lord to forgive me and to give you a sense of peace?"

"Lord, I bring Carrie's concern to you. Please forgive me for anything I said this morning that misrepresented you."

She thanked me very warmly and returned to her family.

On my right Tom was waiting for me. "Pastor, that was the most amazing sermon I have ever heard."

Again, the Lord warned me. *Be careful.*

I chuckled at the sheer irony of the totally opposite assessments of my sermon. The man sensed my hesitancy.

"Please, look where I was sitting. I brought fourteen people today and they were all touched deeply." To my amazement they were embracing each other, praying, laughing, and weeping—having some kind of major reconnection.

Bob Mumford preached a sermon entitled "How to Handle God's

Glory." He said compliments are trophies. God deserves the credit for anything we accomplish. Because He loves us, He loans His trophies to us for the day. We should return them to Him by day's end.

I thanked Tom for his kind remarks. When he walked away, I thanked the Lord. "Lord, I know that trophy belongs to You. I will carry it joyfully the rest of the day and then return it to You. I do have a question, Lord. What was that all about—Carrie's frustration about the sermon, and then, Tom's delight?"

You are not as bad as she said and you are not as good as he said. However, you pleased Me today because you preached exactly what I told you to say. Have lunch and enjoy the rest of your day.

I was lighthearted all afternoon, knowing His evaluation of me was all that mattered.

Questions to Consider

1. Has anyone given you a compliment lately that was too grand to believe? Has anyone criticized you, pointing out what, in his or her opinion, you lack? Do you accept the opinions of others as a valid measuring stick? Do you use God's word(s) to evaluate their comments? Romans 12:3 (NLT) says, "Because of the privilege and authority God has given me, I give each of you this warning: Don't think you are better than you really are. Be honest in your evaluation of yourselves, measuring yourselves by the faith God has given us."

   - Measure by the standard of your God-given faith. In other words, evaluate what you have done or said according to the word(s) God has given you, not by someone else's opinion. Simply put, did you do or say what He told you to?

2. A two-part standard of measurement:
   - Did I do (or say) what He said?
   - Did I do it (or say it) for "the glory of God"?

3. Do you teach your children to rely on God's evaluation of what they do and say? Colossians 1:10 (AMP), "That you may walk (live and conduct yourselves) in a manner worthy of the Lord, fully pleasing to Him and desiring to please Him in all things, bearing fruit in every good work and steadily growing and increasing in and by the knowledge of God [with fuller, deeper, and clearer insight, acquaintance, and recognition]."

    - What have they done recently that pleased God? Did you point it out?
    - What is the fruit produced by their service to others?
    - Has their knowledge of God increased?

CHAPTER EIGHTEEN

THE DAD WHO GOT AWAY

SINCE I WAS "ZERO FOR two" with dads, I watched the men in the church intently. We attended a small church in Ness City, a farming community eight miles from the farm. The list of single men was short. One elderly farmer stood out. His old, out-of-style suit coat and his comfortable, dark green corduroy shirt were not impressive. He was solid, built like an oak tree, but most of the other farmers had the same durable and weathered look. What he said always sounded so simple. Nevertheless, he stood out.

One of the church's Sunday morning traditions was testimony time. White-haired Sister Paulette, wearing her sky-blue, every-Sunday dress, always stood first. She waved a lacey white hanky. "I just praise His holy name." That was all. With a very satisfied smile on her face she would sit down.

During the week Mother would mimic Sister Paulette.

The milk cow hit Mother in the head with her bony tail loaded with cockleburs. Mother got off her milking stool and tied the cow's tail to the barn wall. Then, she waved an imaginary hanky in the air. We boys sang out. "I just praise His holy name."

When the skunk sucked the goodies out of all the eggs in the hen house, Mother had a response. "If I had an every-Sunday, sky-blue dress, you know what I would say?"

We both laughed and joined in.

"I just praise His holy name."

The tension always went away.

Dad's response was more practical. He did not want to frighten the hens—they would stop laying eggs. Instead, he waited for hours outside the hen house and shot the egg-sucking intruder, a full-sized mama skunk.

During the testimony time Sam Watkins testified second. He always wore overalls and a red or blue flannel shirt. He reminded me of the Currier & Ives poster hanging in the school library. He just needed a pitchfork in his hands and a wheat straw sticking out of his mouth to complete the picture.

"Some folks thank the Lord for divine healing. I thank Him for divine health. I haven't been sick for years." His report never varied and he was always healthy, dressed in his best Kansas wheat-farmer clothes.

When seventy-five-year-old George Cook stood, he would sing part of a hymn. It was on key but they never asked him to sing a solo. It was worship, not entertainment. For me it was the best part of every Sunday service.

"Rock of Ages, cleft for me. Let me hide myself in Thee." Then he would testify with a far-off smile. "The crop failed and I was plowing it under this week. I turned the corner near the dried-up pond and my tractor broke down. I was tempted to be angry but as I sang, great peace came over me. I remembered God has promised to give me all I need for life and godliness." His contented look said more than his words.

Before he left church, I overheard him talking to the pastor's wife. She had made a last-minute dinner invitation.

Brother George replied, "I apologize. I can't come to your house for Sunday dinner. I am going to visit the elderly this afternoon."

I ran to the car so I could report what I had heard.

"Mother, Brother George doesn't know he is old. He is visiting the elderly instead of eating Sister Noreen's roast beef and rhubarb pie."

She just smiled. "I know. I heard it, too."

I was quiet for the rest of the ride home.

I thought about George every day. One day I shared my theory with my stepdad.

"I think I have figured out why George Cook is so cheerful. Apparently, he has never had a really bad day in his life. I know he had a crop failure and the tractor broke down but that happens to everyone."

Dad leaned on his pitchfork and stared at me.

"George lost his only son in a terrible car accident. A few years later his wife died after a long, lingering bout with cancer." He paused, a thoughtful look on his face. "He, also, has devoted much of his adult life to raising Lucille, his mentally-challenged daughter. You have seen Lucille so you know what I am talking about."

Dad walked away. I could not hold back the tears. I wanted to be like George but his response to life completely puzzled me.

That evening I talked to Mother. "I don't know if I have what it takes to be like George."

"God will help you. I will pray that when you're a man, you will figure out what George knows!"

"That will take a miracle."

Mother hugged me and laughed. "You look like you have another question."

"I do but I don't want to upset you."

"It will upset me more if I don't hear your question."

"Okay. Did you ever think about marrying George Cook?"

She sat down at the kitchen table and motioned me to sit across from her. "So you think he's the Dad who got away? You think I missed the chance of a lifetime?"

"You said you wanted to hear my question."

"I did say that. To tell you the truth, even though Gladys joked about it, I didn't think anyone would ask me to marry him. So no, I never thought about marrying George Cook or Fred Keller or any other name you want to put on the list. I just assumed any proposal would be prompted by God Himself. Actually, I think you thought it was the right idea, too."

I shrugged my shoulders. I didn't know what to say.

"Well, I have a question for you, Mr. Deep Thinker. What do you think George would do if he were in our situation?"

I think God gave me the answer to her question.

"He would get that faraway look, sing another hymn, and tell us God would meet every need." I didn't want to be happy with that answer but after I said it, I felt a great sense of peace.

Mother patted me on the arm. "Sounds like you have a little bit of George in you already."

Reflections

God sent George Cook to model living well and loving well. He spoke many times about God being his source. Because of that faith he rejoiced more over a slice of bread than most people do over a five-course banquet. Despite his fifty-five-year-old daughter's limitations with learning and communication, she always looked like someone who was deeply loved. He was the best sermon I ever received at the Ness City church.

Knowing that he would turn to God, his unfailing source, and tell about it during the Sunday service both inspired and puzzled me.

One Sunday morning Brother George quoted Philippians 4:19 (NIV), "And my God will meet all [my] needs according to the riches of his glory in Christ Jesus."

I asked, "Brother George, how can you know whether that verse is true or not?"

"I know who made the promise."

Knowing the answer is on the way is deeply satisfying to me. George Cook was more grateful for an answer that hadn't come yet than I was over the best gift I had received. He was kinder to his daughter with all her challenges than I was to Phil, my brother who had a good mind and a good heart. His life and love challenged me.

During my middle school years, I foolishly wondered why God had not sent us to George's house instead of grasping that God had come to our home.

Questions to Consider

1.   Think of something you have prayed to receive. Would you be willing to pray, "Thy kingdom come; thy will be done. Send whomever or whatever is best for me"? Is it possible God has already sent the gift that's best for you, but your heart wasn't open? Invite Him to come again.

2.   Aunt Cora had unsightly varicose veins. I didn't want to go with Mother to visit her. Mother said, "You don't have to go. You get to go. Someday you will be older. Perhaps God will remember this visit and send a child to visit you." Aunt Cora

and George Cook were about the same age. God placed both of them in my life—for entirely different reasons. Who has God sent to you? Perhaps, a senior citizen who will inspire you or another who needs your love?

3.   Is God your source? If He is, what are the first action steps He would prescribe?

   • Ask God to forgive your lack of trust.

   • Pray that He will help you dismantle strongholds-the habitual thought patterns of trusting whatever or whomever more than fully relying on Him?

   • Learn what He has promised—wisdom, resources, the Holy Spirit interceding for you, healing inside and out.

   • Ask for grace (i.e., the capacity)
         a. to believe in your heart what He has said and
         b. to obey.

3.   Have you examined your priorities?

   • Matthew 6:33 (New Century Version—NCV) says, "Seek first God's kingdom and what God wants. Then all your other needs will be met as well."

   • Are you asking for what you need or what you want?

Luke 12:15 (AMP) says:

   And He said to them, "Guard yourselves and keep free from all covetousness (the immoderate desire for wealth, the greedy longing to have more); for a man's life does not consist in and is not derived from possessing overflowing abundance or that which is over and above his needs."

CHAPTER NINETEEN

THE CARDINAL SPEAKS

Every Sunday "The Ride-Home-from-Church Comedy Hour" began as we pulled out of our parking stall. Mother was a comedienne and Pastor Dell provided very good material.

One Sunday he wore a new suit. Mother called it "distinguished gray." He added a fire engine red tie and hanky. With his square shoulders and wavy brown hair Mother said, "He is a picture waiting to be taken." She leaned forward just before the opening prayer and whispered,

"He would stand out if he were sitting down."

With his bright red additions on display, Pastor Dell said the title of his sermon was, "Immodesty, a Word of Caution." His targets were women and their sleeveless dresses and shapely ankles. He used 1 Timothy 2:8-10 (KJV) as his sermon text:

> I will therefore that men pray everywhere, lifting up holy hands, without wrath and doubting. In like manner also, that women adorn themselves in modest apparel, with shamefacedness and sobriety; not with broided hair, or gold, or pearls, or costly array; But (which becometh women professing godliness) with good works.

Mother coughed loudly three times during the service. That always meant she really wanted to say something.

At twelve o'clock sharp Sister Lillian closed her pocket watch with a loud click. The service was officially over. The pastor closed with prayer. It was a brief prayer because no pastor ever had the courage to challenge Sister Lillian.

Dad backed the blue Buick out of the parking stall in front of the church. Mother did not waste a minute.

"That was such a fine sermon by Pastor Dell. My farm wife ankles are scratched and swollen. I would have never guessed they were a problem for men."

Dad said the same thing every week. "Mildred, watch yourself."

Nothing stopped Mother when she had a great topic.

"Oh yes, watch myself and every other woman in the church. Be on the lookout for short-sleeved dresses. I may see bra straps exposed. We all know how dangerous that is."

"Mildred, you are distorting what the pastor said."

She ignored Dad and treated us to a perfect imitation of Pastor Dell.

"Brothers and Sisters, you may wonder about my bright red tie and hanky. Have you seen the male cardinal—eye-catching red color with fancy plumage? God also made the female cardinal. Please notice she is plain and brown, drawing no attention to herself. The message is obvious. Even the female cardinal dresses modestly. Clearly, God uses nature to illustrate His principles of conduct."

Mother sighed.

"Well, if I had a bright red hanky and a matching tie, my humility would be on display too. Fred, I am so happy. That particular hanky and tie solved the mystery. We are just a small country church but we have a cardinal for a pastor."

Suddenly, Mother's hands shot into the air.

"Oh no, I put that poor chicken out to thaw. It is naked, lying on the kitchen counter. Those exposed thighs and legs may be tasty when they are fried but that chicken is as naked as a newborn baby. What was I thinking? When we get home, I want you boys to stay in the car until I have concealed all that immodesty."

We boys tried every trick we knew to keep from laughing out loud and incurring Dad's anger. He knew he could not stop her but he could threaten us.

"Do not encourage your mother by laughing. She is mocking the pastor."

Mother let out a long sigh. I think that gave Dad hope. He made one more feeble attempt to regain control.

"How do you think women would dress if the pastor did not give some scriptural warnings?"

"Oh, that is easy. They would wear red dresses and red shoes. Red lipstick and a red rose in their hair. Short-sleeved blouses with underwear exposed and skirts that revealed shapely calves and ankles. All you male cardinals would have a meeting to decide when to hand out brown uniforms with long sleeves. When that day comes, do not forget the brown stockings and brown shoes."

Suddenly, Mother grabbed her Bible and rapidly turned the pages. Dad accepted the bait.

"What are you looking for?"

"I am trying to find lessons from the animal kingdom in the Bible. If we copy the Cardinal's dress code, what do we do about our milk cows? No short sleeves and bra straps there. Just fully exposed teats. I do not know when I am going to have time to make dresses for all those cows."

She looked like it was too much for her. She closed her Bible and laid it on the seat.

"I am really looking forward to Cardinal Dell's next sermon. Maybe next week His Eminence will warn us about the dangers of 'broided' hair. I don't even have time to tell you all my thoughts about that."

Phil always sat right behind Mother.

"What is broided hair?"

"I don't know, Son, but I'm sure it's a problem. If King Jimmie and the translators included it in the Bible passage he read this morning, it must be worth a warning."

Dad turned into the driveway.

"I am sure glad we didn't invite the pastor to lunch. And Mildred, please do not bring up the naked chickens again."

Dad went upstairs to change his clothes. I set the table while Mother started preparations for dinner. She began talking to herself.

"Oh, is that a genie in a bottle? Well, thank you very much. Yes, I do want all three wishes. Absolutely, I am ready." She paused dramatically. "My first wish: I'd like to meet a man who is as concerned about his vanity as he is about my modesty." She rolled the chicken in the flour and continued her conversation with the genie. "No, I do not need more time. My second wish: I want a pastor who doesn't think his job is to fix every woman he sees." She put the lid on the skillet and turned to me. "My third wish is that you become that kind of man."

The humor ended. The chicken fried to a golden brown and lunch was ready. Before we ate, Mother prayed.

"Lord, give Louie humility and common sense by the time he's a grown man. Thanks, also, for letting me laugh. If I hadn't, I would have had a headache all day. Oh yes, thanks for the food."

She opened her eyes and looked at Dad. "I apologize for my comments about Pastor Dell."

Dad never knew what to say in those moments.

I could hardly wait for the ride home next Sunday.

Reflections

Mother's sense of humor taught me to laugh when I was disappointed, insulted, overlooked, or worse. Her comedic view of life showed me there was almost always a different way to view injustice or injury. Seeing myself as a victim was not the only option. Hopelessness is not a word in God's vocabulary.

When Pastor Dell preached about women being immodest, Mother wanted a hero to step forward. She suspected that his daughter was the target for his sermon. Did any man have such clarity he could urge the pastor to parent his daughter at home? Who was the man who would defend all of the innocent women in the church?

I laughed and laughed on Sunday but inside I knew Mother was a would-be champion. She would not get a chance. In her generation only men were recognized as possible champions. Part of her comedy routine on the way home was letting off steam; part of it was a plea for me to become a heroic man—at least by the time I grew up—who could see clearly what was really happening, hear God, and make it better.

As I listened to her humor, I realized that I wouldn't be heard if I didn't speak up. I knew I needed to be memorable when I had a chance to express my opinion, my feelings, or my suggestions. I didn't realize until later that I had taken up her offense more than once. I spoke up but I lacked a sense of God's timing. I didn't know how to be effective with humor. All I had learned was to speak in a funny, unforgettable way.

Mother encouraged me to gain language skills so what I said would stand out. Having skill without wisdom was like giving a kid a loaded gun but never requiring him to learn gun safety.

Her humor taught me disrespect, also. Humor masks boundary violations—people laugh even when you hurt them deeply. If they don't laugh, others will. A group laughing at you can be overwhelming.

I learned to use humor and language as weapons of retaliation or intimidation. It fostered pride when I outwitted others, especially those who hurt me or abandoned me. It rarely occurred to me that I was seeking vengeance, which the Lord had said He would handle.

Beyond that, humor and language became a sanctuary I ran into when all else failed. I didn't cry or hit others—except for Phil. I simply used humor and then hid behind it.

As an adult I was slow to learn the toxic powers of a funny story. I knew in theory that humor has the power to express vital truth or to inflict great damage. One Sunday after I preached, four couples approached me one at a time. They all had the same concern.

"You were funny this morning but you insulted Beverly."

"Thanks for telling me what bothered you. I don't think you're right about Beverly but I promise I will ask her."

After lunch the boys took a nap, giving the two of us time to talk.

"Bev, in the sermon this morning did my funny story about you insult you?"

"I knew you didn't mean me any harm but, yes."

I had been more interested in getting a laugh than in protecting Beverly's dignity and identity.

The next Sunday morning I addressed the congregation. "I wish we had the same crowd today that we had last week because I need to apologize. Four couples acted out of integrity last Sunday morning, telling me my story about Beverly insulted her. What was worse than the humor? I had not realized my story caused any discomfort.

"Beverly, you graciously admitted I hurt you with my story. My dear Beverly, I am sorry.

"All of our friends who are here today, I am sorry.

"How will I move forward? I have asked a member of this congregation to critique my humor in the weeks ahead. He will offer his opinion to me, pointing out when my funny stories inflict pain (or not) and whether the humor connects to the major points in the sermon. He, also, will pray with me, asking for a change of heart and behavior."

Humor can be costly but it has the power to lift spirits, say what could not be said otherwise, and provide hope for the next painful moment.

Questions to Consider

1. Who is the funniest person at your house?

2. What lessons does that person need to learn?

   - Personal humor is humor directed at a person. Learn to laugh with, not at, others.
   - If you are the only person laughing at your funny story, it is not funny—at least not in that setting.
   - If you are offended, instead of using humor as a weapon, speak to your alleged assailant in a clear, calm, God-prompted way.
   - Don't use humor as a cover up for disrespect.
   - Ask yourself, "Am I using humor for God's glory?"

3. How can humor be effective? How can it affect change?

4. Don't throw out humor. Use it well.

CHAPTER TWENTY

THE BROTHERHOOD OF FARM KIDS

I WAS IN THE MIDDLE SCHOOL library, sailing down the Mississippi on a barge with Huck Finn when Vicki floated in. I got light-headed when she looked at me. Sadly, she was unattainable. It wasn't because of her piercing blue eyes. It wasn't her long blonde hair—but I would have given two months of my allowance—if I had had one—to run a comb through it one time. It wasn't her perfect skin—but if I had touched her just once, I would have never washed my hand again. It was her status. Vicki only talked to varsity athlete upperclassmen.

I was a guard on the ninety-nine-pounds-and-under midget basketball team. I had another serious liability, way too many zits. People don't even see little guys with acne.

I complained to Mother. "Why doesn't the stuff I do count? I can load ninety hay bales on a truck in forty-five minutes. I milk eight cows by hand twice a day. I cultivate our stupid garden almost every evening. But none of that counts at school."

I didn't know Vicki knew I existed. She stopped in front of me and adjusted her bra strap.

"Are you staring at—?" and she pointed to her chest!

I was but midgets never admit crimes against angels. I knew death was imminent

Instead, she said, "I am 36B."

I prayed that I would never awaken from this dream.

"What is 36B?" I croaked in a stage whisper.

She obviously saw my bewildered look, "It is cup size."

"What is that?"

"You are unbelievable? You really don't know anything, do you?"

Wearied by my ignorance, she explained. "Cup size is bra size. Okay? A is small—for beginners—like grade school. B," she said sweeping her arm in a grand gesture, "is perfect! At least that is what my boyfriend says."

I managed to make sounds. "You have a boyfriend?" *You are only in the eighth grade.*

"Yes, dummy—Brian, the quarterback from Ransom High School. He's a sophomore." She paused dramatically. "What do you think of that?"

I muttered, "I wish I were Brian."

"That's funny."

Her laughter sounded like chimes joyfully ringing. "Do you want me to continue?"

I nodded gravely.

"Well, C is very large and D is enormous."

This was undoubtedly my only chance in life to ask the other question. I could barely speak.

"What does 36 mean?"

Now my ignorance was becoming annoying. She said with a dismissive gesture, "You use a tape measure and measure around your bust—36 inches!" To finish her performance she did a curtsy and sailed out of the hall library.

I was in a daze. Points of perfection! The school bell interrupted my daydreaming.

Nick, our school bus driver, only waited five minutes for us to be on board. He was a no-nonsense guy who had driven tanks in Korea. He told one of the dads, "The North Koreans did not stop me. Weather will not stop me. No kid is going to stop me."

With no time to spare, I slid into my assigned seat next to John Moss. He lived two farms over. We had been seatmates for three years.

His sister Sharon always sat behind us on the bus. She was two years older, a sophomore—much older. Sharon never talked to me but she would occasionally smile. I wasn't invisible; I just wasn't high priority. Sharon was close by when lightning struck the family horse but she survived. She nursed her favorite calf back to health when a rattlesnake bit it in the nose. And, she never stopped doing her chores after she fell out of the hayloft and broke her arm. She knew I existed; she simply had bigger challenges.

To our complete surprise she leaned forward and ordered John, her brother, "Move across the aisle."

He was so startled he nearly jumped to the other seat.

She gripped the back of the seat and spoke to me.

"I heard you talking to Vicki today and I am totally ashamed of you!"

Tears squirted out of my eyes. I knew my life was over. When news of "the cup size talk" got out, I would be demoted from invisible midget to village idiot.

Sharon used her I'm-in-charge voice. "Look at me. If you have a question about stuff like that, you ask me."

That directive was as startling as Vicki's revelations. It would have never occurred to me in a thousand years to ask Sharon about bras.

She was not finished.

"Farm kids do not talk to girls like Vicki. Do you understand me?"

I did not understand but I nodded anyway. Until that exact moment I had never thought of farm kids as an elite group.

She leaned forward one more time.

"I talked to Vicki and warned her. If she tells anyone about your talk in the library, I will give her a cup full she has never seen before."

She motioned to John to move back across the aisle.

Apparently, Vicki was afraid of Sharon or I had become invisible again. Whatever the reason, she did not talk to me after that, so it was easy to follow Sharon's instructions.

Days later I told Mother about the talks in the hall library and on the school bus.

"Louie, what if God knew you did not have a dad so he sent Sharon instead. Pay attention, Son. God uses whoever is available to speak. Are you listening?"

Mother was probably right but I was afraid to admit it. I hoped God sent a different messenger in the future.

Reflections

Nothing had prepared me for Vicki and her revelations. I wondered how to get our boys ready by the time they began to notice girls (or be noticed by girls). I knew middle school and high school physical education and gym classes were hotbeds of misinformation and boyish fantasizing about sex. Outside the locker room, inappropriate words and acts could catch them off guard anytime or anyplace.

What would our strategy include? They needed vigilance 24/7, thoughtful preparation, relevant support, and prayer.

We wanted to state principles with memorable and understandable language. These principles would be a foundation for everything else:

1. Sex without relationship will disappoint you unless you are very shallow.

2. Marriage without heart-warming intimacy is a contradiction. God intended the first to be accented by the second.

3. The Bible answers questions about sexual intimacy.
   - Who? A husband and wife.
   - When? After you are married.
   - Why wait? To develop delayed gratification and impulse control.
   - What is the goal? Sexual intimacy in marriage should be *agape* love at work—meeting each other's needs in an other-centered way.

4. Intimacy without commitment is misleading. Commitment preserves intimacy; intimacy enhances commitment.

5. Don't do things that excite for the moment but you have to pay for the rest of your life.

6. Avoid an act or comment that will hurt your future mate's heart and totally confuse your children.

7. Your peer group does not represent the norm. God's way is normal even if you are the only normal kid in the room.

8. *Everyone's doing it* is never true. The question, "Is it worth doing?" always applies.

9. Pressure to be intimate is a warning sign. If it is love, you will not have to hurry or be leaned on to be intimate. At the right time and with the right person, give yourself as a gift.

10. Listen to your conscience. If the comment or act feels wrong, it probably is.

11. Pornography is pictures of someone's daughter and sister. Would you want anyone to stare at pictures of your sister or daughter without clothes?

12. Nothing good happens after midnight. If it is worth doing, do it in the light of day so you can see what you are doing.

13. If you have to conceal what you are doing or if you feel huge pressure to lie about it, stop! Pray! Seek advice and move toward people who help you think straight.

14. If anyone hurts you or touches you inappropriately or makes you feel uncomfortable or urges you to conceal a matter (or threatens you not to tell), run as fast as you can to the safest adult in your life and tell them your story.

    To the safe person (when a child tells you his / her story):

    • If you doubt the truth or objectivity of the child's story, hear all of it before you draw conclusions. Don't defend the adult offender even if he has been nominated for sainthood. If it is the truth, get help immediately. If it is not true, get help immediately—just different help.

- At least once a month ask your kids, "Is there one (or are there more) of the fourteen on the list we need to discuss now?"

- Tell them, "If I ever fail to take time to hear your story or to rejoice over your victories before the day's end, ask for an explanation. If that doesn't satisfy you, talk to your mother. If neither of us hears you, ask both of us what you are to do when you are not heard."

- Ell them, "When you ask a question or confess a sinful act, I pledge not to judge you (Matthew 7:1, NCV, "Don't judge others); and I pledge not to exasperate you (Ephesians 6:4, NIV, " ... don't exasperate ...")."

- Why are these pledges by the parents important in a parent-child discussion about sexuality?

Questions to Consider

1. What characterizes your family's approach to sexuality? Fearful? Thoughtful? Clueless? Aware? Spirit-led? Scriptural?

2. How do you prepare your children for life? Family meetings? One-on-one talks? Family prayer times? Reading a book together? Arranging for your child to talk to a trustworthy friend of yours?

3. If you are a parent, are you clear, forgiven, and healed? In other words, are you free from your own youthful mistakes? If not, where can you get help ASAP?

CHAPTER TWENTY-ONE

DAD'S MATH

DAD BELIEVED WE SHOULD TITHE. One morning he interrupted Bible reading to explain. Most of the time he was like a block of granite, silent and almost impossible to figure out. So, when he talked, we listened.

"Tithe isn't ten percent of the profit. Tithe is ten percent of everything that comes in. We tithe because the Bible tells us to. Ten per cent is a minimum requirement. Beyond that, we should give an additional ten percent out of gratitude. It does not please God to do only what is required.

"If we buy a bushel basket of peaches and can twenty jars for the winter, we take four to the pastor. Two are the tithe; the other two are a thank you to God.

"We have fifty egg-laying hens. If they lay fifty eggs, five belong to God and five are our gift. The book of Malachi says to take the tithes to the storehouse. I believe the church is the storehouse so we take our tithes there." His brief remarks ended as quickly as they began. He opened his Bible as he did every morning and read a chapter aloud to the three of us.

I was speechless. I had so many questions. When we moved to the farm, I thought this new dad would speak wisdom on a regular basis. This was the second time he told us what he thought about deeper issues. I was very pleased.

Not long after that we paid a trucker to take our grass-fattened, two-year-old Hereford steers to the cattle auction in Wakeeney forty miles away. Dad and I in our ancient Chevy truck followed the semi-trailer truck, loaded with our cattle.

This was high adventure. We watched the cowhands unload the truck, twenty steers weighing about one thousand pounds each. The crack of the bullwhips and the shouts of the men frightened the cattle. They quickly moved down the ramps and into the stockyards. The cowboy hats waving, adrenaline pumping, cattle bawling, plus the smell of fear, wet leather, manure, and damp straw provided a rodeo atmosphere. When the last steer came out of the truck, we walked a short way to the sales arena. About eight rows of stadium seats, positioned at a steep angle, surrounded the wire that enclosed the corral. The corral was large enough for several cattle to mill around, giving the buyers, seated in the eight rows, a good look.

Many farmers brought their cattle to be sold that day. We waited about thirty minutes until it was our turn. My heart raced with anticipation. Finally, the cowhands brought in our steers, four and five at a time. The auctioneer introduced the offer and then began his sing-song.

"We have four range-fed, two-year-old steers, sold as a lot. I got twelve, now thirteen, now fourteen. Who'll give me fifteen? I got fourteen. Who'll give me fifteen? Fourteen and a half? Fourteen and a half? Sold to Benson Packers for fourteen."

It only took fifteen minutes to auction off all our cattle, but I was drained when the last steer left the sale ring. Dad said we got a decent price. We waited at the cashier's window for our payment, a total of $2,000. Dad paid the trucker and the sale barn $1,600.

Dad said he was hungry. I wanted to eat in the stockyards café but Mother warned me not to ask. She had explained. "We don't have any money!"

I thought, "How can $2,000 be no money?"

I quietly ate the peanut butter sandwich we brought along.

On the way back to the farm Dad was very pleased. "We have enough to pay the preacher!"

Using Dad's math for giving, the tithe plus an additional ten percent for generosity was twenty percent of $2,000 (the gross). That equaled $400, the amount we had left. He happily took that to the pastor. We had sold our cattle and the money was completely gone.

I didn't realize until I was an adult that no one I knew agreed with Dad's tithing theories. They would have tithed ten percent of the $400 profit (or $40). That is, no one appreciated his math except God.

One day, huge, black storm clouds approached from the west. They looked like they were full of hailstones. It was a few days before western Kansas farmers would begin harvesting their wheat. Dad had a simple approach to life: he trusted God. He knelt in the edge of the field, faced the approaching storm, and prayed.

"God, this is Your field. If You choose to destroy it, it is Your field. If you save it, it is still Your field."

He stayed there on his knees, waiting for the black clouds to pass over. The hail leveled the fields on all four sides of Dad's wheat as the storm slowly moved past. Clearly, God liked Dad's math or was it his generous heart?

He never took me with him again to the auction. Each year Mother asked. The answer was the same every time. "There is work to do. Do you want to spoil him? If he gets done with hoeing the weeds in the garden, he can always check on the fence line. We can't let the cattle get out."

My heart was quiet. I had had my day. I had seen Dad bless God and God bless Dad.

Reflections

The passage most referred to when pastors teach about tithing is Malachi 3:8-11. The Amplified Bible says:

> Will a man rob or defraud God? ... [You have withheld your] tithes and offerings. You are cursed with the curse, for you are robbing Me, even this whole nation. Bring all the tithes (the whole tenth of your income) into the storehouse [my note: the churches we attended said the current storehouse is the local church.]... and prove Me now by it, says the Lord of hosts, if I will not open the windows of heaven for you and pour you out a blessing, that there shall not be room enough to receive it. And I will rebuke the devourer [insects and plagues] for your sakes ...

God takes our giving—or lack of giving—very personally. While the tithe is a specific amount—ten percent—it is not just the amount that's important. The heart attitude and the thought process are very important.

2 Corinthians 9:7 (AMP) says:

> Let each one [give] as he has made up his own mind *and* purposed in his heart, not reluctantly *or* sorrowfully or under compulsion, for God loves (He takes pleasure in, prizes above other things, and is unwilling to abandon or to do without) a cheerful (joyous, "prompt to do it") giver [whose heart is in his giving].

Dad read and reread these verses, determined to please God with his giving. He concluded that we should give what is commanded and then add an extra ten percent out of gratitude. In other words, our family tithed ten percent off of the gross and gave an additional ten percent in offerings.

Money was not our best gift. We were hospitable, frequently inviting other people to come for a meal. When the crops failed, we still had the garden. Mother was generous with our guests, sharing homegrown vegetables. She, also, gave of herself, practicing acts of kindness to others, especially elderly relatives.

Deuteronomy 12:6, 11 (AMP & NIV) expands the topic of giving, saying to bring burnt offerings, sacrifices, tithes, special gifts (also called "choicest offerings"), freewill offerings, the firstborn of their herds and flocks, and a first gift from the fruits of the ground. Giving was obviously a very important part of their lives.

Deuteronomy 26:12 (NIV) adds the idea of benevolence:

> When you have finished setting aside a tenth of all your produce in the third year, the year of the tithe, you shall give it to the Levite, the foreigner, the fatherless and the widow, so that they may eat in your towns and be satisfied.

The year of the tithe was a time set aside to honor God's generosity by blessing those in need. Many Christians I know think like accountants who lack compassion. They reveal their heart attitude: "In that year of the tithe, am I *required* to give an additional ten percent?"

From time to time I hear the argument, "Tithing is an Old Testament idea so it no longer applies." That ignores what Jesus said in Luke 11:42 (NIV):

> Woe to you Pharisees, because you give God a tenth of your mint, rue and all other kinds of garden herbs, but you neglect justice and the love of God. You should have practiced the latter without leaving the former undone.

In those verses Jesus affirms tithing. However, God seems to be asking, "Will law and obligation or gratitude and compassion set the tone for our giving?"

Malachi wrote that tithing gives God a chance to demonstrate his generosity: "... prove Me now by it, says the Lord of hosts, if I will not open the windows of heaven for you and pour you out a blessing, that there shall not be room enough to receive it."

For Dad the proofs of God blessing us were everywhere. Phil fell through the Dempster drill at the exact moment Dad looked back. He stopped just in time to save Phil's life. I had my own scary accident. I fell off of the certified seed platform onto the handle of a pitchfork, catching it just below the ribs. I couldn't breathe normally for what seemed like an eternity and couldn't talk for eleven hours. I fully recovered. We could not name a dollar amount for two lives being saved. In addition, it was a startling exception if our cows did not have healthy calves. The Hereford bull was bitten in the nose by a rattlesnake and survived. Our two water wells never ran dry. We were almost always in good health. Storms never kept us from going to church (but Dad towed the car to the road with the caterpillar tractor one snowy morning). We had freedom to worship and to vote and to plant what we chose to plant. God loved us and Jesus died for us. Who needed to get out a calculator to see whether we had received as much value (reward, benefit, blessing) as we had given?

Dad and Mother were cheerful and purposeful givers. That was one of the best parts of the legacy they passed on to us.

Questions to Consider

Take one more look at Malachi 3:8-11 (AMP).

> Will a man rob or defraud God? ... [You have withheld your] tithes and offerings. You are cursed with the curse, for you are robbing Me, even this whole nation. Bring all the tithes (the whole tenth of your income) into the storehouse [my note: the churches we attended said the current storehouse is the local church]...and prove Me now by it, says the Lord of hosts, if I will not open the windows of heaven for you and pour you out a blessing, that there shall not be room enough to receive it. And I will rebuke the devourer [insects and plagues] for your sakes...

God uses strong language in this passage. He, also, makes an extravagant promise. Why? It must be important to Him and to us.

- God calls it robbery when we do not tithe.

- He has promised He will pour blessings on us if we do.

- He has declared that He will remove any curse affecting us when we do.

For this chapter I have only one question. Why would anyone who reads these verses not tithe? Beverly and I do and we can assure you God more than meets the challenge, repeatedly proving His generosity.

CHAPTER TWENTY-TWO

THE CALL OF GOD

I PREACHED MY FIRST SERMON WHEN I was twelve. Our church's Sunday morning attendance was fifty or sixty, including the children. Because the church was small, the teens and young adults, ages thirteen through thirty-five, formed a combined group. It was called "BWT" (Be one! Win one! Teach One!). Half the church was in this age group.

When Mother heard that BWT would include twelve-year-olds the next year for the first time, she knew immediately who the leader should be. My twelfth birthday was coming up. The timing was perfect. The group could elect me, the kid with the call of God on his life, as the group's president and speaker. At least that was Mother's idea.

Mother talked to everyone who had a vote.

"Wouldn't it be amazing if the BWT elected Louie? You know he has the call of God on his life. Please, give him an opportunity to begin his life's work. When he becomes a full-time pastor or missionary, he will look back and thank each of you for this chance."

She had answers for their questions.

"You are probably wondering what will happen if you vote for Louie. I will help him prepare his sermon each week."

One curious member said, "Preach a sermon? Twelve years old?"

Mother had an answer. "No matter what age he is, if it is in a church, behind a pulpit, and based on God's Word, I will call it a sermon."

They elected me unanimously and then, reelected me to serve a second one-year term. I didn't understand why they selected a kid, but the election gave me a walking-on-the-clouds feeling.

I became the leader of the group the first Sunday in January. That night I spoke in public for the first time. The two dozen who came made me feel very grown up. I wrote down two of the compliments.

"Your mother said you are going to be a pastor. I can believe it."

"Good message. Before long you will be speaking on Sunday morning."

That was the first of a hundred sermons I preached to the BWT group over the next two years. The sermons were really Mother's but I delivered them after repeated practice sessions.

The sermon preparation added great pressure to both our lives. On a typical weekday afternoon and evening I got off the school bus, hoed weeds in the garden (a task I hated), took the dogs we were training to get the cattle at four o'clock (I loved those dogs), milked eight cows by hand (twice a day x 365 days), sometimes with Mother's or Phil's help, cranked the separator to pull the lighter milk from the heavier cream, fed the chickens, ate dinner, did homework, and rehearsed the sermon for the following Sunday. I was always tired.

I was happy to team with Mother. Most weeks, I enjoyed the challenge and the nice things people said afterwards. But, the best part each week was Mother's confidence in me.

"I have to say it again, Louie. You are definitely fulfilling your purpose in life."

Each week Mother would read the Bible, a Christian book, or *The Capper's Weekly* ("A Newspaper for People of the Plains"). She would prepare a simple, three-point outline. Human interest stories in *The Capper's Weekly* offered down-to-earth illustrations. For instance, one farm couple drank eight glasses of water when they were angry at each other. It stopped the argument every time. Mother thought that was a funny, but practical way to live out Ephesians 4:26, "Be angry; don't sin."

I asked Mother, "Don't you think we should make some progress with anger here on the farm before I preach about it?"

When Mother picked a topic, she was unstoppable.

"We will learn right along with them."

In one of our practice sessions we tried to drink eight glasses of water, but she stopped at five and I gave up at six.

For that sermon Mother and I had our own creative idea. I brought three small bags of marbles that Sunday night. I offered to give away two bags of marbles to the first two volunteers who would join me at the front. I stuffed my mouth full of marbles. Everyone laughed as my volunteers, Frank and Wayne, filled their mouths, too. I held up a sign.

"When you are angry, try this."

Sometimes, Mother puzzled me when she told me the topic for the Sunday night sermon. For instance, she wanted to use dog training as a way to talk about "Train up a child in the way he should go. When he is old, he will not depart from it" (Proverbs 22:6, KJV).

I objected. "I am not a parent. I feel weird talking about raising kids."

"We are the only family in the church who trains cattle dogs. Kids need the same training as dogs. The BWT will love it."

And they did. We brought pictures of our trained cattle dogs, beautiful black-and-white English Shepherds. Mother coached me and I talked about the various steps in the training:

- **Timeliness.** We were careful to preserve their lives as puppies. We did not begin working with them until they were at least six months old.

- **Consistency.** We trained them to round up the cows every day at 4 p.m. In addition, we used the same commands every time: "Sit. Stay. Heel. Down. Go. Slow Now."

- **Self-control.** We taught them to go slow so the cattle would walk, not run. Peaceful cows give more milk.

After the sermon, the entire group talked about dog training for children. Mother admitted afterwards, "I thought the teens might be offended." Instead, the story of Toby, our male cattle dog, inspired them.

After years of training, Toby went after the cattle every day at 4 p.m. without prompting. Dog lovers, ranchers, and dozens of people who heard the story in *cafes, after church*, and at high school ball games sat in our driveway on cloudy days, during light snowstorms, and in the middle of a thunderstorm to see if Toby's internal clock would still work. He amazed them every day at 4:00 p.m. People offered Dad huge sums of money for the black-and-white sire. Dad always said, "No."

According to Mother, the Bible was a picture of God at work in daily life. The 23rd Psalm was our photo album of "Four Times When God Is Present" (Verses 2-5).

- Verse 2: God is with us when we are in green pastures and beside still waters. We used wheat harvest in a good year as a practical example.

- Verse 3: He leads us in paths of righteousness. The annual church revival in August was our snapshot.

- Verse 4: He comforts us in the valley of the shadow of death. I talked about Dad abandoning us at the Bible school in Waxahachie, Texas, but God was still there.

- Verse 5: Even when the enemy surrounds us, the Lord feeds us and holds the enemy at arm's length. Our best picture of this was the recent hailstorm that flattened every field but ours.

After the group heard our personal examples, they shared openly about their life stories.

In my opinion, Mother chose many sermon topics because she thought the material would develop my character. For example, Charles Sheldon's book *In His Steps* told a story about a local church. The members of that church pledged not to do anything for an entire year without first asking the question, "What Would Jesus Do?"

I accepted the challenge. I was a junior-high kid, trying to live by the standard "WWJD" for an entire week. Normally, I was the class clown. When I did not disrupt class for five days, I puzzled my English teacher.

"Louie, you haven't said a word all week. I am happy about the change but I am worried about you. Have you lost your voice?"

I told her and the class about WWJD. Unfortunately, I was the same old me the following Monday. Mother said I was a work in progress.

The BWT practiced WWJD that week, as well. Most of them told us about one time when they asked the question, "What would Jesus do?"

Gary, an unusually strong high-school senior, could lift the edge of a four hundred pound pool table. He stopped to help a lady who slid off the road and into a ditch with her Volkswagen. He used a fence post for leverage and single-handedly pushed the car back onto the road. He said, "I almost didn't help her because I wasn't sure Jesus could have pushed that car back onto the road." He was so serious we all had a good laugh.

Oswald Chambers' book *My Utmost for His Highest* was a treasure chest of devotional thoughts. Anytime we were unable to come up with a fresh topic, we would use one from Chambers' book. For instance, three different devotionals talked about laziness. Once again, I asked Mother if I was the best one to talk about laziness. She assured me people would be busy, thinking about their own failures.

Not all of Mother's ideas worked. One Sunday night I reported on the biography of Smith Wigglesworth. We all talked about his unique way of life, never reading any book but the Bible. After a twenty-minute discussion, Wayne summarized almost everyone's thoughts.

"You have to admire the guy but it wouldn't work in Ness City."

Mother would tell me week after week, "We want to catch their attention right away, use Scripture as a pattern for life, and tell them stories that will help them remember the main points." Later on, Mother added a fourth goal—use phrases that will stick in their minds and help them remember. Before long we heard all the BWTers quoting Mother's one-liners.

"God always shows up. Sometimes he looks like your next-door neighbor."

"God is singing your song [Zephaniah 3:17]. What music are you listening to?"

"God is not late. When he shows up, reset your clock."

During the second year I was BWT president, Mother announced a Lincoln-Douglas debate between Mr. Brooks—the church called him Brother Wayne—and me. The topic would be, "Who was the greatest disciple, Peter or John?"

Mr. Wayne Brooks was a thirty-two-year-old college graduate. He owned his own store. He served as chairman of the Ness City school board, president of the Chamber of Commerce, and president of the Rotary Club. He knew how to talk and he knew how to debate. My credentials were limited. I was a teenager who presented Mother's messages. She said I was a good speaker.

I thought, "Why not debate?"

Mother invited the entire church and almost everyone came. Many of them brought friends and neighbors and other relatives.

The Lincoln-Douglas format gave Mr. Brooks the opening seven minutes. He presented Peter as the greatest apostle. Then, I had eleven minutes to declare that John was the most amazing apostle ever. Finally, Mr. Brooks had four minutes for rebuttal.

He destroyed my best points. I said John was the disciple Jesus loved. He pointed out that John said that about himself in the Book of John, a book he wrote. Therefore, according to my opponent, it didn't count.

I said Peter betrayed Christ but John served the Lord.

Mr. Brooks had a question.

"If John was so great, why was Peter chosen to preach the message at Pentecost?"

I said, "Furthermore" (Mother added a few big-sounding words that I would never use on my own), "John was one of four biographers, chosen by God to tell the story of Jesus' life on earth." Mr. Brooks said Peter was the star character in the book of Acts. Peter spoke on the Day of Pentecost. Peter led the first church. Peter was a man's man. Surely, his life's work was a greater book for all men to read than if he had written a fifth Gospel.

Mr. Brooks said everything well. On the other hand, I sounded like a thirteen-year-old from a farm that had seven crop failures. I wasn't the president or chairman of anything.

Mother was very happy because she had her dream-come-true, large crowd. People said it was the best entertainment the church had ever had.

Thankfully, Mother hadn't picked any judges. Everyone could make up his own mind about who won. In a variety of ways they declared that Mr. Brooks was the winner.

"Hey, Louie, you did your best. Your day will come."

"Remember, if you can keep your head up in defeat, you'll be a better man."

"What did you expect? A junior high kid could beat the chairman of the school board?"

They patted me on the back and smiled but their comments humiliated me. I felt stupid and small. I wanted to disappear. I moped around for a full week. The next Sunday evening during BWT, I was still having a pity party.

"Mother, no one wants to hear me. I got killed at the debate."

When I got to the church, I walked out the front door, crossed the street, and hid in the bushes by the county courthouse. I could see the church clearly but no one knew where I was. I am not sure what Mother said to the group, but the next week they acted like nothing happened. I didn't know whether to be happy or sad.

There was one change. Mother listened to my heartache.

"You said I had a chance to win."

"I did say that. That was my pride talking and I am truly sorry. I didn't know Mr. Brooks would be that good at debate."

She continued.

"On the plus side we had a large crowd. I think everyone enjoyed it—except you. Both you and Mr. Brooks helped people think about two disciples. And you did your best without any formal training in debate. Don't let one debate define you."

Toby, our best cattle dog, decided that was the perfect moment to lick my face. He knew exactly what I needed.

Mother continued. "By the way, did we both need to learn some humility?"

I had to think a while before I answered.

"I hear you and I am sorry. I did think more about me than anything else. I hate to admit it but losing probably was good for me."

For two years I had trusted Mother's assurances that God called me to be a preacher. Despite all I was learning, I was having doubts.

"I think I have a lot to discover about the call of God."

"What are you saying?"

"I think you are the one God has called. You have whatever it takes. Defeat doesn't defeat you. Me skipping out was just a bump in the road for you. If you are not called, what is it?"

"The call of God is a personal invitation to serve in the church or community. I believe I have been called, but it is a behind-the-scenes invitation to serve others. I think God has invited you to use words and stories and questions that make people think."

"I hope it is that simple."

At the end of the second year we were both worn out. Mother thought it was time for someone else to lead BWT. I thought I was off the hook. I had no idea how determined God would be to clarify my calling.

Reflections

The call of God confused me for many years. Romans 11:29 (KJV) was the scriptural basis for my misunderstanding of the call. "For the gifts and calling of God are without repentance."

What did the translators mean by "without repentance"? The Amplified Bible (AMP) came out in 1954 and it offered some clarity about the two words.

> "For God's gifts and His call are irrevocable. [He never withdraws them when once they are given, and He does not change His mind about those to whom He gives His grace or to whom He sends His call.]"

For clarity I combined the two translations: "Without repentance" meant God would never turn away from the person He called nor take back the call. If God never changed His mind, it was very important that I understood exactly what He was calling me to do.

Mother was sure God had called me to pastoral ministry. Hearing that, the adults in the church treated me with respect. They took it for granted that Mother was right, that I would say, "Yes," and that I would go to Bible school to prepare for pastoral ministry.

I wanted to be a schoolteacher. As far as the people of the church were concerned, what I wanted didn't matter. Mother said God called me and that was enough.

My freshman year of college I enrolled at Southeastern Bible College in Lakeland, Florida. I only stayed one year. Some adults at home assumed that I was rejecting the call of God and avoided me in church as much as possible.

During that first year of college I had a very clear sense that God wanted me to be a teacher. I transferred to Fort Hays Kansas State College, graduated with a B. A. in English, and immediately began teaching high school in Russell, Kansas. I was where I belonged!

Confusion about the call persisted, also, because of what Beverly and I were passionate about and what worked well. We were avid readers, determined to have a different kind of marriage. Despite our love for each other we argued daily, judged each other, and lived with a lot of tension. During that time we were busy serving in the local church (teaching Sunday school, leading a small group, accepting responsibility for the youth ministry, offering janitorial help, caring for babies in the nursery, leading worship and playing the piano, singing solos—and just about anything else the pastor asked us to do). Despite our struggles God blessed the ministries we led and the places we served. The success was puzzling. We thought we would receive judgment because we argued every day. Instead, God gave us grace again and again.

My Sunday school class grew to over seventy. We maxed out the room and no one else could get in. Our small group for marriage began with four couples and grew to eighteen. Trinity Presbyterian Church invited me to teach their youth group early on Sunday mornings. Twenty high school students came the first week and eighteen of them were born again the first Sunday (the other two left early because they were the church musicians). People came when I taught, followed when I lead, and accepted my counsel. They believed God had called me because He blessed what I did. Beverly was a living example of that favor. She announced that God had sent her to support the ministry God gave me.

If I had only been successful in one area, there would have been no confusion. However, I was successful as a teacher, too. The Junior Chamber of Commerce honored me as the "Outstanding Young Educator in the District." Early in my career the school district promoted me to English department head and then to curriculum coordinator for grades seven through twelve. I successfully negotiated with the school board for all teachers in the district for two years. I was an officer in the teachers' association. Success in teaching did not surprise me because I felt a clear sense of the call of God to be a teacher.

If God didn't change His mind once he called us, how could I have two callings at the same time—teacher and pastor?

My understanding of Ephesians 4:11-12 (KJV) added to the confusion.

> And he gave some, apostles; and some, prophets; and some, evangelists; and some, pastors and teachers; For the perfecting of the saints, for the work of the ministry, for the edifying of the body of Christ:

I thought God gave five gifts to the body and two of them were pastor and teacher. As the years went by, many thoughtful leaders suggested that there were four gifts to the body—pastor and teacher were combined. I was a pastor/teacher. I had always been a caregiver and I had always thought about how to teach any concept, any time, to anyone. My life-long passion was to care deeply and to communicate scriptural truth clearly and simply. Unfortunately, I could not fully grasp the scriptural truth about the call of God until He dealt with my internal turmoil.

All of my life I had struggled with a fear of abandonment. My insecure conclusion was that I had failed with two dads. I could not disappoint God. I had to get it right.

I wanted the call of God to be dramatic, like Saul of Tarsus being knocked off his donkey. Mark 3 (NIV) was a disappointment to me:

> Jesus went up on a mountainside and called to him those he wanted, and they came to him. He appointed twelve—designating them apostles—that they might be with him and that he might send them out to preach and to have authority to drive out demons.

No thunder and lightning, no choirs of angels, no surprises, just "Peter, come with me." I assumed that anything as important as the call of God would include high drama. Anything less and it probably wasn't genuine.

The Twelve had the advantage of seeing Him and hearing Him speak their names out loud. A personal audience with the Lord qualified as high drama. How would I know for sure if He called me? Would it be convincing?

One year, teaching at Manhattan High was particularly difficult.

As the new English department head, I implemented team teaching. The transition did not go as planned and the teachers blamed me. Because of the difficulties at school I thought I was failing to fulfill my calling. I desperately needed perspective. Our good friends Bob and Marianne agreed to pray with Beverly and me at 10:00 p.m. each night.

We did not announce the 10 o'clock prayer times. It was very surprising when people asked us if we ever had prayer times at our house. We said, "Yes," and one by one they joined us. One night thirty-seven people filled our family room at 10:00. We met every night for almost two years. Sometimes the praying ended after midnight but we were not tired the next day. What's more, the prayer was saving my sanity.

I did not try to grow this group numerically. For me it was simply a time of prayer. God multiplied this gathering. For instance, one night a National Guard trainee from St. Louis, Missouri, came. He had inquired at a Conoco station about three blocks away. None of us had ever gotten gas at that station. Nevertheless, the attendant told him about our prayer gathering and gave him perfect directions to the house. Without the Holy Spirit drawing thirty-seven to pray, we would have numbered four. Without Him refreshing us daily, we would have been physically exhausted.

In sharp contrast to the difficulties at school, the prayer time was wonderful. The group grew. Prayers were answered. I received clarity and encouragement and I made it through the school year.

All who came to the prayer time said God chose me to lead. Because I was overwhelmed at school, I did not feel called to any additional leadership. For me, the miracle of growth in the group was a historical fact, not evidence of the call. The enemy's fog machine was working.

Sister Jean, a Spirit-filled nun, shared the leadership responsibilities the second year. Several people thought we should prayerfully designate one person as the leader for the sake of clarity. The Catholic bishop located in Salina, ninety miles away, knew nothing of our small gathering. However, the day after we decided to choose a leader, he transferred her to Salina. Another dramatic intervention, but I believed I was a schoolteacher not a pastor. I was so sure God called me to be a teacher, I could not imagine Him changing His mind and calling me now to pastoral ministry.

During this season I led a Bible teaching and worship time each Friday night. That, too, was growing. We moved each time the group outgrew a location, reaching a weekly attendance of 270. While we were meeting in the Lutheran church basement, a group of about two dozen approached me.

"You are our pastor and this group is our church."

"Oh no, I'm just a schoolteacher."

It did not occur to me that two dozen thoughtful, praying Christians could be God's messengers, giving voice to the call.

I tried to short circuit their idea.

"We would need money for salaries to start a church. You can appoint a treasurer but you can't take up any offerings." *That should stop it.*

People gave like they knew something. Before long they had enough funds to hire three of us as full-time staff. They had no doubt God called me to be their pastor.

My hidden fear was that at any moment I might displease God and He would remove the call anyway. Twenty-four people entreating me was dramatic but it didn't remove the lifelong sense of abandonment and disapproval I felt.

God used a funny story to help me be clear. Beverly and I were attending a church of about 170 in Manhattan. The pastor was very pleased with his wonderful, unilateral discovery: he was an apostle. According to him, three of us were elders, not deacons. He believed the small church was going to grow dramatically as the people embraced this new revelation.

I came early to a monthly deacons' meeting so I could entreat him not to continue this sermon series. Many of the members thought he was full of pride and confusion if not deception, calling himself an apostle. They, also, doubted that we three deacons were elders. When I got there, he immediately invited me into his office. He repeated his new understanding of roles. Then he asked me what I thought.

I had asked the Lord for a thoughtful and respectful warning.

"Pastor, if you call yourself an apostle, people will resist it. If you do the work of an apostle, I think they will call you by your right name."

He wrote on the margin of his sermon notes, "They will call you by your right name."

Moments later, Larry, who rarely said anything at the deacons' meetings, walked in. As he passed the pastor, he said "Hi, Dumb Dumb."

I had never before heard him disrespect anyone, intentionally or unintentionally. The pastor didn't call himself an apostle again.

Had God really called me to be a pastor? I didn't want to be called "Dumb Dumb." So I served the best I knew how to, carrying a lot of self-doubt.

As I prayed one day, I said, "Lord, it feels like you tricked me into ministry."

Have you ever asked me if I called you to be a pastor?

"No, Lord!"

I knew your mistakes, your character flaws, the struggles you have with a few interesting people in the church, your sense of abandonment because of your childhood, and I still chose you.

I was speechless and greatly relieved.

I believed that if God called me to be a teacher, He would never change His mind about my vocation. He would not deny His word and at a later date call me to be a pastor. I know now that He called me to be a pastor but He chose an educational setting for me to practice pastoral care.

Except for the year we experimented with team teaching, I was very happy, teaching high school English. I had many opportunities to share my faith. My last year at that high school fifty-two kids accepted Christ's sacrifice and confessed Him to be their Lord. Many people contributed to that harvest. I received this as further loving confirmation of God calling me to be a pastor. That was the last year I taught in the public schools. I accepted God's and the church's call to be their full-time pastor.

Now, after seventy years, I know God wants all of us to be clear about our calling. As a loving father, He will affirm and confirm the calling. We are chosen and He will never abandon us.

- He will bless what we do. He will, also, allow difficulties to increase our trust in Him.

- He will give us clear perspective. He will, also, allow confusion to enter so we will seek His wisdom.

- He will send gifts (residing in people) that complement ours. He will, also, let Judas make an appearance.

1. You can be at peace about the Call of God. When God calls you, He will make it clear that He has chosen you—if you ask. The confirmation of your calling may look and sound unlike anyone else's.

2. You do not have to hold God to His word. He will do that for Himself. If he seems to be violating Romans 11:29, you are the one who is confused.

3. People will call you by your right name. Perceptive Christians have clear sight about your calling. Others will call you by a wrong name. That will be accusation and, therefore, false.

4. You can avoid much confusion by developing a relationship with an older person who has clarity about his calling.

Questions to Consider

There's a richness and fullness to God's plan for my life. It is the Call of God+ [plus].

First, I am an example of His craftsmanship. Beyond that, what has been lost because of sin has been recreated [born anew] in Christ Jesus. I am chosen and appointed. I have an inheritance and a life purpose.

There are meaningful and good works for me to do. God has prepared a path for my life. He has made ready a good life for me to live. He is involved, working out everything in agreement with

His counsel and according to His purpose. Ephesians 1:11 (AMP) and 2:10 (AMP).

Ask for revelation about one or more of these promises? If God promised to explain these two verses in Ephesians, what questions would you ask?

1. "God's [own] handiwork"—why do I need to understand, embrace, and even celebrate the way God created me? Appearance? Physical abilities? Mental and physical limits? Why celebrate?

2. I have been re-created. Sometimes, I don't act like it. How can I walk each day as one born anew?

3. How can I embrace the truth of being chosen and appointed? I know how to live as one not chosen and with little sense of being appointed. How can I walk as one chosen, fulfilling His appointment for my life?

4. My inheritance? life purpose? good works? the path for my life? and the good life God has prepared? If you want more, please ask the Lord how to understand and then, receive all He has for you.

    For we are God's [own] handiwork (His workmanship), recreated in Christ Jesus, [born anew] that we may do those good works which God predestined (planned beforehand) for us [taking paths which He prepared ahead of time], that we should walk in them [living the good life which He prearranged and made ready for us to live]. Ephesians 2:10 (AMP)

    In Him we also were made [God's] heritage (portion) and we obtained an inheritance; for we had been foreordained (chosen and appointed beforehand) in accordance with His purpose, who works out everything in agreement with the counsel and design of His [own] will.. Ephesians 1:11 (AMP)

CHAPTER TWENTY-THREE

AROUND THE MOUNTAIN AGAIN

I N MY LIFE GOD AUTHORED a well-defined pattern. Each success was followed by a lesson in humility.

My junior year in high school I enrolled in a year-long speech class. One of the class requirements was to enter the league speech contest. I memorized a humorous reading, "The Fisherman's Daughter." Two of my classmates, Ann and Doug, also entered the humorous reading competition. That created a dilemma. Only two of us could go to the district speech contest. Our class instructor, Mrs. Floyd, made the obvious decision. "The two of you who rank the highest at the league contest will represent the school at the district meet."

Our class instructor, Mrs. Floyd, made the obvious decision. "The two of you who rank the highest at the league contest will represent the school at the district meet."

Before the league contest weekend, I presented my humorous reading for church and civic groups. They all greatly affirmed my performance. I felt very confident.

After each competitive category, league officials posted the results on the wall outside the auditorium. Each student received a rating from I to IV. I received a number I rating and both my classmates did as well.

The next day Mrs. Floyd offered a solution. "The three of you will present your humorous readings in the school library auditorium. There will be three judges—Mrs. Linn, Mrs. Munroe, and me. We will choose the best two to go on to district."

I could hardly wait to get home. When the school bus stopped at our driveway, I ran to the kitchen.

"Doug, Ann, and I are going to present our humorous readings to three teachers—Doug's mother, Mrs. Floyd; Mrs. Linn, who told the class not to vote for me; and Mrs. Munroe, whose dog tried to bite me."

"So, you have already lost?"

"That's how it feels."

"Louie, is that what you hear the Lord saying?"

We prayed. I got my sense of humor back. That helped me do my best the day of the break-the-tie competition in the school library.

Mrs. Floyd told me what the three ladies decided. "Louie, we think it would be easier for you to memorize another reading. We would like you to present 'The Telltale Heart' by Edgar Allen Poe at the district contest. It is a dramatic reading so you will compete in a different division than Ann and Doug."

I embarrassed myself by crying, but at least I did not respond in anger. For the next several weeks Mrs. Floyd showed me great kindness. She tutored me at school, at her husband's office, and at her home.

At the district speech contest in Hays, Kansas, her son Doug received a number II rating; Ann, a number III rating; and I received a number I rating, which qualified me for the regional contest.

My district triumph was really a miracle. The rules were unbending. No presentation could go over eight minutes. At precisely eight minutes I stopped speaking because I could not remember my lines. I froze in place. The timekeeper thought I was done and turned off her clock. Seconds later my memory returned and I delivered the last thirty seconds of my reading. She admitted afterwards she was afraid to tell the judge she had turned off the clock, so she didn't report that I ran over. I would have been disqualified. Instead, the judge gave me a I rating.

At the regional competition I again was awarded a number I rating. At the state contest, the final rung on the ladder, the judge shocked me completely with a rating of IV. He said he didn't like the British accent I used for "The Telltale Heart."

I wanted to find a hiding place so I wouldn't have to tell everyone the results. When I finally phoned home, Mother offered a helpful perspective. "You rejoiced about the three number one ratings, Mrs. Floyd's kindness, and the timekeeper's mistake. Why stop rejoicing now?"

Once again, success was followed by a lesson in humility. Mother didn't let up. "What is the Lord teaching you?"

"Why did I get three number one ratings and then a four? Every time something really good happens, I get hammered. It feels like God is resisting me for unnamed offenses. If God wants me to be a public speaker, the debate fiascos, the unfair run-off for speech competition, negative responses—judgmental remarks, for instance, and damaged relationships seem like failure. How do they confirm the call of God on my life?" [My note: I can't focus on me and my failures and find God's supernatural peace or direction. If I simply enjoy His presence and wait for His timing to deal with the enemy, life is very eventful. His presence takes on new meaning.]

"Louie, I have heard a number of pastors and missionaries talk about the call of God. I don't remember them telling us how God prepared them to fulfill their call. We missed the journey from the call to the fulfillment."

"I think this is really hard."

"That's true but His way is also kind. I do not think He called you to succeed or fail but to bring glory to Him. If you miss that the first time, he lets you go around the mountain another time so you can learn the lesson."

"Around the mountain another time. That is definitely my story."

Reflections

One of my students, a high school senior, said, "Why don't you just give me an F and get it over with?" I was helping him write a paper worthy of a higher grade.

"Bill, I am not going to give you an F. You and I, working together, are capable of writing a decent paper."

He trembled and a tear ran down his cheek. "I thought you were just trying to be nice."

"If I ever give up on you, I will give you a pass to the library and recommend a good book."

"Well, if you are not going to send me to the library, show me one more time how to write a thesis sentence."

Bill did not object to my correction because I gave him acceptance. I was merely passing on what I desired for myself.

For years I thought maturity is the point at which you no longer need correction. You have learned your lessons, acquired the needed skills, and developed a harmonious network of relationships.

When I had to redo, retrain, reacquire, reorder, or revise anyone or anything, the unspoken accusations of failure and disapproval increased dramatically. That prompted a dark symphony of rejection and abandonment. I was drawn repeatedly to join that orchestra.

Jeremiah 30:12-17 (NIV) was a breakthrough passage for me.

> This is what the Lord says: "Your wound is incurable, your injury beyond healing. There is no one to plead your cause, no remedy for your sore, no healing for you. All your allies have forgotten you; they care nothing for you. I have struck you as an enemy would and punished you as would the cruel, because your guilt is so great and your sins so many. Why do you cry out over your wound, your pain that has no cure? Because of your great guilt and many sins I have done these things to you. But all who devour you will be devoured; all your enemies will go into exile. Those who plunder you will be plundered; all who make spoil of you I will despoil. But I will restore you to health and heal your wounds," declares the Lord, "because you are called an outcast, Zion for whom no one cares."

Verses 12-15 say that I am wounded, sick, vulnerable, and abandoned. God has punished me and I deserved it. No surprises, so far! Verse 16 describes total grace: without an explanation, He emphatically states He will defend me. Verse 17 declares that He will heal me and restore me. These six verses are the story of my life. I deserve punishment over and over but the God who cares affirms that He will restore me.

I offered Bill a chance to rewrite his paper. Because of God's grace I, too, get more than one second chance? If I stop at verse 15 (the response of a just God to my failures), rewriting my paper is pointless. I deserve an F, which I will receive. Verses 16 and 17 (God's declarations that He will defend and restore me) astonish me and compel me to repent and relearn how to be a son. The One who loves me most has decided to act on my behalf. That's acceptance! When He asks me to rewrite, I know it is an unexpected, undeserved opportunity to learn what I missed the first time.

Romans 8: 20-28, 35 repeats this theme—sons subjected to frustration and frailty, groaning while they wait for adoption. They don't know how to pray. In the middle of this, the Holy Spirit intercedes for them. He knows God's thoughts. If they line up with those thoughts, God will work in all things for their good. The chapter has a glorious ending: nothing will ever separate them from God's love.

He doesn't have me repeat something because He's angry with me. He asks me to do it again because what I have been doing lacks fullness. That's not His plan for my life. He intends for me to line up with His will and then, all things will work together for good, for His redemptive purpose. That will be the best possible result.

A couple of months ago I had thirty-seven radiation treatments. At an early hour on day #1, the Lord was training me how to think in this cancer-treatment setting.

I have work for you to do. Do not misinterpret this day. Do not focus on yourself after the radiation.

After the first day's treatment, I returned to the waiting room, looking for a divine appointment. I entered the lobby and saw an eight-year-old girl standing by a jigsaw puzzle. She was alone and not moving. I sat down at the puzzle, picked up a piece, and handed it to her without looking at her. After a long moment, she put the piece where it belonged. I handed her another with the same result. Then, she dropped to her knees beside the low table and began putting pieces in the puzzle.

Without saying a word to each other, we worked together for about twenty minutes until her parents reappeared. The mother had wheeled the dad to the back of the treatment center in a wheelchair so he could receive chemo. The little girl, left alone, needed someone. God arranged for me to be at that place at that exact time.

I had to drive in heavy traffic for thirty-eight minutes, partially undress before three very gracious nurses, and lie still while I was radiated. While the machine whirred around me, I remembered the terrible, possible side effects from radiation. That affected my stamina. The oncologist, also, mentioned typical side effects such as grumpiness and depression. I wasn't grumpy but I did struggle with depression many mornings.

In the middle of the radiation treatments, the hormone therapy caused additional side effects: hot flashes, abdominal cramping, and joint pain. Hearing about the impact of the hormone shot, my friend Noreen had a question.

"Did this increase your empathy for your wife?"

"Noreen, it increased my empathy for every woman who has ever lived."

Before one particular crack-of-dawn drive to the Cancer Therapy & Research Center (CTRC), Beverly asked me, "How are you doing?"

"God is retraining my eyes," I told her.

Eighty people each day receive radiation at CTRC. That gives the enemy a huge opening to question everything: *Are you a child of God and here for radiation? What happened to healing? If the Lord truly loved you, wouldn't He heal you?*

If we don't tell the Enemy to get lost, he accuses us of bringing this on ourselves. *What did you do this time? Parkinson's plus radiation for your prostate? Well, you can be sure of this: it's your fault.*

He waits for us to hear the forty zillion possible side effects of radiation added to the possibility of the treatments failing.

Did you hear that? You may have permanent damage to the organs near your prostate. That is really scary, isn't it? You need to stop ministering to others and focus on yourself. That is your only hope.

When he tempts me, I don't always know what to say. Then, the Holy Spirit reminds me that He is interceding for me and nothing can separate me from God's love. I move into the next situation, knowing I will need additional training. For instance, before this diagnosis, I had no idea the CTRC existed. I had never seen this part of the battlefield.

I told Beverly that day, "My eyes are wide open and I am okay."

After we left the Ransom Hospital and moved to the farm, I vowed to never go back to a hospital again unless it was feet first. As a pastor, I could not avoid hospital visits, but they have always been a struggle for me. The Lord has shown me how that vow was not His idea. I need to be vulnerable—and that includes hospital visits—if I am to love well. The training on "how to serve in a war zone" is costly. I am realizing how little I knew of others' struggles with cancer. Now, I am an undercover agent, learning increased empathy.

Most importantly, God is present. I asked for healing and He gave me His presence, His favor, and divine appointments, but He has not removed the Parkinson's. He is healing my eyes (the eyes of my heart) and increasing my compassion. I am honored by that. Clearly, He still has work for me to do.

Last month Beverly and I went on a transatlantic cruise aboard the Queen Elizabeth. Our dinner assignment was table #500—in my opinion, the worst table in the elegant dining room. It was close to the entrance so everyone walked by the table. It was a long way from a view of the North Atlantic. The marvelous view of the ship's wake and the setting sun blessed others at the table nearest the fantail.

The second night I looked for a divine appointment. The man ahead of us was pushing a cart and walking with great difficulty.

(I did not have a nifty cart, but walking was hard for me, too. In fact, I had balance problems before we got on the ship.) The Lord is training me to be empathetic, so, I connected with the man. As he and I waited side-by-side for the doors to open to the dining room, I asked, "How are you doing, sir?"

His speech was halting, "I'm ... not ... doing ... very ... well." I surmised that Parkinson's was slowing his speech.

"You are not doing very well," I repeated. "What do you need?"

"They gave us table #599 at the very back of the dining room. I am having a hard time pushing my cart in and around so many tables. I need a table close to the entrance."

"You have met the right person. I have the table just inside the entrance. I will talk to the maître d' and see if we can swap."

My new friend Colin, hobbled by Parkinson's and struggling to walk, traded us table #599 with its awesome view of the ship's wake and the setting sun. Chris, the main server for that table, had the most seniority in the dining hall. He had been on the Queen Elizabeth since the first day she sailed. (We had not enjoyed the server at table #500, the table we gave away.) When Chris saw my hand tremors, he told Beverly, "My father died of Parkinson's four months ago." He was honored to serve us and we were delighted to nurture him.

I have a new goal. I want to line up with God's purpose each day and see Him work in everything for good. He has trained me to think that way and then, He has loved me so deeply I want more of His purpose. Being trained and retrained and then, being drawn into His redemptive purpose by His love intrigues me. It challenges me every day to learn, to grow, and to follow His lead. All that offers rich fellowship with Him.

If He heals me, and I am praying that He will, my purpose will be the same. *Draw me into your redemptive purpose every day. Train me, retrain me, or not—whatever pleases you!*

Questions to Consider

1. Are you a life learner? How are you discovering what's next: Prayer? Classes? Books? Your mentor? Or do you prefer the alternative—retirement with no more training?

2. Do you have a plan to apply God's Word to your life day by day? Are you memorizing scriptures? Have you prayed, asking the Lord what life-giving verse He has in mind for you this month?

3. When God has an assignment for you, are you available for service? Have you had your divine appointment today?

4. Are you learning to love Him and to receive His love for you? May He train you and retrain you until your relationship is all He intends.

CHAPTER TWENTY-FOUR

YOU WILL HAVE AN IMPACT

I SAT ON THE FRONT ROW at church every Sunday. Because everyone could see me, I learned to sleep sitting straight up. One Sunday morning in the middle of the sermon, I had a nightmare. I leapt out of my seat, landed near the altar, and let out a mighty shout.

Pastor Satterfield and the entire congregation laughed and laughed. Finally, the Sunday morning crowd settled back into their seats for the rest of the sermon. That's when the pastor made a fatal mistake. He looked at me again. When he did, he began laughing and could not stop. He motioned everyone to go home. He plopped into his seat on the platform and continued his out-of-control chuckles.

My leap totally embarrassed Mother and Dad. "Louie, wait until the pastor heads out the door. You must apologize," Mother said.

About thirty minutes later he was nearly calm. He walked to the back of the church.

"Pastor, please forgive me," I asked.

"Oh, you don't need to apologize. I haven't had such a good laugh in years." He patted me on the head and walked out the front door, laughing again.

Mother couldn't resist a comment. "Well, son, I have always said you would have an impact on any church you attend."

Dad did not see the humor in my mighty leap. He thought I had had enough impact.

That wasn't the way it turned out. I dumbfounded the adults again at an impromptu Sunday afternoon church business meeting. Our particular denomination encouraged every member to participate in the government of the church. An important example was the selection of the pastor. The candidate would preach and then the congregation would vote. Two thirds of the members had to vote "for" the man they had just heard in order for him to be approved.

Pastor Satterfield had resigned and the church was eagerly looking for a replacement. The district headquarters encouraged the congregation to invite Pastor Dell to "try out." When our would-be pastor finished his sermon, Brother Russell, the chairman of the deacon board, announced we were going to have a church business meeting immediately so we could vote for or against Pastor Dell. To be sure we did everything right, he asked if anyone had a question. For a moment no one responded.

I had a question. I didn't know I had to be eighteen to be a member and have the freedom to speak during a congregational meeting; I thought his invitation included me. I asked, "Is it possible we are moving too quickly? Should we wait at least two days while we ask the Lord for direction?"

After a very awkward pause, Brother Russell had an answer.

"Brother Dell is on a tight schedule. He and his wife drove here this morning all the way from Oklahoma. He believes that if he is the man for this job, we will vote in his favor. He is asking us to have a brief prayer, hear God, and make a decision. If two thirds of the congregation approve him, he will accept the invitation and head back home immediately to pack and load the rental truck."

Close to one hundred percent of those present voted "Yes." Two weeks later Pastor Dell and his family moved into the parsonage.

Mother explained the arrangement. "This is a small church and we don't pay much. But the pastor does get free housing."

During his first year there Pastor Dell annoyed or confused almost everyone. Many of the members invited him and his wife for a meal. Each time, the meal ended with an argument about some small point of scripture, the church, or daily life. The church and the new pastor simply did not work well together.

I protested to Mother. "I was right. We should have waited a while."

"Louie, you were right. Now you face a test. Can you forgive all of us? Let God redeem this story."

Brother Russell had one more upside-down encounter with me. He offered to teach the high school boys' Sunday school class. To make his task as easy as possible, he had a teacher's quarterly, which included extra information and explanations about each of thirteen lessons. What he didn't know was that I, also, had a teacher's quarterly. Mother bought it for me. She told me what she expected. "I want you to be super prepared because God has a calling on your life."

I could hardly wait for the class to begin. Brother Russell prayed and then told us the story of the life of Moses. I had read and reread the story. His version was different from the story in the Bible. I questioned him, asking which verses he was referring to.

He paused.

"I guess I owe you boys an apology. I didn't have time to prepare for this class, so I went to see the movie *The Ten Commandments*. Charlton Hesston was Moses."

Brother Russell resigned after the class. The church strongly objected to its members attending movies. (Mother and I always wondered if he told the pastor how he prepared for the class.) When the pastor asked him why he was resigning, he said, "Louie asked too many hard questions."

I had ended a morning service with my leap. I spoke up in a congregational meeting when everyone expected me to be quiet. Now, a Sunday school teacher resigned because of my questions. If this was impact, I did not want it.

"Mother, you said I would impact any church I attend. I think I am just driving people crazy."

"I know you. You are probably wondering what a dad would say about your impact. Louie, you don't need a dad today; you just need an honest mother. It is time for me to come clean. You jumping out to the altar embarrassed me. I knew you didn't do it on purpose, but I could not believe you did it. I think I missed the point. The pastor and everyone else enjoyed a good laugh.

"When you said we should wait and pray before we voted, I was thinking the same thing. I did not speak; you did. I was a coward; you were brave. It did not take a year for me to know you were right; it just took that long for me to speak up.

"And about Brother Russell's resignation ... I knew he would not inspire you and I doubted that he would prepare for the class. That is why I gave you the teacher's quarterly. With that I knew you would learn. It is definitely not your fault that he quit. It was wrong, totally wrong, that he would fail to prepare and then blame a kid.

"I do not know when you will make a difference in the church but I can honestly say you are impacting me. Now, Louie, get out the Chinese checkers and I will *impact* you."

Reflections

Mother's assertion that I would have an impact in the church stirred both fear and pride in me. Fear that it would never happen. Pride that the dads who had abandoned me, the adults who disappointed me, and the kids who rejected my friendship would all be speechless on that day of great impact.

I was, also, acting out of a sense of entitlement. Surely I had suffered enough.

"Please, Lord, have somebody say it."

Just off the stage to the left a deeply resonant voice spoke, "Give the kid a break!" That was my dream: me, center stage, making a difference; God, stage left, cheering me on.

Our church met in what used to be a feed and grain store. It was low rent. God didn't seem to object to the setting. He came to the feed store on Sunday nights.

Ten or twelve people stayed to pray every Sunday night after the service. There was such a sense of God's presence that I have never forgotten it. My heart changed. I began to want Him to impact me more than I wanted to impact others.

How could I ever forgot the joy of His presence? From time to time like every sinner, I did. In morning family devotions we read the parable about the shepherd leaving the ninety-nine sheep in the fold and going out to get the one lost sheep. I was that wandering one. How many times had He said He would never leave me or forsake me? He found me and I was moved to tears. Once again I was in His presence!

He saved Phil's life. We were keenly aware of His presence that day.

Less dramatic moments were critically important, too. We drove eighty-eight miles to Garden City for a youth rally. In a way I still remember, God was with us during the worship time. Our worship invited Him and He was present. "Yet you are holy, enthroned on the praises of Israel," says Psalm 22:3 (NLT). "You sit as the Holy One. The praises of Israel are your throne" (NCT).

The times of worship touched my heart: He was impacting me. That was the goal. When I focused on me having an impact, the results were mixed. Some of what I did and said produced good results—some bad. When I prayed that God would be with us, impacting us, the results were surprising and delightful.

Mother (1921-2010) has been gone almost three years. I am glad she is no longer in pain, but I wish we could talk about impact one more time. This is what I would say, "Me, impacting the church, is no longer my goal. I pray instead that the Lord will impact me each day."

She would disagree and I would explain, "Responding to what He does is my primary and satisfying purpose. What I initiate is not my central focus."

John 3:29-30 (MSG) expresses my thoughts: "That's why my cup is running over. This is the assigned moment for him to move into the center, while I slip off to the sidelines."

Questions to Consider

President Harry Truman once said, "It is amazing what you can accomplish if you do not care who gets the credit." I would add, "It is even more amazing what you can accomplish if God gets all the credit."

1. In practical terms how do we do that?

2. I like the term, "a confident humility." If you use that to describe someone's state of mind, what would you mean?

3. How can you (or do you) humble yourself?

4. Have you experienced Him "lifting you up"? (See 1 Peter 5:6.)

5. Was it "in due time"?

CHAPTER TWENTY-FIVE

NOT PHYSICS!

OTHER DECIDED WE SHOULD SELL fresh eggs in town. Since Mrs. Munroe was one of the high school teachers, Mother encouraged me to ask her if she would buy our eggs. I seriously objected but Mother wouldn't take "No" for an answer.

To my dismay, Mrs. Munroe said, "Yes, bring a dozen fresh eggs on Thursday."

When I took the eggs to her house, her son Benson opened the door, smirked, and shouted over his shoulder, "Eggs!"

I hated him for his scorn.

Then, their large bulldog growled at me. Benson gave me a condescending look. "He won't hurt you."

His mother gave Benson the money for the eggs and he handed it to me. I turned to leave and the dog jumped at me. I had a large wallet in my back left pocket. The dog clamped his teeth over the wallet. I screamed, Benson laughed, and the dog let loose. I never delivered eggs to their house again. I had no love for the Munroe clan and I imagined they felt the same about me.

Unfortunately, Mrs. Munroe was the only physics teacher in the high school. I struggled with physics. I wasn't the only one having difficulty, but Larry and Ann received help from her during the class. It was totally unfair.

Mother said to me many times, "Don't jump to conclusions. Give people a chance to do the right thing."

I prayed for courage and then asked Mrs. Munroe a respectful question.

"Ma'am, could you take a look at my lab experiment?"

"You will have to come in before or after school."

"I ride the school bus, Ma'am. It gets here five minutes before school begins and leaves five minutes after—with or without us."

She shrugged and walked away. I followed her.

"Can you help us during class?"

"I said before or after school."

Her sharp answer enraged me. Why was she helping some kids and not others? It seemed clear to me that she had favorites. Beyond that, she must not care about bus kids. Ignoring the bus schedule seemed like clear evidence.

It was time for some detective work. First, I questioned Larry.

"Does your family go to the same church as the Munroes?"

"We don't go to church."

"Do you hang out at their house?"

"My mother plays bridge with Mrs. Munroe."

Aha, good detective work.

Ann's answer was worse. "My mother is Mrs. Munroe's bridge partner."

I had solved the mystery. That was why she favored Larry and Ann.

I gave great thought to an appropriate response. When she handed out the next exam, I drew a large zero on the front of the test. I added a note. "My performance on this test will be an exact reflection of your teaching ability."

She quickly read my note and stomped out of the classroom. I imagined smoke coming out of her ears.

During the next class period Principal Harry Linn called an impromptu assembly. All of the 150 high school students met in the school library. The principal motioned to me to sit on the front row—alone.

He stood in front of me but did not look at me. In a well-measured tone he began. "This school has some very bright people who think they are witty. Their humor is totally misguided. I will not tolerate it." The longer he talked, the more passionate he became. The sermon continued for at least fifteen minutes. He listed every penalty that was available to him— removal from extracurricular activities, forfeiture of all honors and awards, no credit for one or more classes, a hearing before the school board, suspension, expulsion—the list seemed unending.

Mr. Linn's threats did not move me. I had been bullied before. Dad had beaten me with a bullwhip for lying when I had not lied. At home and at school I wanted to be treated fairly. He could punish me but my cause was just.

He closed with a dramatic but slightly altered reading of Galatians 6:7. "Be not deceived; this school will not be mocked: for whatsoever a man soweth, that shall he also reap."

He never asked before or after the all-school assembly to hear my side of the story. Many of the 149 students questioned me.

"Why were you on the front row?"

"What did you say to make him mad?"

"Is he going to expel you?"

I told them about the note. Their responses varied from total horror to sheer admiration. I was very pleased with myself.

I was sure Mother would hear my story and defend me. Instead, her response totally surprised me. I wanted to be seen as a champion. What I got instead was correction.

When I got off of the school bus, I ran to the house to tell Mother about the injustice and the abusive school assembly in my honor. Dad listened quietly as well.

Mother had one question.

"Did you write that note to Mrs. Munroe?"

"Yes, I did."

"Why would I protect you from the consequences of something you did? If you thought you were right, trust the outcome. If you are telling me you were wrong, how can you make it right?"

They sat quietly while I thought.

"Mrs. Munroe was wrong but I did not like act like a Christian when I wrote the note. I will not drop physics and I will apologize."

I thought she would soften when she saw my change of heart. Even though I maintained a C average for the rest of the year, she gave me an F as a final grade. [I know now the heart God wanted to change was mine.]

My high school diploma recorded 3 A's, 2 B's, and the F for my senior year.

I thought that was the end of the story. Eighteen months later I joined the navy, went through boot camp in San Diego, and reported to advanced training at the Memphis Naval Air Station.

The first class was a terrific shock. Aviation electronics technician training began with physics. In sheer disbelief I turned to the fellow trainee next to me. "Are we starting with physics?"

Before he could answer, the instructor, a petty officer first class, quickly walked to our seats. He had a question for the guy next to me. "Are you my replacement? Did they send you without notifying me?" He removed his sailor hat and scratched his head. "Why didn't you tell me you were here to take over?"

His use of irony was not lost on me. However, he totally mystified the guy next to me.

"No, Sir, I am not your replacement. I am just one of the students."

"Well, that is a great relief. I still have a job. But, why did he ask you his question?"

"Sir, I have no idea."

"At least we cleared up who the teacher is."

He never spoke directly to me but I had no doubt who the target was for this lesson in misdirection. Unlike my high school physics teacher, this instructor always helped us with our lessons. He did not tolerate any disrespect nor was he ever disrespectful. And he had no favorites.

I wrote a letter to Mother.

Dear Mother,

I completed the basic aviation electronics course with an eighty-four percent average. It included physics. You remember my troubles with that course. *After high school I said I would never study physics again. God must be laughing at me.*

Love,

Louie

Mother wrote back:

Dear Louie,

Is it possible your Father in Heaven chose a navy man to deliver His Dad message this time?

Thoughtfully,

Mother

Reflections

In my opinion, most people overlooked injustice. As a result, I took up other people's offenses.

Mrs. Parmley, the 11th grade English teacher, always called on Julius and Murphy first and second After they had humiliated themselves with consistently wrong answers, she would turn to Ann and me to give the correct answer. I decided it was time to show support for the guys in the back of the room. They needed a champion.

Mrs. Parmley assigned the class a twenty-five-sentence exercise about predicate nominatives (a noun or pronoun that follows a linking verb and renames the subject). We were to underline the predicate nominatives in each of the twenty-five sentences. In the sample sentence at the top of the page, the word to be underlined, the predicate nominative, was one and one-half inches from the start of the sentence. I drew a line from the top of the page to the bottom and underlined whatever word in each sentence was one inch from the start, guaranteeing the answer would be wrong. [That measurement had absolutely no grammatical significance; it was simply part of my complicated joke.]

I was sure Mrs. Parmley would quickly figure out that someone was playing games with the exercise. Teachers generally had their warning systems set on high alert. That would lead to an interesting conversation when she discovered the clever sabotage of the class assignment. Then, I would heroically defend the guys she always called on first.

I asked everyone to have a little fun with me. Each of the other twenty-four students underlined the same incorrect answers.

At the start of class the next day Mrs. Parmley began as usual.

"Julius, sentence number one, 'The car is a red Cadillac.' What is the predicate nominative?"

"Ma'am, I underlined *red.*"

She had not expected a correct answer. Murphy?"

"*Red.* Same as Julius."

It was time for her to demonstrate how well she had taught the college-bound students.

"Ann, sentence number one, please."

Ann played her part well. "I know you are not going to believe this, Mrs. Parmley, but I underlined *red*, also."

I was her closer, the ninth-inning specialist.

"Louie, please give us the right answer."

"Hmmm, we must not have understood the assignment. I marked *red*, also."

Mrs. Parmley aged ten years in front of our eyes. With slumped shoulders she turned to the blackboard. She had a terrible task ahead of her, teaching ignorant farm kids about predicate nominatives.

I turned and looked at the rest of the class. I had not gained any compassion for Julius and Murphy. Ann was angry because I had drawn her into the plot. I had crushed Mrs. Parmley. In the eyes of the class I was not a champion, just a smart kid with a misguided sense of humor.

"Mrs. Parmley, wait just a moment. I was looking at the wrong sentence. You said number one? The answer is Cadillac, the noun in the sentence following the linking verb that is interchangeable with the subject. Ann knows the answer to that, too. I think we understand predicate nominatives. Would you like me to show Murphy and Julius the right answer?"

She had a look of pure relief on her face.

"No, let's move on to direct objects."

I had tried and failed to rescue Julius and Murphy. Instead, my plan did more harm than good.

I wish I had learned my lesson that day but I tried to rescue many other times. The results were never good but there was so much injustice and so few would-be champions.

Questions to Consider

The Bible is very clear. We are not to avenge ourselves. Romans 12:19 (AMP),

> Beloved, never avenge yourselves, but leave the way open for [God's] wrath; for it is written, Vengeance is Mine, I will repay (requite), *says the Lord.*

Hebrews 10:30 (AMP) emphatically repeats the theme,

> For we know Him Who said, Vengeance is Mine [retribution and the meting out of full justice rest with Me]; I will repay [I will exact the compensation], says the Lord. And again, The Lord will judge *and* determine and solve and settle the cause and the cases of His people.

1. Vengeance, an eye for an eye, makes sense. Why shouldn't we settle our own problems, arrange a favorable settlement when we have been sinned against, and demand a terrible price to serve as a deterrent against future attacks? Why doesn't vengeance work?

2. Forgiveness, letting the perpetrator out of your jail and turning it over to God, doesn't make complete sense. Why doesn't it? However, it does work. Why does it work?

How are we to respond to injustice? When your children tell you someone has mistreated them, you are not supposed to judge the abuser or get even. What can (and should) you do?

Look at the four problems.

- Problem #1: *Limited authority.* God is the only one totally authorized to judge or to exact revenge. He instructs us not to act as judges. No matter how skilled, we are not authorized.

- Problem #2: *Limited sight.* Paul, writing in 1 Corinthians says, "We see through a glass darkly." Dark sunglasses 24/7 clearly limit what we see. Unless we trust His sight and insight, we see part of the problem; He sees it all.

- Problem #3: *Limited skills.* We cannot match God's skill set. He, alone, has the capacity to judge a man's thoughts and intentions.

- Problem #4: *Limited information.* He is omniscient, knowing all.

3. The question: considering our natural and spiritual limitations as judges and avengers, why don't we trust God?

CHAPTER TWENTY-SIX

GOD'S MICE

I SIMPLY COULD NOT MISS MY first student council trip. I got up at 3:30 a.m., milked the eight cows by hand, ran the cream separator, fed the chickens, and put on my Sears Roebuck catalog, black suit with a razor thin, black, clip-on tie. It was my best look.

I told Mother, "I think I can walk to the high school in two hours if I go down Star Route to the highway. I cannot cut across country because I will be sweaty and dirty when I get there."

It was eight and one-half miles to Ness City High School. On the bulletin board the activity bus schedule read, "Student Council Conference—Leave for Goodland, Kansas at 6:30 a.m."

I left on time at 4:30 a.m. It was a cool, cloudy morning. The first four miles of Star Route were gravel and hard to walk on. Highway 96 was asphalt—easy to walk on. Both roads were devoid of traffic. By 6:15 a.m., fifteen minutes until departure, I was two miles from the school. Veraging one mile every sixteen minutes, I was going to miss the bus.

I prayed desperately, "God, help me! God, help me! God, help me!"

There is not a word in the English language to describe that morning's despair. I felt that my parents and God had abandoned me. I wanted to scream and weep but I knew everyone would see my tear-streaked face when—and *if*—I got on the bus.

A Catholic family who lived one mile east of us drove past.

In our town there were two grade schools, a private school for Catholics and a public school for Protestants. State law allowed the public school bus to pick up Catholics but they had to come to the nearest road. In other words, the bus did not go out of its way for Catholics. As a result, the neighbors seldom rode the bus. I barely knew them.

To my amazement they recognized me, picked me up, and took me to the high school. I was very grateful but so angry I could not speak. When we got to the school, I nodded to them and waved good-bye. I got on the bus. One minute later the driver closed the door and drove out of the parking lot.

I finally fell asleep on the school bus. When I awoke, I felt weary and numb. The past few days played in my mind like a film with no "off" switch.

Summoning all my courage, I had asked Mother on Sunday night, "Can you help me milk the cows Tuesday morning?"

I was going to ask for a ride to town, also, but Dad interrupted.

"It is not our fault you are in student—whatever! We have a farm to run. Milking those cows is your job every day. Do not ask us to give you a ride. You figure it out."

This was no ordinary request from me. Mrs. Floyd, my English teacher, nominated me for the student council. Step two was the election, students deciding who would represent each class.

My candidacy annoyed Mrs. Linn, my Latin teacher. She and I had almost constant conflict. Edie, as we called her behind her back, had the disconcerting habit in Latin class of calling on me to recite first every day.

I decided to cure her. I prepared a made-up translation of one day's Latin assignment. True to form, Edie called on me as soon as she finished taking attendance.

I read with a halting voice, pretending to have difficulty with the translation.

"Aeneas … got in his boat … and sailed … around the tip … of Italy." I paused for dramatic effect.

Mrs. Linn demanded, "Louis! Where are you reading?" (She

always called me "Louis." She insisted Louie was common and undignified. Latin class was her opportunity to civilize me.)

When she stopped me, I was smiling on the inside.

"I'm reading from page twenty-one, today's assignment."

She gave me her most disapproving look.

"Karen! Will you please translate?"

Mrs. Linn never called on me again. She found another way to reassert her control. Later that day we had a Junior Class (Class of '59) meeting. The student council election was the final item on the agenda. Mrs. Linn addressed that topic.

"You know that Louis is one of the candidates. You may not know that he is very busy and probably will not have time to fulfill the student council responsibilities. Besides that, he rides the school bus and has no way to get here for morning meetings."

She nodded to the class and gave me a stern look.

Her editorial compelled me to act. I knew this attempt to keep me from office frustrated the other invisible kids in the class as well. To them and to me it was personal. The world ignored each of us for different reasons. I was a zit factory. Clearasil had no discernible effect on my blemishes. I hated to see my record-setting pimples in the mirror.

Julius was another kind of invisible. Mrs. Linn never did learn his name. She called him "Who-lee-oo" or "Julian" or "Last Seat— Row 4" and one time, "Geronimo." That time we all laughed until she said, "You know your name. Please recite." For once, Julius was silent as well as invisible. That day he became my ally.

Mrs. Linn's public assault, telling the class not to vote for me, gave me visibility. Everyone waited, knowing I would not ignore her speech.

I put together a class roster. After each student's name I marked "I" for *invisible* or DNM for *"doesn't need me."* I did not say to invisible students, "Please vote for me," but I launched a silent election campaign. For instance, I gave Connie and Sue birthday cards.

They both laughed and protested. "It's not our birthdays!"

"I know that but I want to be the first to wish you Happy Birthday!"

Invisible people love that kind of surprise.

In Mrs. Linn's class an unsharpened pencil was a no-no. No pencil was worse—a capital offense. Brenda, who sat across the aisle from me, hardly ever said a word. For some unknown reason no one ever asked her for a date. That qualified her as an "I." One day in Latin class she could not find her pencil. She gave me a palms-up, helpless gesture. I gave her my pencil. When Edie discovered I did not have a pencil, she ordered me to go to the library for the hour. Edie banished me for the day but I was Brenda's friend for life.

Because I noticed details, I told Carol, "Your blue and gold dress perfectly matches your azure eyes and honey-blonde hair." I became a walking greeting card. She could not believe that anyone had actually seen her.

Julius and Murphy were train wrecks in English class. It only took a few moments for me to underline the direct objects in their workbook exercise. Mrs. Parmley could not believe their answers were perfect that day.

Finally, the day of the election dawned. I could not stop trembling. When the principal announced the results, Harold received the most votes but I beat out Ann by two votes, making me the other class representative to student council. Edie had a very grim look.

Edie's opposition and Mrs. Floyd's support inspired me. I had to be on the bus to Goodland. After the Catholic neighbors rescued me and gave me a ride, I wanted to hate Dad for refusing to take me to the school that morning. Mother's warning kept ringing in my head.

"Don't drink the poison! When Dad is hard on you, you still have a choice. Don't drink the poison!"

For Fred Keller, my stepfather, life was simple. It consisted of two lists: things you should do and things you should not do. If you chose from the wrong list, a painful whipping would help you remember the next time. I struggled with life in his black and white world. Worse yet, I didn't know what was on each list. Why was a ride to school on his list of things I shouldn't ask for? He did not use the bullwhip but refusing to give me a ride was worse. My back ached. My feet were sore. My head throbbed as the bus headed to Goodland.

The all-day conference ended. We survived the three-hour trip back to Ness City. I dreaded the thought of walking eight miles home. Two blocks from the school, the faculty sponsor stopped, smiled, and offered me a ride home. Two miracle rides in the same day!

Mother waited up for me. She was sitting at the kitchen table, reading her Bible. A slice of pecan pie, my favorite dessert, was waiting for me. She poured a tall glass of ice-cold milk.

I could not eat. I was still in terrible turmoil about the day. My questions poured out.

"Mother, what was wrong with asking for help with milking?" I wept until my heart was empty. "Was it sinful to ask for a ride? Was God punishing me?"

She had no answer. The chimes on the grandfather clock in the next room rang twelve times. I had one more question. "Why didn't you fight for me?"

She hugged me before she answered. "I honestly do not know."

As Mother listened to me, it quieted my heart. I needed someone to hear my pain. Calm slowly returned. Then, laughter came.

"Mother, you know God sent mice to pick me up?"

I told her about the neighbors picking me up on Highway 96. Their last name was Meis. We both laughed.

I was still puzzled. "It was a miracle for them to pick me up, but it was a scary, last-minute miracle. If God loves me, why did He put me in that desperate place, two miles to go with fifteen minutes left?"

Sometimes, God is confusing. I believed He prompted the neighbors and later, the faculty sponsor, to pick me up. But why would He allow my parents to fail so miserably in the first place, refusing to take me to school?

God sent mice in the morning, an observant teacher in the middle of the day, and pecan pie at night. I was grateful but I wanted answers. I fell asleep with my clothes on. Maybe life would make sense tomorrow.

Reflections

For most of my life surprises were painful. As an adult I began planning the next year's vacation as soon as we returned home each July. I covered every detail over and over. As the months passed, half or more of my enjoyment was the anticipation. If someone else planned my birthday celebration, I was restless. I felt left out, tempted to fear that the celebration would not be satisfying.

Being elected to student council was a rarity, a surprise that was truly satisfying. I wanted my parents to be happy for me. When they refused to give me a ride to town, it was mind numbing. They were not alongside me, relishing the thought of my first student council activity; they were not involved at all.

When Dad returned from the war, his lack of connection with Mother and me was a painful surprise. Him leaving jn the night was the prizewinner for *worst surprise ever* until the early morning walk to catch the student council bus. As I headed to town that morning, I had two hours to recall every major, agonizing surprise of my life. By the time the neighbors stopped for me, I was so upset I had difficulty thinking straight.

I couldn't recall any scripture commanding, or even suggesting, that we enjoy surprises or avoid them. However, I did find verses that said to trust God and to ask for wisdom. The scripture passage that brought peace was Isaiah 55:8-9 (NLV).

> "For My thoughts are not your thoughts, and My ways are not your ways," says the Lord. "For as the heavens are higher than the earth, so are My ways higher than your ways, and My thoughts than your thoughts."

I prayed, "Lord, you know what is really going on. I need to follow your lead because I can't see the big picture. Please forgive me when I become afraid and angry instead of turning to you. Thank you, Lord, for sending all the grace I need."

2 Corinthians 9:8 (AMP) says,

> And God is able to make all grace (every favor and earthly blessing) come to you in abundance, so that you may always and under all circumstances and whatever the need, be self-sufficient [possessing enough to require no aid or support and furnished in abundance for every good work and charitable donation].

For years I was fearful and self-protective. As I have learned to trust Him, He frequently surprises me. On our last cruise, a Ft. Lauderdale to New York City to Southampton, England trans-Atlantic crossing, we read an announcement about a daily Christian gathering in the Admiral's Lounge every morning at 9:00 a.m.

A young missionary couple who got on the Queen Elizabeth in L.A. and off at Ft. Lauderdale had requested the room and time. The cruise ship granted their request and reserved the Admiral's Lounge for the daily meetings. They got off in Ft. Lauderdale and we boarded there so we never met them. Four Christians who were continuing to New York City bridged the gap between those leaving and those getting on.

New and old met at the Christian gathering our first morning onboard. Like us, others came out of curiosity. By the time we left NYC three days later, nine to ten interesting people showed up each morning. We shared struggles and discoveries. We prayed together and talked of meaningful scriptures. It was unexpected and very meaningful. I am relishing the thought of the next surprise because I trust the Lord.

Questions to Consider

1. What was your best or worst surprise? Did it prompt fear or joy?

2. If your answer was fear, how can you give it to the Lord? Ask Him how He views your bad surprise? How will He work in that surprise *for the good*?

3. We taught our children to ask where God was in an activity or comment. In other words, was He present? Then, we asked Him for grace to celebrate or strength to overcome.

   - Consider a surprise that puzzled you. Where was God in that moment?
   - If you had asked, what do you think He would have told you to do or say?

CHAPTER TWENTY-SEVEN

THE LOCKED DOOR

I RAN FOUR MILES ACROSS COUNTRY to catch the basketball team bus to Jetmore. I made it with two minutes to spare. I didn't have to stick to the roads because I was not wearing a suit and tie. Besides that, the basketball players would not care if I were sweaty.

Earlier that day I tackled a task that was much harder than the four-mile run. I needed permission. It was my only chance to go to the basketball game with the team.

It was 5:30 in the morning and we were eating our typical breakfast of Cheerios, eggs, toast, and bacon. I had to milk eight cows, run the cream separator, get ready for school, and then catch the bus at 7:30. Mornings were always hectic. It probably was not a good time to ask but I could not summon the courage to ask the evening before.

"If I get the cows milked in time this evening and I figure out a way to catch the basketball team bus, can I go to the game in Jetmore?"

Both Dad and Mother stared at me before Dad answered. "We are not wasting gas on any foolishness."

"I understand."

I think they were too caught off guard to ask any more questions. I put my breakfast dishes in the sink, grabbed my cap, and ran to the barn before they could change their minds. The entire day was a torment, wondering if they would say "No" when I got home. Curiously, neither of them said a word.

Mother could milk the cows in about thirty minutes. She was gentle with the cows so they relaxed and let down their milk quicker. It usually took me about an hour. I hoped the cows understood I did not have that long on this day. How could I get the cows to cooperate?

"Daisy, Millie, Three Spot, I need your help. I am in a super hurry. Please do not give me a hard time today." They turned their heads at the sound of my voice. Maybe it would work.

I milked in record time and walked briskly from the milking shed to the washhouse. I couldn't run because the two five-gallon buckets were full. Mother understood my dilemma and helped me run the cream separator.

At 5:35 p.m. I dashed out the door and headed straight east. The nearest eastbound county road was one-half mile to the south. I didn't have enough time to add that extra half-mile and stay on the roads. I worried about the two creeks intersecting my path, but there was very little water in either of them. I was able to cross on fallen trees. My last obstacle was the Stewart farm. Would their dogs let me cross their property? They were huge, fiercely protective, mixed-breed mongrels. I knew that because we attended the same church as the owners. Miraculously, I was downwind from the dogs. They didn't get my scent so they ignored me. I reached the highway near their farm as the school bus, carrying the basketball team, rounded the curve south of town a mile away.

I could not be on the team and participate in the practices because of evening chores, but the coach agreed to let me be the statistician. I kept track of everything, wanting to prove my usefulness.

Both the B team and the A team played in Jetmore so we didn't get back to Ness City until 11 o'clock. The coach asked if I wanted to be let off at the Stewart farm. I said "No" for several reasons. The thought of being dumped on the open road in the dark was scary. I hated to admit I was afraid of the Stewart's dogs and the creek crossings in the dark. My most frightening thought was I would be no match for coyotes hunting in pairs.

Gene, another farm kid, offered me a ride home without me having to ask. Until then, I had a really bad headache and my stomach was in turmoil. Gene's offer felt like an Alka Seltzer.

When I got home, our dogs greeted me warmly. I could always count on Toby and Sandy. They licked my hand, jumped up and down, and ran circles around me. I petted them and hugged them. They followed me onto the porch as I tried to open the kitchen door. It was locked. I tried it several times, thinking maybe it was stuck. When I couldn't open it, all the tension of this day plus the exhaustion made the locked door the final straw. I began sobbing and pounding on the door. The dogs knew something was wrong. They began barking furiously.

I screamed over and over again, "Open the door."

Within moments Mother unbolted the door. My anguish silenced her. I followed her up the steps to the bedroom, sobbing.

"Why? Why lock me out?"

She climbed back into bed with Dad.

I wasn't done. Between sobs I confronted them. "You gave me permission. I milked those darn cows. I ran four miles across country. I did not waste one gallon of your gas. I am a good kid. I was not having sex. I was not doing drugs. I was not drinking. I was the statistician at a basketball game. I didn't do anything wrong. If you ever lock me out again, I will get a sledgehammer and knock that door into a million pieces. You will not need to get out of bed to let me in because there will not be a door there anymore."

I went across the hall to my bedroom, slipped off my shoes, and slid under the covers fully dressed. I didn't have any tears left.

The next morning Mother awakened me. "We are both very sorry about the locked door. Dad simply was not thinking. It was the end of the day so he locked the door. We both are grateful you are a good kid. Please forgive us."

By that time Dad was standing right behind her, looking surprisingly remorseful.

I mumbled, "I forgive you."

I did not know how to tell them how deep my despair was. I tried to be glad that Dad hadn't locked the door on purpose. But, for him to forget me, to forget that I wasn't home, left me feeling very empty. It was a deep wound. I wept off and on all day, aching for a dad who would at least remember me.

My English teacher saved the day. Thankfully, she didn't ask any questions. She told me I could stay after class, sit in her tiny office, and read. I stayed the rest of the day until the school bus came.

Finally, someone noticed me. *Her door was not locked.*

Reflections

The effects of child abuse, physical, verbal, or emotional, take a heavy toll. For me, beatings were bad but the fear of beatings was worse. The whippings lasted for a few moments; the fear haunted me day and night. However, nothing was as painful as being ignored or forgotten. Refusing to celebrate with me about the student council election was devastating.

When I became a parent, rediscovering Ephesians 6:4 (AMP) was life changing.

> Fathers, do not irritate *and* provoke your children to anger [do not exasperate them to resentment], but rear them [tenderly] in the training *and* discipline and the counsel *and* admonition of the Lord.

My boys were ages ten, eight, and four when that verse became alive for me. "You know that you are to honor and obey me. If you do not, I point it out and you receive consequences. I am making a covenant with you today. From this day forward if I exasperate you, you are to tell me. I will hear you and ask God how to respond, how to make it up to you."

We had never talked about exasperation. They were smart kids and I wanted to know if they understood.

"Boys, do I exasperate you?"

Greg surprised me totally. "Yes, you do!"

I had no idea how naïve my next question was. "Do you have examples?" I taught the boys to give honest answers to hard questions.

"Would four be enough?"

That was more candor than I expected. Greg's answer shocked me and that must have been completely evident.

"Dad, are you okay? Should I not have told you?"

"Give me a moment to get a glass of water. I need to breathe deeply, too. Now, please give me the four examples."

"You interrupt us when we are talking. When you are upset, you tower over us. Sometimes, you give us an answer but we haven't gotten to the question. You sound angry when you disagree with us."

Everything Greg said was true. I felt sick. I really did want to be a great dad. If I continued to exasperate them, I knew I would do long-term damage. The Lord spoke to my heart.

They are not capable of perfect obedience either: these boys will dishonor and disrespect you from time to time. No matter hard you try, you will exasperate them. If you and your sons come to me with honesty and humility, I will heal your hearts and teach you another way to live.

My leadership role and job as Dad was to be the first to repent and the first to seek God. They were to follow my example and to do so respectfully. God always responded when we asked for help and it became a much better way to live.

Questions to Consider

1. Explain to your children what *exasperate* means. Tell them you really do want honest answers. (Don't punish them for being candid and straight forward.) Then, ask when or how you have exasperated them.

   If they are adults, it is not too late to clean up past offenses with honesty and humility, and, wherever needed, to ask for forgiveness. Don't rebuke them, distance yourself from them, or lash out at them for honest comments.

2. Why would God give us an impossible task—to never exasperate our children? Do you think the answer is *to teach parents to rely on Him?*

3. Would you be willing to type Ephesians 6:4 on a 3 x 5 card, carry it in your pocket or purse or wallet, and pray for a heart change every time you see the card? Who would be the best person to intercede for you as you make this change?

CHAPTER TWENTY-EIGHT

MR. BROOKS

EVERYBODY NEEDS A MR. BROOKS. My Mr. Brooks owned a clothing store on Main Street in Ness City. People from all over the county shopped there. The front window displays were attractive, reflecting the current season. The clothing offered for sale displayed the current styles from the market in Kansas City. However, most customers came because Mr. Brooks knew their names, offered old-fashioned customer service, and had an endless supply of funny stories.

He was a fascinating salesman. A woman came into the store and asked for a spool of thread. I paused with my broom to watch the sale.

"Arlene, we have a dress in that same shade of blue."

The color and the size were perfect for her. She tried it on and bought it.

"You know, Arlene, you will need new shoes to go with that dress." His tone conveyed genuine care.

She purchased the shoes and a scarf that matched the dress. He did not stop there. She added color-coordinated earrings, a bracelet for accent, and a necklace to complete the picture.

He did not overlook the basics.

"No new outfit would be complete without appropriate undergarments."

They were added to the sale. All that started with a spool of thread.

The next customer was a man who had been asked to be a groomsman in an upcoming wedding. Mr. Brooks already knew the family reserved First Methodist Church six months earlier. In fact, he had anticipated outfitting the groomsmen. He gauged by sight the exact size and the style that suited the man's body type.

"This style will fit you perfectly. Let's see, you're a size forty-two short. Right?"

The suit could not have fit better had it been tailored specifically for this customer. He left the store with the suit, a matching tie, and black shoes and socks to complete the outfit.

Mr. Brooks startled the next lady.

"Naomi, I am so glad you came in. When we were at the clothing market in Kansas City, we ordered a dress just for you."

She couldn't wait to try it on. We could hear her from the dressing room.

"I look amazing in this dress. The color is perfect for my skin tones. My hubby will be speechless."

She wanted to give Mr. Brooks a tip for his thoughtful order. He had a better idea. "Let's just see what else you need to go with the dress."

He clearly enjoyed serving people, helping them look their best. I was watching a servant at work and a joyful one at that.

I didn't need an excuse to go by his clothing store. Unless he had a customer, he always stopped what he was doing and we talked. He was honest about problems at the church. He was thoughtful about politics. He was transparent about struggles with people. Mr. Brooks told stories between customers.

One of his funniest stories was about a mistake. He said, "I helped a lady find what she needed. Meanwhile, we talked about names for children. I told her there was only one name I would never ever name a child—Phoebe."

He realized he had never met this lady and he did not know her name. "By the way, what is your name?"

"Phoebe."

"For once," he admitted, "I had nothing to say."

In all these conversations he was never condescending. He didn't act like he was doing me a favor by talking to me. He seemed to honestly enjoy having me drop in. Other adults responded to me as the boy destined for a promising future or reacted to me as a precocious pain in the behind. Mr. Brooks avoided those extremes. With him I was a teenager who came by for good talks.

He inspired me to pay attention to people. I think he knew the names of all six thousand people in Ness County.

"Louie, do you remember Marla Whipple from Utica?"

I was sure I had never seen or heard of her.

"She was in the store on Tuesday when you were here. She has a peculiar way of brushing her hair out of her eyes."

With that clue I remembered Marla. I realized he worked at remembering people. It wasn't the gift of memory as much as it was the fruit of paying attention.

Top quality work was a passion with him. For instance, he experimented with different ways to sweep the floor. Everyone who worked for him learned this one-best way to sweep the store. One-best way? His insistence seemed controlling. After I followed his instructions, I had to admit his way really was best.

Inventory was another opportunity for excellence. He did not have computers so people who helped with inventory needed a good memory and a keen sense when things were not right. For instance, he asked me to count the number of overalls in stock. I counted and said, "276."

He said very calmly, "Your count is off."

I counted again. "277." I am not sure how he knew I was wrong but I was painstakingly careful after that.

He did express frustration one time. "How long did it take you to paint this wall?"

"I started when I got here today and I worked through the lunch hour."

"No matter how much I pay you, I cannot afford to have one wall take more than a half day."

I was sad about disappointing him. I did not know what to say.

He dipped the brush in the paint, showing me how much paint should be on the brush.

"Use long, firm strokes. Then, dip it in the paint again. You are painting a wall not a work of art, so don't be so careful."

He handed me the brush. "Now, you do it."

I didn't have his strength so my strokes did not compete with his. However, they were better than I had done before.

He finished the lesson.

"I don't want any excuses, just improvement. I bought this apartment above the store for storage. No one is going to live here. But, that is not the point. Anything worth doing is worth doing well."

He patted me on the back and went down the stairs to the store.

For my last two years of high school he was my friend. As my friend, he offered acceptance and expected my "A" game in return. He thoroughly defeated me in the Peter versus John debate at the church, but it did not change our friendship. It was just one more example of him believing in me and expecting the best in return.

However, when I wanted to date his daughter, he assumed a new role: the protective father of a teenage daughter. The friendly dialogue was over. It was time to worry about the prospective son in law.

Thankfully, he raised a daughter who extended grace. She believed in me and that was a welcome and affirming surprise.

Thanks, Mr. Brooks. You and your daughter are gifts to me.

Reflections

A couple came to me for pastoral counseling. Rosalie wanted to talk about her difficult father. For almost thirty minutes she told stories of his heavy-handed and abusive interaction with her. When she stopped, she held both palms up in a "what's next?" gesture.

I asked, "Did your father ever sin against you?"

"Oh, my, no. He had a hard life so I understood why he was mean. We kids came early before he was twenty years old. He dropped out of college and never had a chance to be a forest ranger. Mom had her car wreck. That cost a lot of money and he had to take care of her. So I would say, "No, he didn't sin against me."

"That's interesting. Are you familiar with Romans 3:23 (NIV), 'for all have sinned, and fall short of the glory of God.'"

"Well, if that's the standard, everything he did was sinful."

She wept. She groaned. She pounded on the table. For twenty minutes she talked about the ways he sinned against her.

"Rosalie, if your dad just had a bad day, there is very little we can do. That was in the past so you could carry the wounds and try to forget. On the other hand, if he was a sinner, the cross offers great help. We can forgive him and pray that he will repent. If you have judged him, you can repent, remove your black robes, turn in your gavel, and take the gold nameplate off the door. Close your courtroom and we will take him down the hall to the Lord's courtroom. He is the only one authorized to judge. Only He can change hearts."

I appreciated her response very much.

"After we pray for Dad, we need to pray for me. With my anger I sin against my kids almost every day. Wait! It is more than almost. I sin against them every day."

We ended with an amazing prayer time.

Questions to Consider

1. In what ways did your parents sin against you? Have you ever asked the Lord to forgive them and heal your heart?

2. In what ways do you sin against your children? Have you ever asked the Lord to forgive you and heal their heart(s)?

3. Find a support group, a mentor, or a book that will help you parent well.

4. Take off your black robe, dispose of the gavel, and remove the gold nameplate (mine read Judge Louie) from the door. Lock the door and throw away the key. You have completed a significant first step.

   Then, take the one who hurt, offended, betrayed, abused, ignored, or abandoned you down the hall to God's courtroom. Believe it or not, He knows them and their sins better than you or I do. When you get there, you kneel before God. Confess your own pride and stubbornness and your failure to trust Him. Ask Him to forgive you for trying to take His place as judge.

   Turn the one who wronged you over to Him. Be free from the burden of being the sheriff, the warden, the avenger, and the bookkeeper who records all offenses and logs the actions you have taken.

CHAPTER TWENTY-NINE

THE HOUSE THAT RULES BUILT

N ESS CITY HIGH SCHOOL WAS four stories tall with stairs everywhere, beckoning with open arms, "You must run! Up is good; down is better!"

The institutional gray paint on the stairs was not a deterrent. On the contrary, the slick surface and stark coloring offered a high-speed racing surface. Crowds of students on the stairs, moving from one class to the next, were merely obstacles to be overcome. Posted on an outdated metal sign at the top and bottom of each stairwell was the rule, "No Running!" That only slowed down new or timid speedsters. One and only one stop sign could not be overcome—Miss Brungardt. She stood at the top of the fourteenth step with her arms folded across her chest and a storm-clouds-are-coming look.

The local hardware store must have had only one color of paint—institutional gray. Janitors mopped the plain gray floors every day. The smooth surfaces, the result of many layers of paint, were ideal for tennis shoes with studs on the bottom. The rounded metal balls, pressed into the soles, provided inexpensive skates. Any student, male or female, who had appropriate footwear and a need for speed could slide forever. Once again, the administration posted a sign completely lacking in color or imagination—"No Sliding!"

The signs were not enough. Law and order only had a chance when Miss Brungardt patrolled the halls.

Cream-colored, plastic venetian blinds covered the massive windows, which extended from a student's waist to the ceiling. As the shades aged, the rich cream of another era faded to a very tired yellow. This yellow did not brighten the gray floors and stairs. Dust accumulated on the blinds, eliminating any hope of cheerfulness. Boys waited until the teacher left the room. They dashed to the long, long cords and pulled the shades to the ceiling. A cloud of dust slowly settled on everything and everybody. Without fail, when the teacher returned, she demanded, "Who opened the shades?" The "keepers of the rules," as usual, caught and punished the culprits. Another sign appeared—"Do Not Open the Shades!"

The administration failed to notice that Miss Brungardt, the poster girl for rules enforcement, was the only sign that worked. She dressed for the part. Her school wardrobe featured two dresses, a plain brown, calf-length selection and an equally somber, no-nonsense black. She wore one color for an entire week and then the other for the next. She had one pair of shoes—black. Her hair was drawn back in a tight bun. No scarves. No foolishly expensive jewelry.

The girls noticed the total absence of color. When they complained to their parents, they all heard the same answer, "What do you expect? She's a teacher."

It was mid-October before the students saw color. One high school senior lit the trash can on fire in typing class. The bright red didn't last long but it offered weary students a combination of sheer excitement and terror. Of course, Miss Brungardt returned to the room, grabbed the fire extinguisher, and put the fire out. Within moments, she identified the fire starter, escorted him from the room, and demanded he be expelled. The next day there was a new rule posted in each room—"No Fires!"

I thought I detected a hint of human kindness in Miss Brungardt. I frustrated the other do-it-by-the-numbers authority figures, so how was she different? How should I respond to these faint signals—like smoke signals on a windy day? Ah yes, humor. That was my baseline strategy when I detected a hint of a desire for friendship.

One day when she was on patrol outside the study hall, I stopped in front of her, did a smart left face, saluted her, and said, "Reporting for duty, Sarge."

Her lips quivered and she nearly cried. She looked really sad.

Why did I think she would think that was funny? Why do I have to learn everything the hard way?

Mother and I talked about how to make it right. The only flowers in full bloom on the farm were sunflowers. I put one in a large vase and placed it on her desk with a note attached, "From a misguided, repentant comedian."

She said, "What is this?"

"There's a new rule at this school. If you try to be funny and you're not, you have to bring a sunflower and place it on a teacher's desk. Terrible consequences follow if you do not do it within twenty-four hours."

I thought I saw a hint of a smile.

"You better go, Louie. There is another rule. Be on time for your first class of the day."

Reflections

The institutional feel of that small town high school did not stop students from distinguishing themselves. In a two-year period Mrs. Munroe prepared students who graduated from MIT, Harvard, Stanford, the University of Kansas and Kansas State University. Five out of a class of fourteen had remarkable success in fields dependent on physics.

Perhaps there is a footnote somewhere that says, "Louie eventually had modest success in Physics, completing a class called Naval Aviation Electronics," but I doubt it. (My degrees were a B.A. in English and an M.A in English.)

Obedience was demanded at Ness City High. Entrepreneurial thinking was not encouraged. Conformity was praised. Uniqueness, creativity, and originality were allowed but rarely highlighted. Discipline was inconsistent and dictatorial. I do not recall one instance of a student being asked for his side of the story when he was sent to the principal's office. Teachers openly played favorites. Physical comfort was not important. There was no air-conditioning so classrooms were extremely hot in September.

Why did I thrive in that environment? Mrs. Floyd always encouraged me. Miss Brungardt routinely challenged me. Coach Nichols offered empathy. They believed in me and, as a consequence, I believed there was hope for me.

Mrs. Floyd chose me to be the editor of the school paper my senior year. I am quite sure other teachers opposed that idea. She was always encouraging and she taught me to communicate clearly with the team, meet deadlines, and be diligent about details.

Miss Brungardt, my typing teacher, was the champion of no shortcuts. She accepted nothing less than the best. She wanted me to take first place in the league typing contest. She was the first person, other than my mother, who believed I could be a champion.

I could type seventy-six words per minute with no mistakes. At the league contest all of the typing desks were designed for girls. My knees did not fit under the desk so I had to reach out and type with my arms extended. She objected on my behalf but the contest judge said she had no other tables. I could not recall another adult not named Mother, fighting for me as she did that day. I did not do well but I never forgot her faith in me and her advocacy.

Coach Nichols noticed that I showered last every day in gym class. One day he walked into the showers and saw the huge welts on my neck, shoulders, and lower back.

"What on earth caused that?"

"I fell down."

"As soon as you are dried off, come to the first aid room and let me dress your back."

He was very gentle as he applied first aid cream and bandages. He didn't ask any more questions but his actions touched me deeply.

In the days that followed, he looked out for me. One night after an away game I did not have a ride home. I dreaded the thought of an eight-and-one-half-mile walk without a flashlight.

"Hey, Louie, my wife and I are going for a drive in the country. We can let you off at your farm if you'd like."

I was too young to realize his wife probably did not want to go for a ride in the country after 11 o'clock at night. He drove by their house. She came out in her nightgown. They drove eight miles to our farm and dropped me off at the driveway. If he had turned around immediately, I would have known this was not "a ride in the country." I climbed the windmill and watched. He drove on three quarters of a mile before he turned towards town. I was not a pity case. His wife had actually wanted to go for a drive. That's what Coach Nichols wanted me to think and that's what I thought until I had a wife.

Questions to Consider

1. Who were your most inspirational teacher(s)? I sincerely regret that I did not personally thank each of them, preferably face to face, while they were still living. Please do not make the same mistake.

2. Encouragement is important but truly believing in someone and then encouraging them is far better. Is there anyone God wants you to believe in and encourage?

3. Ness City High School was very plain and its structure was very rigid. In that environment three teachers changed my life. Is there any parallel in your life? Did you have very plain surroundings and seemingly insurmountable obstacles? Has God sent anyone to help you rise above the colorless setting and the limitations? Perhaps you are the one He has sent as a missionary to that setting!

CHAPTER THIRTY

DANCING LESSONS

FATHER DAVID, THE LOCAL CATHOLIC priest, taught me to how to dance. He obviously did not have the same concerns my church had about dancing:

- The musical beat stirred deep, sinful urges inside.
- The lyrics encouraged impure thoughts. Holding a girl close for two to four minutes for each song was sure to arouse lust.
- The lights were turned low. Darkness concealed secret, unrighteous thoughts and behaviors.

But I had seen Sheila and I was willing to risk all.

The dancing lessons were a totally unexpected follow-up to my question, "What do you think about me dating a Catholic?"

"Do you attend a local church?"

"Yes."

I didn't say more because I was embarrassed. I went to a small Pentecostal church, located in an old, run-down stone building that had been a feed and grain store in another lifetime.

He didn't press for details. Instead, he gave me a thoughtful look.

"What do you have in mind?"

"I want to dance with Sheila at the high school dance."

"I'm guessing you are an amazing dancer."

"No, Sir. I don't know how to dance."

"So, her Catholicism is not your only problem."

I nodded my head. If any of this surprised him, he certainly didn't let me know it.

"Have you asked her to dance with you?"

"No, not yet."

I wasn't sure why I felt so comfortable telling him about my romantic idea. We sat in silence. It seemed like an eternity.

He was the first to speak. "What part of this problem can we solve today?" Another comfortable silence. Then, he answered his own question. "I know. Would you like to learn how to dance?"

"You know how to dance?"

He laughed and then I laughed, too, even though I didn't know what was funny.

"I haven't always been a priest. Before I took my vows, I went to every school dance I could."

He put a record on the record player and showed me the two step. Then, he invited me to stand beside him and imitate his dance steps. It felt like a major achievement. I couldn't explain why but the lesson was totally comfortable. Grace, whom he called his "grandmother-in-residence," watched and then clapped.

My official, I-don't-care-if-anyone-knows reason for coming to the Sacred Heart parish house was to deliver the school paper. Mrs. Floyd, the newspaper sponsor, challenged the journalism class to expand the readership and to sell additional advertisements.

"Louie, you are the editor. Who could you persuade to read the school paper? How about the pastors in the city? If they read it, maybe they will ask their congregations to read it."

Other students targeted friends, relatives, and local business owners and employees.

Mother said that I could stay after school and distribute the papers. She would milk the cows. Then, she would meet me at our church at 7:00 for the Wednesday night Bible study.

I walked to the Methodist parsonage, the First Baptist parsonage, and then to the Sacred Heart parish house. The elderly housekeeper said Father David was in. He greeted me warmly and I explained why I had come. He must have sensed there was a deeper reason for my visit.

"Could you stay for dinner? Grace and I would enjoy the company."

"I would like that."

"Your timing is perfect. When you knocked, Grace just told me dinner was ready."

After he thanked God for the food, he said, "Do you have a question for me?" His openness was affirming.

"Why did you become a priest?"

The next hour was a very comfortable conversation between a man and a boy. I felt truly safe and his answers were honest and believable. I finally told him my real reason for coming.

"I have never really had a dad. When we talked about delivering the school papers, I realized the Catholics I know call you Father. I wondered if it was more than a title."

"What is your impression?"

"The title fits you well."

A tear ran down his face. He laughed. "Must be allergies."

That's when I asked him about dating a Catholic. He gave me the short dancing lesson. The clock on his wall said 6:15. It was time to leave. I had to walk two miles to the Wednesday Bible study so I said, "Goodbye."

He called to me as I headed down the street. "Will you deliver the paper next week?"

I stopped in the street. Once again he knew I had another question.

"I would like to attend Sunday mass and then interview you next Wednesday."

"I will look forward to it."

I knew I would have to have an amazing explanation for the folks to allow me to attend the Catholic mass. When I told them I was doing a feature story for the school paper, they said, "Yes." I was even more surprised when they allowed me to attend the mass at 11:00 a.m. instead of our church.

It was a puzzling morning. First, the finger bowl in the entryway confused me. I thought it was placed there to receive coins. Someone saved me from putting my only two coins in the bowl. They dipped their fingers in the water and dabbed in on their forehead. I had no clue why they did that.

Kneeling and standing was a nightmare. I stood when they knelt on the pull-down altar rails, knelt when they sat down, and sat down when they stood. Finally, I gave up and sat motionless for the rest of the hour. Thankfully, no one seemed to notice.

Afterwards, I had a pressing question.

"Father David, only half of your congregation took Holy Communion. I have always thought Catholics were very committed."

He laughed comfortably.

"I asked them to fast breakfast—skip breakfast—so they could take Holy Communion. Obviously, half of them ate before they came."

"What will you do about that?"

"Oh, my new friend, I am the pastor, not the sheriff. I lead them but I definitely do not control them."

I had other questions about the wine, the wafers, and the offering baskets that were at the end of a long pole. All of his answers were thoughtful and kind.

Finally, my notepad was full. It was time for my bad news. My hands shook and one or two tears ran down my face even though I squinted to stop them.

"I cannot come back because of chores each evening. Mother covered for me both Wednesdays but she is already complaining. I am so sorry!"

His "Goodbye" was gracious. The high school newspaper received a warm "Thank You" for the paper being delivered in person.

Mother asked me about the interview.

"Was it what you expected?"

"No, it was much more. It was like opening a package on Christmas morning, a very happy surprise in September."

Reflections

Paul wrote in 1 Corinthians 4:15-16 (AMP),

> After all, though you should have ten thousand teachers (guides to direct you) in Christ, yet you do not have many fathers. For I became your father in Christ Jesus through the glad tidings (the Gospel). So I urge *and* implore you, be imitators of me.

I think Paul was saying, "Many men can teach you what they know. I shared the good news of salvation with you. Since I had a significant role in your rebirth, we have a special father-son bond. Don't just do what I say—do what I do."

Paul was a part of something being birthed in them. Beyond that, because of his exemplary life they could imitate his walk with the Lord. That's what he meant by fatherhood.

- Who are the men who have been part of what God wanted to birth in me?

- Whom should I imitate as a father in the faith?

God sent George Cook, the young-at-heart but elderly farmer, who lived the message of the hymns he shared when he testified. I wanted to be like Brother George. Bob Mackish, the camp counselor and former boxer who became a missionary, offered correction with kindness and he got on my level to do it. I wanted to imitate Mr. Bob. Coach Nichols paid attention, realized what was happening to me, and dressed my back. He did not refer to himself as a Christian but he was fatherly towards me. We did not have a connection through the Gospel, but when I grew up, I wanted to do for others what he did for me. In college, Ward Williams fathered me on the run, answering my unending questions as we walked across the campus. He modeled a love for and total reliance on God's Word to answer all of my questions. It birthed in me a life-long love for the Word and a deep desire to see that passion grow in others' lives. An addition to the fatherly men in my life was Father David, the priest who taught me to dance. He practiced empathy, coming alongside me, hearing my heart, and responding in a way I would want to imitate.

Later in life, God sent another father in Christ, Richard McAfee, who invested two years in teaching me to ask better questions. He taught me a skill and inspired me to pattern after his teachable heart.

I had many teachers, but it is fathers in Christ whom I have joyfully tried to imitate. When I remember all the fathers God has sent, I think *I may be the richest man I know.*

Questions to Consider

1. Do you have a special connection—a father or mother-in-Christ relationship—with the one who prayed for you to be born again? Ask the Lord how to view that and how to respond.

2. What Godly discoveries or character traits or connections have been birthed in you because of the father (or mother) in Christ God sent? Are you to imitate any aspect of that person's faith, character, or connections? How can you become one who assists in kingdom birthing and/or who lives as an example worth imitating?

3. Does God intend for you to be joined to others He has sent? Whether they are called "father" or "teacher" or just "the one whom God sent today," how have they helped birth character, connection, and purpose? How has their example been helpful? Some possible applications:

   • Find them and thank them.

   • Explore whether God has more in mind with those connections.

   • Express your gratitude by modeling what you have received—pass on the legacy. How and for whom should you do that?

CHAPTER THIRTY-ONE

AN ODD FIT

"Dad, can we hurry up? I was hoping we could go to the state fair."

"If we get everything done today, there will not be anything left to do tomorrow."

Did he say what I think he said? That's unbelievable. "Why would we save work for the next day?"

"You are always in a hurry. What good does it do you?"

The conversation was over. Dad hadn't heard a question he wanted to answer. I had to guess what the answer was to my question.

So that means we can't go to the state fair?

Dad did everything at a slow, deliberate pace. My high energy, always-on-the-run approach to life mystified him.

"Why do you run to bring the milk cows in? You have to walk them back slowly."

I couldn't tell him, "Running makes me feel free." He would think I was speaking a foreign language.

We were opposites in the vegetable garden as well. When he hoed weeds, he swung the hoe with an easy, relaxed motion. He and his sister Emma cultivated five acres of fruit trees during their childhood. They developed amazing skills with a hoe. As an adult when he finished a row of radishes, every weed was gone. He hadn't damaged a single radish. I flew down the row with my hoe, getting two thirds of the weeds and destroying far too many radishes.

His advice was always the same.

"Slow down. Relax. Rock back and maintain a consistent stroke. You will get the weeds and it will save your back."

Hoeing was a Catch-22. To save the vegetables, I put on knee pads, used a short-handled hoe, and crawled down each row on my hands and knees, slowly and cautiously removing weeds, not radishes or cucumbers. The alternative: hoe standing up, damaging plants, missing weeds, and destroying our food. I just couldn't hoe like Dad.

Someday I will leave this place and never come back!

Dad and I disagreed about the horses as well. I thought God created horses for speed. Dad thought horses should earn their right to stay alive by being useful. Otherwise, sell them to the rendering plant. Our farm had two horses, a well-trained cutting horse and a mean mustang. Dad loved Dexter, the cutting horse, and his remarkable ability to lock onto one steer visually and then, quickly cut him out of the herd. Dexter was amazing but he was up in years and almost always slow and deliberate. I rode him when we moved cattle from one pasture to another.

Once, someone—probably me—left the gate open and the steers got out. Just for fun I let Dexter act like a cutting horse. He flew across the plowed ground, young again, zeroing in on a single steer and cutting him from the herd. I had never seen him move this quickly. Suddenly, the steer he was chasing made an abrupt right turn. Dexter turned right instantly and I went straight. Fortunately, the plowed ground was a good place to land. When Dexter's reins fell to the ground, he stopped instantly, the way he had been trained to respond. I got on, quit playing, and rounded up the steers.

For the sheer joy of riding I always chose Star. I slipped a halter on his head and leapt on bareback. After a slow, warm-up trot down the hard-packed, three-sixteenth-of-a-mile lane, we would turn for home.After trying a couple of times to bite me, Star ran like the wind. Riding Star when he was flying made me one happy farm boy. When we reached the corral, going at top speed, the stallion would always brush the gatepost, trying to throw me off. I rode bareback so I could lift my right leg out of the way.

"Nice try, Star!"

Dad would watch with obvious irritation. "Someday that horse is going to kill you!"

At least I'll die happy!

I knew Dad wanted to send him to the glue factory. Mother intervened and Dad sold him to Corliss, a would-be horse trainer and a distant relative.

Mother and Dad had the same push-pull about pace when we loaded bales on the truck. The oblong-shaped bales weighed about fifty pounds each. The baler left them in rows the length of the field. Mother always drove the ancient Chevy truck at a furious pace, picking up the bales. They flew up and then off of the bale loader attached to the side of the truck. Dad and I stood on the truck bed, grabbed the bales, and stacked them as they came up the conveyor belt.

I couldn't say out loud what I was thinking. *At this pace even loading bales is fun.*

Each trip Dad hollered at her. "Mildred, slow down! Slow down!"

When the truck was full, she would say with an innocent look, "What were you saying?"

"I said to slow down."

"Oh, I couldn't hear you."

I walked around the truck so Dad couldn't hear me laughing.

The fast-slow drama continued every Sunday. I don't think we ever arrived at the church on time.

I joked with Mother. "I wonder what they do at the start of those church services?"

Every Sunday we turned down the gravel road, eight miles from town. Dad drove the 1950 Buick at thirty miles an hour, his predictably slow pace. Mother said the same thing every week.

"Fred, can we speed up a little?"

"Mildred, we can't make up time on the road!"

Phil and I would listen in the back seat and then silently mimic both parents, repeating their seemingly memorized lines.

Mother knew what we were doing.

"What's so funny, boys?"

"Oh, nothing! We were just thinking about funny people."

Mother always laughed. Dad always corrected us. "Quit making up stuff!'

From the back seat came two: "Yes, sirs!"

One Sunday evening we were fifty-nine minutes late for an hour-long service. When we entered, the pastor was leading the congregation in prayer. Everyone's eyes were closed so they didn't see us come in.

"Lord, the Fred Keller family is always here. We do not know what the problem is tonight but we pray nothing bad happened on the farm. We pray they did not have an accident on the highway. Keep them safe until we meet again. Amen."

They opened their eyes and saw their prayers had been answered. Almost everyone had a good laugh. I thought it was more embarrassing than funny. Dad drove home thirty miles per hour.

Dad and I disagreed totally about milk cows, too. This mirrored the fast vs. slow conflict. Milking shorthorns had small teats and stubborn personalities. However, Dad insisted, "If I say she is a milk cow, she is a milk cow."

Several of the cows did not agree with Dad. His reluctant subjects had to have the halter on their head fastened to the side of the stall. Another rope encircled the cow from front to back, also attached to the wall. Hobbles, a chain contraption with a metal cup clasped on the back of the cows' hind legs, kept them from kicking us. We sat on one-legged stools beside the tied-down cows and pulled on their short teats, extracting small amounts of milk.

One day I asked, "Why don't we get one Holstein, Dad? She would give more milk than all eight of these stubborn fools."

Dad sighed.

"What would the neighbors say if we had one black and white cow in a pasture and all the others were red and white?"

I wanted to say, "They would say we knew the difference between a milk cow and a beef cow." I didn't say more because I did not want another lecture or a beating.

When Dad wasn't at the milking shed, Phil and I sprayed the cats with milk. The grateful cats licked the milk off of their coats and came back for more. They did not care what color the cows were.

I asked Dad, "Did you ever spray the cats with milk when you were a kid?"

"Why would I do that?"

Have you ever done anything just for fun? You missed it, Dad. These cats are hilarious.

It was time to change the subject.

In the entryway to the house there was a plaque, honoring Dad for graduating from Central Business College in Sedalia, Missouri. He didn't fit with most Ness County farmers because of his education. None of his rural classmates had gone to college. When he graduated, he got an accounting job in the Kansas City stockyards. He said it was a perfect fit.

"Dad, why did you come back to the farm?"

"To honor my father. I was the oldest son and he asked me to take over the farm. I couldn't say, 'No.'"

"I don't understand. Your younger brother Bill loved farming. You loved accounting. Why didn't your dad turn over the farm to Bill and let you be the happy accountant?"

"It just wasn't done that way."

So, Dad was an odd fit for the farm and I was an odd fit for Dad.

Reflections

Dad and I judged each other continually. If he failed to fit in, I condemned him in my court. If I forgot or resisted or stumbled, he sentenced me quickly. Praising each other for a job well done rarely happened. I know now there was much for me to commend.

- Dad read from the Bible to the family every morning. He read so slowly it was almost impossible to stay awake. I should have been more grateful that the head of our home loved God's Word.

- He did drive slowly but every piece of equipment on the farm was in excellent running order.

- No one trained cattle dogs to perform better than Toby. Toby was amazing but he learned everything he knew from Dad.

- Dad gave generously to the church and shared his limited food with anyone who came to the house.

- I didn't realize until I was grown that his hands were crippled with arthritis. I never heard him complain, not once.

- He was always kind to Mother and my sister Janell, born three years after we moved to the farm.

- Many people criticized him for marrying a divorced single mom. He never ever retaliated.

As a child I did not know what to do with the conflicting thoughts I had about Dad, but now I sincerely regret judging him. By God's grace I was able to sit by his bed during his last days. I asked for forgiveness and he nodded. Near the end I was one of a few he still recognized. That was a gift. Our hearts were quiet. We did not need more words.

Questions to Consider

1. How does God view the one(s) who hurt you? What did you miss? Ask God to soften your heart. Looking back, I remember Dad quoting scriptures. He honestly thought his beatings were saving me from being stoned in the city gates—a metaphor for living a life of crime that ends badly. More than that, he wanted to be sure I went to Heaven. I still think his approach to discipline was wrong but Humility insists I, too, have committed many well-intentioned but misguided mistakes. Then, I ask for forgiveness for both Dad and me.

2. When your heart is soft, will it be easier to hear what God thinks about you? What have you missed?

3. There is so much judgment, so much anger, and so much hardness in most people's lives. Hopefully, we will grasp how much grace we have received and pass it on. Who needs you to extend grace to them?

ACT III: THE LAST DAD

CHAPTER THIRTY-TWO

NOT WHAT I EXPECTED

I LEFT HOME AT MIDNIGHT, THE night of my high school graduation. There were no tears. I had served my time in Fred Keller's jail.

I climbed the windmill for the last time. From that lofty height I had looked at the lights of distant cities every night for weeks, counting down the days. On graduation night I could see the lights of Dodge City, fifty miles away. My heart was nearly beating out of my chest.

I packed and repacked the footlocker my first dad brought home from India. The hardest decision was which books to take. Old friends? New adventures? One easy decision was *Exodus* by Leon Uris. I had never been to a refugee camp (the post WWII Israelis, attempting to reach their homeland, were detained on Cyprus), but I understood the need to break out of confinement. I did not know where to find my Promised Land, but I knew it was not on the Keller farm.

At 2 a.m. my footlocker and I left Dodge City on the Greyhound bus, headed for southern Oklahoma. Floyd, my boss for the summer, picked me up in Ardmore a few minutes before noon.

Custom harvesters like Floyd followed the wheat harvest from Texas to Canada. Warm winds ripened the harvest in Texas first, then Oklahoma and Kansas. By the end of the summer the wheat was ready to cut in southern Canada. With his two Massey Harris combines and three hired hands, Floyd's crew harvested individual farmer's wheat. They hauled it in big grain trucks to the large elevators of the farmers' co-ops in nearby towns.

Floyd had stopped by Dad's farm three months earlier to see if we would hire him to cut our wheat when it was ripe. He, also, needed one more crew member for the summer. When Dad said I could go, I threw my cap in the air and shouted for joy. Both men joined me in laughing.

The crew consisted of Floyd, the boss; Galen, a college senior on his third summer tour; Carlton, who would be a senior in high school next year; and me. It was the first summer cutting wheat for both Carlton and me.

That first day the boss took me to his thirty-seven-foot trailer house so I could eat lunch and change into work clothes. This was the traveling summer home for Floyd, his wife Jan, their two children, and the boss's niece Sherri. She helped with the children and the meals for the crew.

On day one when I cleaned up in the trailer's bathroom and ate lunch inside, I did not realize that this was my official, one-time, visit-to-the-trailer greeting. For the rest of the summer, we, the three-man crew, ate our evening meals on a picnic bench outside the trailer and next to the tent. We showered at truck stops or washed off in farm ponds. We slept in sleeping bags on cots in the small tent.

I hurried because Galen and Carlton were running the two combines and there was no one driving the two trucks.

Floyd had no idea how little I knew about machinery. He hired me because he assumed that every farm kid understood basic vehicle maintenance.

"Louie, when we get to the field, I would like for you to change the oil in the blue Chevy truck. We did not have time to get that done this morning before we started cutting wheat."

"I have never changed the oil on a truck."

"You are pulling my leg, right?"

"No, Dad did all maintenance and repairs himself. He said my job was in the field, running the tractor, feeding the livestock, and maintaining the fences."

I wondered what Floyd would think if he knew the rest of the story. Dad would not let me come in the repair shop. He said I would break something or screw up the repairs.

I had just arrived and I was already a disappointment—the story of my life. Floyd grumbled but he did show me how to change the oil. I was so nervous, I only understood half of what he said.

"You do know how to drive a combine, don't you?"

"Yes, we have a 1952 John Deere. Is it like your Massey Harris?"

The look on his face said, *What have I got gotten myself into? This kid doesn't know anything."*

After an awkward silence he showed me the improved features on his brand-new combines. I understood why he was annoyed. I had my doubts, too.

I don't know how to change the oil on the truck. Can I actually drive this complicated machine? I had a sick feeling. *My first real job and I don't even know what questions to ask.*

We finished cutting near Ardmore a couple of days later. The next job was one hundred miles north. Floyd and Galen drove the wheat trucks, carrying the combines. I drove the Ford pickup, pulling the trailer house.

Floyd warned me.

"The pickup brakes plus the trailer brakes, acting together, will not stop you very quickly. Be careful. My wife's best dishes are in the trailer house."

He playfully knocked my cap off and laughed. I thought he was joking about the dishes.

What he failed to tell me was that from sixty miles an hour to a complete stop required a half-mile distance. If I tried to stop quickly, the trailer would fishtail and I would lose control completely. I was afraid he entrusted his wife's dishes to the wrong guy.

The trucks led the caravan and quickly moved out in front. Because of the rolling hills I could not move faster than sixty miles per hour. Floyd kept calling me on the CB radio.

"Hey, you are getting too far behind."

"I am pedaling as fast I can."

"Very funny."

About thirty miles from our destination, I drove over the crest of the hill. A half mile ahead of me the two trucks, carrying the combines, had stopped on the road. They were waiting to turn into a gas station but a car blocked the way. I began pumping the pickup brakes and pulling the lever to activate the trailer brakes. I simply did not know how to coordinate the two and the trailer threatened to fishtail. I let up on the brakes, realizing I could not stop before I reached the trucks. I had less than a minute before four men, the boss's family, two trucks, two combines, and a pickup pulling a trailer would be in a massive pileup.

Moments before I hit them, the car moved and the trucks pulled off the highway. I finally rolled to a stop about a half mile down the road.

Floyd came on the CB radio.

"Hey, where are you?"

"You didn't tell me you were stopping and I couldn't slow down soon enough. I am up the road a ways."

I didn't tell him how close I came to destroying his wife's dishes.

"You want anything from the store?"

"Sure, a Dr. Pepper and a Hershey bar."

My legs were shaking so hard, I walked up and down the road the next half hour to calm down. *How will I learn to pull this trailer?*

I wanted to blame somebody for everything I didn't know. A happy thought calmed me somewhat. *Maybe Floyd will fill that role, teaching me about the stuff I have missed.*

A couple of days later he invited me to ride along on the combine with him. We talked about life and church and raising a family. I breathed a huge sigh of relief. Then, Floyd caught me off guard.

"I know we are both Christians. Your family probably doesn't drink alcohol. I discovered that a beer now and then really relaxes me. I think it would do you a lot of good, too."

The summer was becoming a nightmare with one situation after another that I did not know how to handle. I thought he hired me because we held the same beliefs. In fact, he had said, "I like to hire Christians. When we are all on the same page, we are a better team."

Floyd's suggestion confused me and made me mad. I have an uncle and two cousins who are alcoholics. One is in jail for a nearly fatal, head-on crash. Another almost died from alcohol poisoning. The uncle is always angry. All three lost their families. I do not want to be like them.

"I have never had a drink and I don't want one now."

He immediately stopped the combine. He wouldn't even look at me.

"You will probably be more comfortable in the truck."

So much for Floyd filling the stuff-I-need-to-learn void. I prayed, *God, I have no idea what you are trying to teach me. If this is Your idea of sending a dad, it is not working. What else can go wrong?*

The answer came quickly. I failed to close the oil cap tightly on the combine. The cap fell off and dirt got inside. It took Floyd and Galen an entire day to get the machine running again.

I still had hope. For one evening I thought the craziness would be over. Sherri, the boss's seventeen-year-old niece, went with me to a movie. Galen told Carlton—he thought I was asleep—that when she got back to the trailer, the boss and his wife and Galen quizzed her at length about our time together.

Galen tormented me for days after that. Floyd laughed hilariously every time.

"I guess guys from western Kansas don't brush their teeth before a date."

"I did brush my teeth."

Sherri quickly got up from the table and went to the back room.

"Oh, so the smell came from the other end."

If I answered, Galen added another insult. If I didn't answer, he still made fun of me.

When Sherri served the evening meals, she avoided eye contact with me. That was puzzling and hurtful. We both gave the movie one star out of five, but I remembered our open-hearted conversation on the walk home. It was better than the movie. I had a dozen questions. Away from her aunt and uncle, she talked freely.

"What has been the best part of this trip for you?" I asked.

"I am part of a large family, four brothers and three sisters. At home in Minnesota I get lost in the crowd. Here, people depend on me."

"What is it like to be the only girl, hanging out with three guys?"

We passed under a streetlight and I saw a tear run down her cheek.

"Each of you has made me feel beautiful."

I reached out and took her hand. "I am glad."

It was a peaceful street for a walk home.

When Galen began his trash-the-date comments, I knew she had not insulted me behind my back, but I could not figure out why she was avoiding me.

The next time we had a free evening, Sherri went to the movies with Galen. As they got in the pickup, I saw the satisfied look on Floyd's face. I understood. He greatly admired Galen's skills and enjoyed his friendship. He brought Sherri on the trip to meet Galen, not me. I interfered with the plan when I took her to a movie. I went for a long walk, feeling totally cut off. I could not stop the tears.

"Will there ever be a place for me?"

Rainstorms delayed us for two weeks in Billings, Montana. Each day we went roller skating. I spent an entire week's wages on a pair of skates. I put them on, laced them up, rolled onto the floor, and fell flat on my behind. I limped to the sales counter.

"I can't stand up on these roller skates."

I wanted my money back. Instead, I got an explanation.

"They are speed skates. The wheels are closer together front to back. You can accelerate more easily."

They were wonderful if you knew what you were doing and a total waste of money for a beginner like me. I was too proud to admit my mistake and press for a refund. That provided fresh material for Galen to point out my stupidity.

I had one more near disaster. Floyd took my place on the combine in northern Montana because the fields were full of rocks, big rocks that would dent the combine's header. I drove the loaded wheat truck into town. The county road had an unusual amount of sand on it and the truck was hard to handle. By then, I had a summer's worth of driving experience. I got the old truck up to fifty miles an hour. That was Floyd's goal, to do the round trip as quickly as possible.

As I approached the highway, I slowed down to allow another truck and a combine to pass in front of me on the main road. I was going too fast on the heavily sanded road. When I pressed the brakes, the truck began to swerve. My only chance of survival was to cross the highway in the narrow opening between the truck and the combine. I pressed the accelerator petal down, which straightened out the truck, and crossed over the highway with the engine roaring, passing between the combine and the truck, barely missing both. I took my foot off the gas and the truck rolled to a stop. I was so frightened, my legs and arms shook violently. I got out of the truck to walk around and fell flat on the ground. It took a half hour for me to calm down. I drove the truck slowly to the grain elevator. I was glad to be alive.

"God, I don't know what your purpose is for this summer, but I do know you saved my life again and I'm grateful."

The hazing continued. Encouraged by Galen's ridicule, Carlton joined in. Every day he added another insult. The three of us slept on army cots in a tent. He turned my bed over, dumping the sleeping bag on the ground. Another time he accidentally spilled a Coke on me. He put a banana peel in my boots and crackers in my sleeping bag.

One evening he and I were standing outside the tent. He repeated one of Galen's annoying insults.

"Sherri can't stop laughing every time she thinks about you farting at the movie theater."

Galen reinvented my entire evening with Sherri—me passing gas and pretending I had not done it, spilling the popcorn, trying to kiss her, and asking her to pay for her own ticket because I did not bring enough money.

The truth was far removed from Galen's fiction— buy-one, get-one-free movie tickets, stale popcorn—no spills, no passing of gas, just a shy, quiet girl who hardly said a word at the movie, a nervous guy who never thought of attempting a kiss, followed by a heart-warming walk and talk on the way back, and a friendship that could have been.

I could not listen to their comedy one more time. Despite his size—six inches taller than me—I tackled him, threw him on the ground, and pounded him with my fists.

"I may not be able to stop Galen but you will never insult me again. Do you understand?"

He nodded meekly. I hit him again. "Don't ever touch my stuff. Do not come in the tent with a soda. If you spill one again, you will pay for the laundry and I will knock you flat one more time."

To my amazement he apologized for the insults, the spilled Coke, the banana peel, the crackers, and the dumped cot. I don't know what he said to Galen and Floyd but the hazing stopped.

Our last job was near Shelby, Montana, 1,300 miles from Floyd's winter storage in central Kansas. The thought of pulling the house trailer that distance terrified me. I did not know what to do.

To celebrate the end of the season, Jan invited us to the trailer for a sit-down dinner with man food—thick cut, grilled-to-order sirloins, French fries, homemade bread with real butter and peach jelly, and double chocolate cake with ice cream.

Floyd and Galen brought beer from the cooler in the truck. Galen poured a glass of beer and sat it in front of me. Floyd's wife Jan picked up the glass, poured the beer in the sink, opened a Dr. Pepper, and poured it for me. She said, "Play nice. My party. My rules."

Before the atmosphere could turn sour, she said, "Pick up your drink of choice and let's offer a toast to a successful summer."

We touched our glasses together. "To a successful summer."

When I walked in the trailer, dressed in my best jeans and a shirt starched and pressed at Pilgrim Dry Cleaners, I thought I was going to be sick. Floyd's wife Jan had her best china on the table. "We are hauling my wife's best dishes" was not a joke. During the dinner she explained that this was an annual tradition, enjoying an as-formal-as-possible, end-of-harvest, inside-the-trailer meal. There was more. She carefully unwrapped two other plates, the family good luck charms. The plates had survived a North Atlantic crossing on a pilgrim ship. Jan's ancestors passed them down each generation to the eldest daughter. She had tears in her eyes as she told us the story of high seas, desperately sick pioneers, and two plates that survived out of a crate of dishes. Only I knew how close I had come to destroying those treasured plates.

On our last day in Montana, Floyd and Galen tuned up the trucks.

Carlton and I did serious cleaning of the combines and the trucks. Finally, the three other men left to fill the trucks and the pickup with gas.

Floyd's son brought me a note. "Louie, let's talk. Jan."

I followed the seven year old to the trailer. *What on earth is this about?* Jan had been polite and distant all summer.

"We only have a few minutes before Floyd comes back but we need to talk."

She motioned for me to sit on the couch, not far from Sherri.

"Louie, I owe both you and Sherri an apology. I saw the happy look on Sherri's face when you two returned from the movie in June. I knew she had had a good time. But, Floyd had this huge idea of Sherri connecting with Galen. So, I said nothing as the two men quizzed Sherri. They told her that boys are animals. They want one thing only—sex. If they hold hands on the first date, they are making their move.

"They jumped on the fact you bought only one ticket. Sherri had no chance to explain her ticket was free. The next morning Galen was looking for more dirt when he joked about passing gas and spilling the popcorn. You said nothing so he concluded it must have happened. When he asked Sherri, she began crying and ran out of the room. The non-stop questions reminded her of her older brother, picking on her. Galen completely misread her reaction, thinking her tears confirmed his story.

"I was sure he was wrong but I was a coward and I was silent. I hoped it would all go away.

"Here we are on the last day. I am so sorry about all this. I beg you to forgive me. I will talk to Floyd and Galen tonight. If you like the idea, I will suggest that Sherri ride with you in the pickup on the drive back to Kansas."

My thoughts were a jumble. "I am so glad you told me all this."

I hesitated. I knew what the Lord was saying but I needed His help. "Yes, I forgive you but there is one piece missing from your story."

"Please, tell me."

"The day Galen started attacking me, I told him in the tent that what he said was one big lie. He thought I was accusing Sherri of lying. He told me to shut up or he would shut me up."

"I am sorry. I didn't know. Is there any way I can make it up to you?"

I told her I was really afraid every time I pulled the trailer. Knowing her fine china was a passenger made it worse.

"Have you told Floyd?"

"Twice. The first time he said that I grew up on a farm. I should figure it out. The second time he was very angry. He accused me of trying to get back at him for offering me beer and for exposing me about Sherri. He told me that … [insert four-letter word] was not going to work."

"I am confused. How can I help?"

"After I tell him your china is not safe with me, encourage him to hire another driver."

"That is the least I can do."

We heard the trucks returning. I did not have to talk about Sherri riding in the pickup with me.

Realizing we were out of time, she jumped up and threw her arms around me. "Forgive me, too."

"I did that last June."

I swallowed my pride and talked to Floyd.

"Sir, I have not figured out how to work the brakes together on the pickup and house trailer. I usually roll to a stop. I am asking you to replace me for the drive home."

Floyd was frustrated. "If you leave me one driver short for the trip home, I am not required to pay you for the summer's work."

I had gained a ton of courage in three months. "Please ask your wife if she wants me to drive the trailer home."

I walked away. I prayed off and on all evening. The next day he softened, paid me my wages, and put me on a bus to western Kansas. It was very early in the morning and everyone else was asleep. As the bus pulled out, I wrote in my journal.

"The summer wasn't at all what I expected. I asked God to send someone who would show me what to do and what to say. Instead, He sent someone who showed me what not to do and not to say. But

God was with me, saving my life more than once. I am learning to trust the Lord even if I never find a dad.

A few lessons I learned. Don't ignore what the Bible says. Don't drink just to please someone else. Don't abuse your employees. Don't push people until they are in danger or dead. Don't be a bully. Don't put up with bullies. Teach people what they don't know.

When I drove a fully loaded truck to town, I often waited in long lines to unload the wheat. Drivers from most of the crews would stand beside their trucks and talk until the lead truck finished unloading. Then, we would move the trucks forward one spot, climb out of the cab, and continue the conversation. Four times this summer I heard about guys my age who died in accidents involving wheat trucks and combines. It could have very easily been me.

Oh yes, one more lesson learned. When I took the wheat-harvesting job, I was running from Dad and the farm. I did not know what I was running towards. Dad always moved at a snail's pace. Floyd wanted us to push the trucks and combines to their limits. One extreme was not better than the other.

Vehicle maintenance was part of the job description. Lifting the hood and looking at an engine was a waste of time for me. Did I mention I am not good with machinery? I need to ask better questions the next time someone offers me a job. Moving away from Fred Keller simply required me to face a whole new set of problems. God, help me learn to run towards things, the right things, not from them. I will be home tomorrow."

Reflections

That summer was reality therapy for me—lessons on how life really is away from home:

- No matter where you run, *you* will always be there. The type of people you run from have cousins—the same kind of people—everywhere. It may be easier to learn what God is trying to teach you where you are now.

- Even when you can't see Him, God is there. If you know that and believe it, the summer will be easier.

- Impulsive purchases almost always cost too much, are not what you will enjoy over the long haul, and will dump you on your backside.

- When you have made a mistake, pride will cost you more than you can afford. Admit your mistake. Return the "skates." The momentary embarrassment will pass and you will have $50.

- If your timing is right, Goliath is not as tough as you or he thinks. If it is God's time, the battle will go better.

Questions to Consider

The enemy wants us to believe that our failures, our ignorance, our circumstances, and our critics define us. The Holy Spirit, whom we should recognize and know, is the One we should rely on to discover the truth.

> He is the Holy Spirit, who leads into all truth. The world cannot receive him, because it isn't looking for him and doesn't recognize him. But you know him, because he lives with you now and later will be in you (John 14:17 NLT).

1. What has been your most recent "reality therapy"—the mess God allowed so you would learn what is true?

2.   What did the enemy say was the truth about you and your crisis? What did the Holy Spirit say?

3.   If you do not "recognize and know" the Holy Spirit, who can introduce you to Him?

4.   Have you discovered simple, relevant truths you could pass on? What if God intends your discoveries as a gift for someone?

CHAPTER THIRTY-THREE

FAR, FAR AWAY

I T WAS A SCENE OUT of the movies except this was real life in real time. I ran up the stairs and across the Southern Pacific station platform. The train was rolling slowly. My money, my I.D., a change of clothes, and my favorite books were on that train. I ran alongside, grabbed the steel bar on the side of the passenger car, and swung onto the train.

A startled conductor challenged me. "Do you have a ticket?"

I tried to explain but my heart was racing. No words came out of my mouth. I nodded. I had the ticket in my pocket.

"Welcome aboard!"

I shuddered when I got to my seat. *What kind of a mess would I have been in if I had not heard the train starting to move?*

It happened this way.

I was headed toward Southeastern Bible College in Lakeland, Florida. That was a long way from the farm—fifty hours and three train changes, to be exact. The longest leg on the trip was St. Louis to Jacksonville with a thirty-minute stop in Birmingham, Alabama.

Late on the first night I was wide awake. Every time I saw the conductor, I asked him another question.

"What's the best part about being a conductor?"

"Are there any secret compartments on this train?"

"Do you ever let anyone take a tour of the baggage car?"

The baggage car question stopped him. He took off his cap and scratched his bald head before answering. "I am not supposed to. But, we do have a special guest on board tonight. I guess he is not going to complain if I show you where he is." He moved closer and whispered,

"He is lying down. So far, he hasn't said a word the whole trip. Do you want to meet him?"

"You bet I do."

We moved forward, passing through the rest of the passenger cars. The baggage car was just behind the engine. When we got there, the conductor pointed to his guest. "That's where he is sleeping."

A beautiful casket, securely tied to the wall and floor, was sitting on a raised platform.

"No wonder your guest is quiet."

"I am breaking all kinds of rules to let you in here. When we transport a corpse, we have sheets of regulations to follow—but who is going to know?"

"Don't you have anyone to help you?"

"That's a secret, too. The baggage car attendants are having a drink in the crew's quarters. I don't drink any more. I've been sober for three years." He showed me his AA pin.

As the train rolled on down the track, the conductor explained the rules and regulations for transporting caskets. He showed me how the crew handled the mail and he told stories from the past about train robberies. Eventually, we talked about why he had given me the tour.

"Yeah, I have a son who lives with his mother in Baltimore. I only see him a couple of times a year. I thought if I were kind to you, maybe somebody would be kind to him, too."

He patted me on the arm. "You want a place to sleep? We are deadheading one sleeper car to Birmingham. Come with me and I will make you a bed."

We went to the empty passenger car at the rear of the train. He turned one of the seats around so that it was facing backwards.

Then, he took all of the pillows in the car and stacked them between the two seats. He told me to climb on. He handed me a blanket, turned the lights down low, and said he would wake me up before we arrived in Birmingham.

Just before nine o'clock in the morning, my friend tapped me with his long flashlight and I moved back to my assigned seat. The stop in Birmingham was thirty minutes. Moments after the train rolled to a stop, I looked out the window. I could not believe it. Two porters were placing my footlocker on a luggage cart beside the train. I jumped off the train and told them, "That is my foot locker. I am not getting off here. I am going to central Florida."

"We have to go by the papers we received. The luggage office is downstairs in the basement. Fill out the forms so we can reload your foot locker."

I flew down the stairs and completed the paperwork. It took longer than I thought. All of a sudden I heard my train blow its horn and, moments later, start to roll down the tracks.

"Here is my paperwork. That's my train leaving. Please send my trunk to central Florida."

That is when I reenacted a movie scene and leapt on the moving train. I wondered if I would ever see my footlocker again but it arrived the next day.

The train trip was such an adventure; how could Southeastern top the Southern Pacific?

Early the next morning I joined the line to register for classes. The girl in front of me was a pretty brunette.

"Hi, I am Marilyn from central Ohio."

"I am Louie from Kansas."

"Well, Louie from Kansas, are you on a scholarship or are you going to school by faith?"

"What do you mean?"

"God told me to come here so I am expecting checks in the mail to cover my expenses."

"Does that ever happen?"

It was obvious what she thought of my answer. "Are you even a Christian?"

This was a rocky start. I had such happy thoughts about coming here. I was pretty sure she and I would not be hanging out together. I didn't think she would like my answer but I gave it anyway.

"I have faith for a job."

She gave up her place in line and moved away, apparently looking for someone with her kind of faith.

I turned to talk to the girl behind me. She was as interesting and puzzling as the brunette. She didn't hesitate. "I heard what she asked you. Want to know why I am here?"

I hoped I wasn't about to offend another cute girl. "Yes, I do."

"My parents told me I was dating the wrong person. I could live on the streets or go to Southeastern. Why are you here?"

I really didn't want to tell her my boring reason—I came to Southeastern because I could transfer my credits to Florida Southern; or my honest answer—it was a long way from home, I was broke, and I had made a deal.

Southeastern was not accredited but the school had a working agreement with Florida Southern. Students in good standing could transfer their credits and get a degree. I told people from the church that is why I chose Southeastern. The truth was I had very little money and the school promised to work out a payment plan. No other school made that offer.

Thankfully, it was my turn to register for classes. The registrar called my name and rescued me.

After I signed up for classes, I tackled my next huge problem. I needed a job. I had no car and there were no businesses close to the campus. This problem was certainly increasing my prayers.

Bobby, the guy in the next room, said he was going to Burger Queen. I asked if I could go along. The miracle happened. Burger Queen had a sign in the window, "Help Wanted." I filled out an application. The owner interviewed me and told me to report for work the next day.

It was a five-mile walk one way. I left at 3:30 the next afternoon and barely made it on time at 5:00. My shift ended at 11 o'clock. I walked the five miles back to the dorm. The campus was very dark at 1:00 a.m. Working five hours and walking ten miles round trip each day was going to be really tough.

The next day I left again at 3:30. Will Dowdy, the editor of the school paper, stopped me halfway across campus.

"Louie, right? I've been watching you and the Lord told me to help you. You can borrow my car each day to go to work. But, there are two requirements. Replace whatever gas you use each Friday and never go a single mile other than to and from work."

I was in a daze. "Thank you very much. Only drive to and from Burger Queen? Got it. Fill it up each Friday? Yes, I can do that." He handed me the keys and walked away. I was very happy but I could not stop the tears. Normally, I would have said the old, odd-looking, dark green Nash Rambler was ugly but today it looked like a chariot.

"First, the conductor. Then, the owner of Burger Queen. Now, Will Dowdy. What a week! I am far from home, but God, You are not far from me."

Reflections

I was enjoying myself. I thought doors were opening because I asked good questions—from the tour of the baggage car and having my own sleeper car overnight to finding a job and driving Will's car. In between I leaped onto a moving train, a dream come true. But, I was still restless. *What am I missing?*

I remembered James 4:2-3 (NIV), " ... You do not have because you do not ask God. When you ask, you do not receive, because you ask with wrong motives, that you may spend what you get on your pleasures ..."

I realized that I was asking but I wasn't always asking God. The confusion stemmed from the fact that God blessed me on this trip even though I didn't have my regular devotional time for two days. I asked Him for an explanation. There seemed to be two possibilities:

1. Someone else was praying for me. God was answering their prayers for my benefit.

2. God was extending grace and kindness, drawing me to seek Him first.

I prayed, "God, what could have happened if I had asked You what to say and what to do?"

You might have had an opportunity to share the gospel with the conductor. Possibly, he would have accepted Christ as Savior and Lord. The conductor might have given you his son's name and address. When you got to Southeastern, you could have inquired about a church where the son lives. If that church followed up, there might have been testimonies of forgiveness and healing.

Instead, I used each of my gifts for my benefit without thinking about God's or anyone else's purpose for the day. Later, I didn't wallow in condemnation but I did consider what might have been.

Questions to Consider

1. Why did I feel so good during the train trip, the registration process, and the job search? Was it God's presence or an emotional high prompted by the midnight baggage tour, the private sleeper car, meeting cute girls, finding a job, and receiving Will Dowdy's gift.

The three days of travel and registration were filled with highs. They, also, included my trunk being off loaded in the wrong city and the scorn of Marilyn from Ohio. I chose to be grateful for the good and to not be rattled by the negative. God was present each day. The enemy appeared, too, but he was merely a distraction and inconvenience. Thankfully, my relationship with God was (and is) not based on good or bad feelings or occurrences. Good feelings come and go but the substance of our relationship is intact. I call that joy.

I prayed many times about the long train ride to Southeastern. I have no doubt God was present and the fun things that happened were His gifts. Why? Because I was thinking about Him and grateful to Him. During the train ride I was so busy playing, I did not have my usual devotional time, but He and I talked every day.

However, when the conductor said we were breaking the law by being in the baggage car with a casket, I heard the Lord say, "Don't do this." I was having too much fun so I stayed there. Those good feelings were not from God.

The Southeastern registration process followed the same pattern: seeking God beforehand, being in line next to two pretty girls and then, the problem, Marilyn from Ohio having an extreme notion—in my opinion— about faith and God's provision. I was tempted to think of Marilyn's sharp comment as either ruining my first day at college or a major attack. With God's help I saw it as a minor distraction. I was keenly aware

273

of God's presence. It wasn't a happy moment but it was a joyful morning despite the judgmental comment by Marilyn.

2.   When have you richly encountered God's presence? Do you know the difference between feeling high and enjoying the presence of God? Which of the two do you cultivate? He is present when we worship, when we love well, when we serve, and when we agree. What are other ways we can invite Him to come?

3.   How do you begin each day? Who is your priority? Do you pray, "Lord, Thy kingdom come; Thy will be done"? Or do your prayers sound like "My kingdom come; my will be done"?

CHAPTER THIRTY-FOUR

A NEW ALL-TIME RECORD

"GOOD MORNING, CLASS. I AM Dr. Ward Williams. I would like to welcome you to New Testament 101. Before we begin with Matthew, chapter one, does anyone have a question?"

I raised my hand. "Sir, I grew up in a small, ultraconservative church in western Kansas. They believed that it was sinful for a woman to wear makeup. I wondered what your position is on this subject."

He sat down on the desk, closed his Bible, and ran his fingers through his hair.

"Well, Son, you just set a new all-time record. Students have asked me that question before. No one has ever asked it at the start of day one."

He looked out the window for several seconds. "I guess that is as good a place to start as any. Just out of curiosity, what was their objection to women wearing make up in your church in western Kansas?"

"They said Jezebel painted her face and she was thrown to the dogs."

"Did the dogs eat anyone at your church?"

A few students gasped but most of the class laughed.

"Not that I know of, Sir."
"Let's see what the Bible has to say about women's modesty."
He read 1 Timothy 2:9-10 from the King James Version:

> In like manner also, that women adorn themselves in modest apparel, with shamefacedness and sobriety; not with broided hair, or gold, or pearls, or costly array; But (which becometh women professing godliness) with good works.

You have got to be kidding. He is reading the same verses "Cardinal" Holmes used to talk about sleeveless dresses and shapely ankles. Mother would really enjoy this.

"I think Paul is saying that who a woman is and what she does is far more important than how she looks. As a follower of Christ, external appearances will not adorn her—will not enhance her beauty. Elaborately braided hair, expensive jewelry, and clothes fit for the red carpet are window dressing. Real beauty comes from within.

"Can a woman wear make-up, braid her hair beautifully, clothe herself with jewels and gowns and still have inner beauty and the heart of a servant? I certainly hope so."

He smiled. "You didn't ask but I would address the men as well. In fact, Paul does that in verse 8. 'Therefore, I want the men everywhere to pray, lifting up holy hands without anger or disputing.' That is by definition men acting modestly, appropriately, decently. Modesty in what we do, what we say, and how we look. Modesty for both men and women is from the inside out."

After class my roommate Eddie and I went to the student center.

"Can you believe it, Eddie? He actually answered my question. He didn't treat me like a little kid."

"Have you been treated like a kid?"

"More than once. My size may have caused some of that. I only weighed ninety-eight pounds when I finished junior high."

I was still enjoying what happened in class. "And he was funny—his question about the dogs eating someone at the church."

"Was he actually that good or are you just having a happy day?"

"Both! Oh, did I tell you about the Sunday school teacher who resigned because I asked a question. I don't see that happening here."

"You do know I was in class with you today."

"It was great. Don't you agree?"

"Up till now I thought it was my goofy roommate asking goofy questions about his goofy church."

We both had a good laugh.

"Eddie, thanks for the vote of confidence. Seriously, I have been looking for a dad who will accept me, who has a sense of humor, and who gives answers that make sense. Your goofy roommate feels like he has come home today."

There was a ten-minute window of opportunity each day after Dr. Williams' class while he walked to his office. He parented me during those brief moments, answering my questions about Dad abandoning us and my parents' divorce, about acne and insecurity, about Fred beating me and my struggle with anger, about chronic crop failures, and about God's plan for my life.

Dr. Williams made a life-changing decision for me that semester. It involved Pastor Timothy, a family friend from Kansas. Near the end of the semester, he came to visit me and took me to Titusville. I wrote a letter home about his visit. I wrote a letter home about his visit.

Pastor Timothy was waiting at the dorm when I returned from class. He makes me nervous. I think he is always looking for a handout. He did take me to Titusville to see a rich realtor. He told me to brag on myself because this guy was in a position to help me. went along with it because I did not know what else to do. The businessman asked excellent questions about what I had done well, my goals, and the most valuable lessons I had learned. Y the end of the day I knew Pastor Timothy came, expecting miracles, if not for me, then for him. Our host didn't seem to be reluctant. He gave us money for lunch.

By the end of the day I knew Pastor Timothy had come expecting miracles. He talked nonstop about the ways God was going to bless him and possibly me.

"Oh well, another day in Paradise.

Love,
Louie"

Not long after that, I received a summons to the dean's office. (Dr. Ward Williams, my New Testament 101 professor, was also the Dean of Students.) When I got there, the secretary sent me in to see him immediately.

"Louie," he said, "a wealthy realtor from Titusville, Florida sent a $100 check today, which we deposited in your account." Dean Williams motioned to a letter lying on his desk. "There is more to the offer. He offered you a $10,000, four-year scholarship. I sent back all but the first $100. You have faced difficulties this semester, asked great questions, and overcome obstacles. I thought this much money would do you harm because it would remove the struggle."

I trusted the dean because of his wisdom and his acceptance of me. I did not doubt what he said about the value of facing difficulties.

Dr. Williams never hugged me or even patted me on the back. He never said he loved me. He did not buy me a birthday or Christmas gift. He did not invite me to his home for a meal. But he offered acceptance, humor, and wisdom. I received more from him than the wealthy businessman offered.

I had asked for fatherly care and God had answered my prayer.

Reflections

Why are some people wise? Like George Cook? Mother on a good day? Ward Williams?

Could I become wise?

When God offered a gift to Solomon, the king asked for "a discerning heart" (1 Kings 3: 9, NIV). If I had a similar opportunity, what would I ask for?

First, I had to deal with confusion. Would God ever make that kind of offer to me?

James 1:5-8 (NIV) said He already had:

> If any of you lacks wisdom, you should ask God, who gives generously to all without finding fault, and it will be given to you. But when you ask, you must believe and not doubt, because the one who doubts is like a wave of the sea, blown and tossed by the wind. That person should not expect to receive anything from the Lord. Such a person is double-minded and unstable in all they do.

That sounds like a contradiction. God "gives [wisdom] generously to all without finding fault." But "the one who doubts ... should not expect to receive anything." I struggled with doubts, especially doubts about me and about other people who, in my opinion, needed wisdom. What were we doubters to do?

Hebrews 11:6 (AMP) removed the confusion.

> But without faith it is impossible to please *and* be satisfactory to Him. For whoever would come near to God must [necessarily] believe that God exists and that He is the rewarder of those who earnestly *and* diligently seek Him [out].

God exists. He is the starting point. I had focused on my doubts and received nothing. I needed to rely totally on a wise and responsive God, not a doubting me.

If your starting point is: "I exist and my doubt disqualifies me," you will be double minded, going back and forth between His promise of wisdom and your doubts. You must not doubt God. To clear away the confusion, testify that He alone has the answers.

Start with God.

Questions to Consider

1. Who among men is wise? The answer is either "no one" or "all who rely fully on God as their source." Do you know a wise man or woman? What is the evidence of his or her wisdom?

2. Think of a current (you are in the middle of it right now) chapter of your life. Are you acting wisely?

    • What might the accuser say? What doubt blocks the reward? Turn your back on doubt.

    • What is God saying? What (or Who) will reward you with wisdom?

3. Matthew 25 relates the story of ten virgins—or bridesmaids. Why were half wise and half fools ("foolish")?

    • What was the central focus for the five wise attendants?

    • What characterized the five foolish?

The Last Dad: Looking for Answers When the Dad Piece is Missing

CHAPTER THIRTY-FIVE

ONE OF LIFE'S GREAT MYSTERIES

G IRLS MYSTIFIED ME—SOME MORE THAN others. Lois Randolph, one of our nearest neighbors, sailed onto the school bus my first year in junior high and never looked or spoke to anyone. I prayed that she would talk to me. I made huge offers to God.

"If you help Lois talk to me, I will go to Africa as a missionary. I will milk the cows morning and evening without complaining. I will be kind to my brother Phil. It does not have to be a long talk, God. I am desperate. Please help me."

Two weeks passed. Not one word.

Not even God could thaw that iceberg. There must be other girls somewhere.

I went to the annual Thanksgiving youth convention in Hutchinson, Kansas. There were more girls than guys. That spelled opportunity despite my size and pimples. I introduced myself to Sue. I asked *the* question! "Would you like to sit with me at the youth rally tonight?"

She looked very uncomfortable. "To be honest, I am waiting for Josh to ask me."

I was so angry. She might as well have thrown a bucket of ice water on me. I asked Judy, Mandy, and Sarah, hoping someone would sit with me. I was totally shocked when they all said, "Yes."

Sarah didn't show up. Later on, she said, "Oh, I am sorry. I changed my mind and decided to sit with my girlfriends." I did not realize until later that she said, "Yes," so I would be happy and moments later said, "Yes," to her girlfriends so they would be happy, too.

Judy and Mandy sat on my left and right. We talked forever. Judy would have won a prize for best comedienne. I laughed so much my sides ached.

There was one negative. Afterwards, Judy said, "Shall we get something at the snack bar?"

Time stopped. *Why didn't I think ahead?* I only had money for Thanksgiving dinner, which was the next day. I was half honest. "I am sorry. I left my money at the hotel."

Judy took the pressure off. "We can do it next time."

That answer gave me renewed hope. I said to both of them, "Thank you so much for sitting with me. I had a wonderful time. I hope we can do this again before the convention ends."

Judy answered for both of them. "Oh yes, we had fun. We would love to sit with you again but we have plans for the next two days."

How could anyone have that much fun and not come back for more? It must have been the snacks! I hate having no money. Where should I look next?

Back home, I thought I had a chance with Sheila. Mother objected.

"You will not go to the dance with Sheila. We don't know if she is a Christian. If you try to leave, I will lie down in front of the back door. You will only go over my dead body."

"This is so unfair. You don't even know Sheila. Why don't you trust me?"

I moaned. I wept. I complained. I argued. I ranted and raved.

Mother did not bend. No Sheila.

Who would Mother say "Yes" to? Our church's youth group had three members: Gary, a high school senior, who was 6'5" and weighed 240 pounds; me, the acne-challenged member of the middle school midget basketball team; and Beverly, a very bright and cute fifth grader. She and Mother were good friends. Mother sounded like the unofficial president of Beverly's Fan Club.

"Louie, be nice to Beverly. Some day she will look good to you."

"Mother, she is just a little kid."

That's her best idea?

When Beverly and I were in the eighth and twelfth grades respectively, we took turns leading a Bible study on Sunday nights. We did become good friends, but the four-year age difference was still a huge hurdle.

The night I graduated from high school, I did not go by Beverly's house to say goodbye. I was leaving at midnight to join the custom harvesting crew in Oklahoma. Clueless me. I didn't know she wanted to see me. When I did not come by, she was very sad.

When the summer ended, I went to Southeastern Bible College for a year. After that I served in the U.S. Navy for six months. I would write to Beverly several times in a row and give her hope and then get busy with work or school and not write for three months. The inconsistency confused her greatly.

I never stopped looking. I certainly hoped the girl of my dreams was looking for me, too. At Southeastern, Millie agreed to be my chapel date. I surprised her by sending a dozen roses to her dorm. I worked a double shift at Burger Queen to pay for those flowers. Because no one else received flowers, she was totally embarrassed. I did not know that. I went to her dorm. She came out late and didn't say a word. We walked in silence to the chapel. When the service ended, she went to the front of the chapel to pray. She stayed a very long time, apparently hoping I would leave. I waited because I didn't know what else to do and then, walked her back to her dorm. She nodded and went inside. I was hurt, puzzled, exhausted, and broke.

After my freshman year in college I volunteered as a camp counselor at a Christian camp in Wichita, Kansas. The final camp of the summer was teen camp. My letter-writing friend Beverly was one of the campers.

I was friendly with all of the campers, but I maintained an ethical distance because I was on the camp staff. I did learn every teen's name, hoping that would give them a message of acceptance. One camper intrigued me, a soon-to-be high school senior from Manhattan, Kansas. Sonya and I talked several times.

The highlight of the camp was a Thursday night banquet. Beverly strongly encouraged me to escort Sonya to the banquet. I asked the camp director if that would be a problem. He said, "No, not at all."

We had a delightful evening. One pleasant surprise: both her family and mine were going to a family church camp at Woodston, Kansas on Thursday of the next week. Our family had never been there. Was it a coincidence or was God giving us hints? We agreed that we would spend more time together there.

I enjoyed Sonya very much but I remembered painful moments with other girls. I vowed to be cautious. After the evening service at Woodston, we sat under the massive cottonwood trees on the campground and talked.

"Sonya, I am curious. Do you believe you have a specific calling to full-time Christian ministry?"

"Why do you ask?"

"As a student at Southeastern Bible College, I am asking God to reveal His plan for my life."

"Yes, I think I am called to be a missionary to the Philippines."

My heart nearly leaped out of my chest. I did not know how to respond. I told Mother earlier that summer that I deeply admired Mae Ninemire, an inspirational missionary to the Philippines. I had a keen sense that being a missionary to the Philippines was a likely direction for my life.

After a long, quiet, thoughtful moment I responded. No more caution. "If I have the same calling, what does that say about you and me?"

"I don't know but I am willing to find out."

"Where will you go when you leave here tomorrow?"

"Our family is going to Mount Evans, Colorado."

That stunned me. Our family had never been there. "That is where we are going. That cannot be a coincidence."

We met the next day at Bear Lake, halfway from Idaho Springs to Mount Evans. Sonya and I went for a walk. *This relationship had to be part of God's plan.*

"Sonya, would you do me the honor of wearing my class ring and going steady with me?"

She hesitated but I thought it was just the seriousness of the decision. Whatever she was thinking, she took the ring, put it on, and kissed me. After all the confusion of past relationships, I felt as if my feet would not touch the ground for days to come.

The next day our families traveled together to Steamboat Springs, Colorado. Then, I went back to Ness City to pack my 1950 Buick for the long road trip to college in Florida. The folks had given the car to me in exchange for painting the house earlier that summer. No more fifty-hour train rides.

Sonya's parents were key lay leaders in a church in Manhattan, Kansas. They invited me to speak at their church the following Sunday morning. The church gave me a generous offering to help with my school expenses.

I promised Sonya I would write to her each day. All the way to Florida I thanked God and sang for joy at the top of my lungs. I wrote every day and Sonya wrote every fourth day. Then, her letters came once a week.

A friend of mine from Kansas also wrote.

> Louie,
> I know how happy you have been about your relationship with Sonya. I hate to tell you this but she has been dating your good friend Kent.

I cried so hard I thought I would burst a blood vessel. It wasn't just the loss of Sonya. I thought this might cause me to miss God's plan for my life. I was sadder than I had ever been.

The next day I officially dropped out of school, packed everything I owned in the blue Buick, and drove nonstop to Sonya's house, a nineteen-hour drive.

She was shocked and angry when I rang the doorbell.

"You are supposed to be at Southeastern."

"You are not wearing my ring."

"I am sorry but I don't love you. Everything happened too fast."

She turned and walked into the house. The door was still open but no one had invited me in. I sat on the porch swing, numb and confused. Finally, her mother came to greet me. I did not have to explain what happened.

Sonya's parents continued to believe that she was making a mistake. They thought God brought us together. Consequently, they invited me to stay at their home until I decided what to do next.

I got a job at a charcoal grill. I hoped that Sonya would change her mind but she never did. By the Christmas season three months later, I knew it was time to move on. The navy recruiter was enthusiastic about my math skills. He told me aviation electronics technician would be a perfect choice. They had a slot open in February. With a sad heart I left for boot camp. There were no girls there.

My next stop after boot camp was the Millington Naval Air Station near Memphis. I knew girls would be at church. That's where I met Valerie. She invited me to have dinner with her family. I had high hopes. Life was good. Then, I discovered she was dating Don, a complete loser. That was so confusing I got a headache.

I seemed to make too much or too little out of every interaction with a girl. Judy liked me a lot, she said, but she was going to be a nurse and did not have time for dating. I couldn't tell whether it was an excuse or she had different, can't-be-figured-out priorities.

After six months the navy honorably discharged me and I headed home. The wrist I had fractured years before was a major problem. I could not climb the ship's ladders. The navy doctor signed my release. He said I had a severe arthritic condition in my left wrist. There was no point in me being in the Navy; it was not going to get better. In fact, by my 30th birthday the bones in my wrist would have to be fused or I would have unbearable pain..

The first Sunday at home I realized Mother's words were true. She had told me Beverly would look good to me someday. Bev was now a sixteen-year-old beauty. I borrowed the folks' Ford pickup and we went on a date. I kissed her that night. I knew I must be dreaming and prayed I would never wake up.

It was September but Fort Hays State College accepted my late enrollment and gave me credit for twenty-nine hours from

Southeastern. Beverly was a senior in high school. We continued to date despite her parents' outspoken opposition.

We could not deny their practical wisdom.

"You are both too young. Beverly, you have not graduated from high school or college. Louie doesn't have a steady income."

We did resent the harshness of their words.

"Louie does not care whether you get an education. He just wants to get married and have children. Look at his dad. Do you want to marry someone like that?"

No one taught us how to build a relationship. They only said, "Don't" or "Wait."

In April we broke up. I say I initiated it. She says it was her idea. What we both agree is that her folks said she could not go to Fort Hays State even though she had a scholarship. I lived near the college.

That did not surprise me. In addition to the practical objections to our relationship, my stepdad had publicly insulted Beverly's dad. It happened at our home church. Pastor Farley had a clever idea. He preached about the necessity for change. He proposed as a metaphor for exploring change that everyone give up their favorite pew the next Sunday and sit somewhere else. Bev's parents came early and sat on the left side, second row. That had been our seat for years and years.

So much for the pastor's metaphor of change! Dad was furious. After the service, he verbally assaulted Bev's dad on the church steps.

"Have you forgotten the story of Naboth? He only had one lamb and Jezebel stole it from him. She had so much but it wasn't enough. You are like Jezebel. You have your store on Main Street, your fancy house, and your new car but it is not enough. You had to come early and take my seat. I don't have much but I have always had that seat."

"It was Pastor Farley's idea, not mine. You can have it back next Sunday."

They did not resolve the dispute nor did the pastor ever repeat the suggestion to switch seats. The angry attack colored my relationship with Bev's dad for a long time.

Even though we broke up, I loved her, but I didn't have much hope we would reconnect.

We rarely saw each other that summer. Beverly enrolled at Wichita State. I was incredibly busy, preparing for my second year as a high school teacher. I, also, preached in a number of small churches on the weekends.

In September, Beverly went on a date at Wichita State with one of our friends. All evening he asked questions about me. Beverly thought, "What am I doing with this guy when I like Louie so much better?" When she got back to the dorm, she called me.

"Hi, this is Beverly." She told me about her date that night. Then, she made me very happy. "I realized I would rather spend time with you."

"You are not going to believe this but I was planning to come to Wichita this weekend. My last class ends at 3:15 on Friday. It's about a three-hour drive."

"I can't wait."

We had a marvelous time. At the end of the evening, we pledged ourselves exclusively to each other. There was both joy and peace.

Not long after that Beverly's parents came to Wichita to visit her. When she told her father she had called me, he was furious. He dropped her off at the dorm and drove off without saying "Goodbye."

In the months that followed I went to Wichita every third weekend. We bought rings and made plans for a life together. As the spring semester ended, we began preparations for the big event, our July 17th wedding.

Even though I was very happy for the next two years, the break up with Sonya still puzzled me. It seemed so clear that God had brought Beverly and me together, but what about Sonya and the Philippines?

One evening I was thanking Beverly for two wonderful years. "Sweetheart, the last two years have been the best years of my life. But, I am puzzled about something that happened before we were married. May I ask you about that?"

She nodded and I continued. "Do you remember teen camp—1960 ?"

More nodding.

"Do you remember who I took to the banquet?"

"Sure, I encouraged you to be Sonya's escort."

"I escorted her to that banquet as you suggested. Then, our families had identical plans for the following week—Woodston family camp and a drive up to Mt. Evans. That had to signify something. Next, I heard the miracle that we were both called to the Philippines. I was sure this was God at work. I gave Sonya my ring and she accepted it. Two hearts were in agreement. Our families were both very happy. I thought this was clear direction for my life.

The I'm-in-Heaven part of the story was followed by the heart-breaking news. I wrote Sonya a letter every day until I heard that she was dating Kent. Was I going to miss God's will for my life? I dropped out of school and drove 1,350 miles to Manhattan to confront her.

She was not happy to see me, quickly gave my ring back, and ran into the house. I have been confused about that part of my story since that day."

"I am very happily married to you but I wonder from time to time if I missed some part of God's plan for my life."

Beverly laughed.

"Who knew you were thinking about going to the Philippines?"

"Sonya could not have known. I only mentioned it to Mother—no one else."

"Louie, who did your mother confide in?"

"You and Mother were friends. Did she tell you?"

"Yes, a few nights after you told her, she told me."

Bev filled in the missing pieces to the story. She and Sonya were bunkmates at camp and became good friends, at least for the week.

Suddenly, I understood. "Sonya wanted to go to the banquet with me but you were the one who planted the thought about the Philippines in her head."

I started laughing.

Thank you, Lord. I married the only woman on earth who could explain what actually happened. I thought that I had to figure this all out on my own. Instead, you sent Beverly.

Reflections

God definitely had a plan for the three of us. The story unfolded like a well-thought-out novel. I felt affirmed and my faith in God's plan for our lives greatly increased.

God joined the two of us—me and my serious abandonment issues with a girl from a stable family. (Beverly will have to tell her own story.) This relationship has been a long voyage of conflict and resolution; fear of abandonment and life-giving acceptance; my sensitivity and her tenacity; a night owl and a morning person; a schoolteacher/pastor with a mom/foster home developer. With healing and God's perspective most of the differences have become complementary strengths. Through it all God's plan has continued to unfold.

Questions to Consider

1. God says He has a plan for each life (Jeremiah 29:11). Take time to look for the evidence of God's involvement. Sometimes it is unexpected funding. A fresh insight. A startling interruption. A delay. Another person's assistance. Intercessory prayer.

    - Tell someone the story of God's involvement in your life. Tape it or write it for your children.

2. Have you thought recently about God's plan? Are you in tune with it? Do you pray daily that you will line up with His purpose for your life that day (Romans 8: 26-28)?

    For Beverly and me, our life purpose includes:
    - lining up with His purpose daily (8:27);
    - seeking His redemptive purpose in everything (8:28);
    - looking for divine appointments everywhere;
    - being empathetic—coming alongside others;
    - equipping and releasing Christians for service.

Our jobs and our kids' willing hearts have made it possible to minister to others.

3. Tell your children:

   - God has a plan and it is knowable. Most days it will consist of lining up with His will, enjoying each other, and looking for a divine appointment, an unexpected encounter with someone whom you are to love or serve.

   - The enemy will try to conceal or disrupt the plan. The opposition may be intense but the supreme planner of the universe crafted your plan. Put your trust in Him.

   - If the plan does not unfold for a while, obey the Lord joyfully every day. He is greater than the confusion and the seeming delay.

CHAPTER THIRTY-SIX

NOBODY TO BLAME BUT ME

T HE BOOT CAMP ORIENTATION VIDEO said it and the navy supply clerk repeated it. "You recruits have everything you need for thirteen weeks of basic training."

Loaded like pack mules, each of us staggered up the stairs to our quarters. We chose a bunk and laid our supplies down. Chief Petty Officer Cornell ordered us to stand at attention at the foot of our bunks.

"Now, do any of you have questions before we end this glorious day?"

I had checked. We didn't have everything. "Sir, we were issued two wool blankets for our beds. The sheets are missing."

I became the chief's straight man.

"Please forgive me. I didn't realize we have royalty amongst us. This is a distinct honor. We will have to put in that order for your sheets. Hopefully, they will be here by tomorrow night. I wouldn't think of having you sleep between two wool blankets. Now, Sir, these commoners need their rest. They don't know what sheets are. They are not very bright so we have to look out for them. I am going to put you in charge of safety tonight. You will stand watch to make sure they get their rest. Given your fine breeding, I know you would not want it any other way."

He gave me a clipboard and a flashlight. A page of instructions was on the clipboard—"How to Stand Watch Properly."

Everyone but me quickly crawled between the two wool blankets. For the next two hours I marched in circles around the barracks, twirling my flashlight and watching the men sleep. I was beyond tired when the chief relieved me at 0100.

I could have had two hours more sleep if I had not asked that stupid question about the blankets.

The next morning, my first full day in boot camp, began with a farm boy's delight—a full breakfast. After morning chow we assembled in the large collection area. There were enough benches for a couple of hundred recruits. I grabbed one of the cement benches and immediately fell asleep. Most of the recruits stood and smoked and joked.

I was totally oblivious while eight companies, 639 naval recruits, marched away. When I woke up just over an hour later, I could not figure out where everyone had gone. My heart was beating at a furious pace. I ran out into the street and saw my company's guidon #087 two blocks away, rippling in the breeze at the right front edge of the company. I slapped on my sailor hat and dashed from building to building until I caught up with the rear of the formation. Our company commander, Chief Cornell, was marching near the left front. I ran quickly to the back of the formation and fell into place. I could not believe the chief hadn't seen me join up late.

As we marched, I was very angry. I wanted to blame someone for the question about the sheets, my lack of sleep, and my huge day-number-one morning nap.

The year before at Southeastern I had complained to Dr. Ward Williams. "Sir, how should I respond when I'm clueless? There is so much Dad didn't teach me."

"Has your father enrolled here at Southeastern?"

"No, he is still farming in Kansas."

"Well then, we won't be able to give him a grade on his performance. We will just evaluate you."

Okay, I can't blame Dad for this, I thought as I marched, *but why did I get off to such an upside-down start at boot camp?*

Just twenty-four hours earlier I was sworn into the armed forces in Kansas City. The navy flew me and the other recruits to St. Louis, Los Angeles, and finally San Diego. The last leg of the flight was over the ocean. The plane bucked violently and about forty per cent of the recruits threw up. I didn't vomit but the sounds of sick sailors gave me an upset stomach, too.

We got to the navy supply store around 8 p.m.—2000 military time. The navy issued clothes, a personal-care kit, and bedding. They took a long time to be sure we had the right-sized boots. They knew our feet would swell and blister so most of us received boots one size larger than our normal shoe size.

The process was mind numbing. There were several hundred other recruits in the huge building with its seemingly endless cement floors, steel girders, and massive metal roof. My hometown high school would have fit inside the building.

Chief Petty Officer Cornell introduced himself to us at 10 p.m. (2200 navy time). He was funny and truly insulting.

"Where did you maggots come from? Recruiters must have had a desperate day when they signed you up."

He clasped his hands together in a prayer posture. "God, what were you thinking when you sent me this mess?"

He marched us to the courtyard with its four, long, cement scrub stations. "The navy issued buckets and scrub brushes. Here, we wash everything by hand. Each day you will bring your dirty gear to these tables. Place it on the cement tables, scrub until it is clean, rinse it thoroughly, and pin it to the clotheslines nearby.

You have got to be kidding. So this is what I signed up for.

Our company space was on the upper floor of the two-story, dull-gray cement barracks surrounding the courtyard. We quickly stowed our gear in wall lockers near our beds. On the chief's signal we had thirty seconds to stand at attention at the foot of our bunks. All but two of us were on time. For once I was not the featured recruit. The chief asked them to step forward.

"We want to honor the two maggots who were late. Stevenson and McElroy, fall out and get your wash buckets. Place them on your heads and wear them all day—anytime you are out of your bunks until after morning chow. We want everyone to know you are our first prize winners."

The next morning the chief banged on the bunks with his nightstick.

"What is your problem, maggots? It is 0-500 and you are still in your bunks. I get it. You think this is a vacation. May I be the first to welcome you to your resort, the U.S. Naval Recruit Training Center. At this five-star facility you will be happy to know you have thirty minutes to brush your teeth, shave, dress, and properly make your bunks. When you are ready, assemble in the courtyard and form up in columns. If you are late, bring your bucket so we can honor you."

I nicked myself badly with the new straightedge razor the navy issued me. I put tiny pieces of toilet tissue on each of the places I was bleeding. I was on time but my toilet paper Band-Aids offered all kinds of comedic opportunities for the chief. To my amazement he didn't ridicule me.

"Recruit, fall out. Go to the head (the navy's word for bathroom) and get that bleeding stopped."

I had momentary kind thoughts for the chief until he chose the two tallest members of our company to be Recruit Company Commander, the recruit in charge when the chief was away, and Right Guide, the bearer of the company flag. In other words, at 5'9" I was not a candidate for leadership. I expressed my frustration in a letter home.

> You will not believe how the Chief chose the two recruit leaders. He promoted the two tallest guys. He said the Base Commander would examine Company #087 for performance and appearance. Tall guys at the front look impressive. I thought everyone had an equal opportunity in the U.S. Navy.

Being sleepy every day of boot camp was the norm. One morning at 0200 Chief Cornell banged on our bunks with his nightstick.

"I knew you maggots were trouble but I had no idea you would rape this virgin trash can. I leave it here all shiny and new, thinking you will keep it safe. But, no. You violate it."

With classic navy logic the trash can in our barracks was not for trash. Each night we polished it. He pulled a Juicy Fruit gum wrapper out of it. I was pretty sure he put the wrapper in there.

"I cannot believe what I am seeing. You monsters! You filthy scum! One of you */#^+% lizards put a filthy gum wrapper in her. She will never be the same again. Get out of your racks and stand at attention. We have to find out who did this."

We dressed at warp speed, raced outside, and grabbed our 1903 Springfield rifles from the outdoor rifle racks. He marched us to the grinder, the naval training center's label for the enormous, cement-covered parade ground. He started the music on his portable stereo and we began exercising with the rifles.

"Lift them over your head and then lower them.
Push them to the left and take one step left.
Push them to the right and take one step right."

It was calisthenics with a rifle.

After thirty minutes he ordered us to hold the 8.67 pounds of rifle out in front of us. Within minutes our arms were burning from the pressure. The chief announced that the forty recruits who lowered their rifles first would stay on the grinder for an additional hour. The forty who held their rifles up the longest would be back in their bunks by 0300.

I passed that test and was asleep by 0301. Half of the company exercised another hour.

Sixteen weeks of boot camp taught navy culture and protocol. For instance, we memorized eleven general orders—rules of conduct for sentries. We had to recite them on demand. I was on guard duty in the middle of the day, walking around and around inside the empty barracks. To my amazement two waves (female navy personnel) walked by outside the barracks. I had been on the base almost two months and had not seen a single woman. I stopped and enjoyed the view.

The chief walked up behind me and nearly gave me a heart attack. "Sailor, what in h—- do you think you are doing?"

As a knee-jerk reaction, I quoted general order #2. "I am 'walking my post in a military manner, keeping always on the alert, and observing everything that takes place within sight or hearing,' Sir!"

He thought I was being a smart aleck.

"This is not the time for humor. Standing guard is a serious responsibility. If you ever hope to graduate from boot camp, get serious."

I could not believe I had given such a goofy answer. Why hadn't I said, "Looking out the window, sir!"

I told Pedro Mata, my bunkmate. "All the color drained out of the chief's face when I quoted general order #2. I was doing the exact opposite of #2. I was not walking my post; I was standing still. I did not maintain a military manner the way a sentry would. I was not alert or I would have known the chief was standing behind me. That is not the worse part. The way I answered his question sounded like I was mocking him or the general orders. Pedro, I thought he was going to recommend a court martial for me."

"The chief just said, 'Get serious.' I felt so relieved. My knees were shaking and I could barely finish my rounds. I do not understand me. What to say and do is clear when I am calm but I am in a complete fog when I am under pressure."

At the end of the day I had a talk with God.

Lord, will I ever understand what is going on? When I was ten, you put me in Dad's jail on the farm. I graduated from high school and you helped me get a job with a harvest crew. That was a summer of ridicule and near death. Now I am in the navy and I think You are the one who opened the door to get me here. I ask questions before I think it through. I am too short to be a leader and the chief thinks I am a smart aleck. Will I ever find where I fit?

For a long time I have been blaming Dad for everything. He abused me. He didn't prepare me for life. He forgot me and locked the door. He called me a liar. If I am the judge and Dad is the defendant, there is almost no end to his guilt.

I am beginning to understand, Lord. Since my talk with Ward Williams, I realize Dad wasn't at Southeastern and he is not here either. The navy is not evaluating him. I am the one on the hot seat. God, help me to catch on before I mess up big time.

Reflections

For most of my life I lived with a keen sense of condemnation. Failure seemed more powerful than forgiveness. I could list every mistake I had made and they all seemed to justify condemnation.

Romans 8:1-3 (KJV) confirmed my fears: "There is therefore now no condemnation to them which are in Christ Jesus, who walk not after the flesh, but after the Spirit."

I stopped at verse one. Why read more? In my mind, my many mistakes were ongoing proof that I was walking "after the flesh."

What a difference the next two verses make: "For the law of the Spirit of life in Christ Jesus hath made me free...the law...was weak through the flesh, God sending his own Son...condemned sin in the flesh:"

The Matthew 18:23-25 (AMP) story of the cancelled debt turned the lights on for me.

> Therefore the kingdom of heaven is like a human king who wished to settle accounts with his attendants. When he began the accounting, one was brought to him who owed him 10,000 talents [probably about $10,000,000], and because he could not pay, his master ordered him to be sold, with his wife and his children and everything that he possessed, and payment to be made. So the attendant fell on his knees, begging him, Have patience with me and I will pay you everything. And his master's heart was moved with compassion, and he released him and forgave him [cancelling] the debt.

Someone who knew my struggle asked me, "Are you still living out the Gospel with a credit card?"

Considering the size of my debt [*the* approximate value of my sins], was I making payments—small acts of kindness, words of encouragement, monthly contributions to foreign missions, and more, thinking those small but sincere payments would appease a just God?

The lights went on. The debt is cancelled. It is pointless to pay because it does not exist anymore.

"What if I fail again?"

"The resources of the cross are greater than your sin."

Normally, I would have argued:

- "Isn't there a double penalty for pastors/teachers?"
- "What if I knew it was wrong but I did it anyway?"
- "How can I be sure the Lord isn't saying, 'He will never amount to a hill of beans'"?

God quieted my heart, saying over and over, "The debt is cancelled," until I could not think of another argument.

Questions to Consider

1. If you believed forgiveness for you was total, what would change in your life? Are you or any of your children on the "small-payment" plan?

2. Why would a debt-free man serve, encourage, or pray for others? Out of gratitude? To fulfill his life's purpose?

3. How are we to view mistakes? If they reveal a "system of thought," a habitual way of responding, pray 2 Corinthians 10: 4-5 over yourself. You can "take every thought captive" and demolish any stronghold—any way of thinking that threatens to rule you or define you falsely.

CHAPTER THIRTY-SEVEN

FAITH THE SIZE OF A GRAIN OF MUSTARD SEED

HAPLAIN CHRISTMAN CALLED ME TO the front of the church. "Do you believe God can heal your wrist?"

I was skeptical. "I know He can but I am not sure He will."

"Do you know what it means to have faith the size of a grain of mustard seed?"

"No, sir, I do not."

"If I pray and you are healed, will you know who to thank?"

I had to think about that. *I know the chaplain can't heal me and I can't heal myself. If I am healed, I will have to thank God.* "Sure, I would know."

"That is Faith 101—faith the size of a mustard seed. The one who heals is God. Your faith is in Him. He is the one you will thank."

I laughed and he prayed. It was not a long or complicated prayer but it was obvious the chaplain believed God would heal me.

If He healed me, it would be the final chapter in a long story. I had surgery on my left wrist when I was two. Army doctors at Fort Benning, Georgia made an incision and drained the fluid from my wrist. Years later, other doctors said infection plus that medical procedure damaged the growth center in my hand. As a result, all the bones in my left wrist were [and still are] odd shapes. That limited what I could do with that hand. Since I grew up with the problem, I learned to adjust. I never thought of it as a disability. I did think my wrist could not get worse.

During my eighth grade year I attended Bonnie Carpenter's birthday party at the Ness City Park. Everyone liked her so the entire class came. Several of the boys brought their bikes and we took turns riding them. The bike trails were hilly and dangerous. All of the eighth grade girls watched as we rode. Their concern for our safety was our reward. Our feats became more and more daring. As Harold and Roger approached the edge of one steep incline, they applied the brakes at the last possible moment, slid down the banks of the dry creek, picked up their bikes, and walked up the other side. I rode down the same steep slope, approached the same incline, failed to break in time, slid over the edge, and tumbled into the dry creekbed. I flipped over the handlebars and fell with the bike on top of me. I had a severe compound fracture just above my wrist. The girls gathered around me with obvious concern. I was the center of attention. For one brief moment it was worth it.

Mother and Dad rushed to town and took me to the small, local hospital. The break was so severe they sent us to the nearest orthopedic specialist in Hays, Kansas, sixty miles away. For once Dad hurried. The surgeon set the bones and put on a cast that night.

We prayed diligently that the bones would stay in place. I milked eight cows by hand, morning and evening, and I carried two five-gallon buckets filled with milk from the milking shed to the house. The bones stayed in perfect alignment. We gave God the credit.

The surgeon had another theory. He believed the downward pull of the buckets of milk twice a day for about ten minutes kept the bones in proper position.

His original plan was to open my arm after eleven weeks, re-break and realign the bones, put in rods, and wait another six months for the healing process to be complete. We all agreed that the perfectly aligned bones in my arm were a miracle.

Unlike my arm, the bones in my wrist did not heal properly. Somehow, the eleven weeks in the cast damaged my wrist. The doctor had no explanation for the eighty percent loss of lateral movement. In addition, I lost the flexibility to bend my wrist backwards.

I did not have much faith for healing. Actually, I was not sure what it meant to have faith. Many people told me that I should pray for healing so I did repeatedly. There had been no miracle. I read Matthew 17:20, "If you have faith as small as a mustard seed, you can say to this mountain, 'Move from here to there' and it will move. Nothing will be impossible for you." I knew it was in the Bible but it did not seem to apply to me.

At the end of my freshman year in college, I was broke. I was, also, in love. Sadly, the young lady did not love me. It was time for a change. Would my wrist limit my options?

The posters, "Find a new career in the U.S. Navy," drew me in. I told the recruiter about the problems with my left wrist. He said he would have to have a letter from my doctor, clearing me. The orthopedic specialist who set my broken bones after the bicycle accident wrote the required letter. He did so reluctantly, telling me that there was no way to know whether I could fulfill my duties as a sailor.

The navy offered me a fresh start, far away from my failed dating relationship. I had another, very practical reason for enlisting. I still owed money for my freshman year at Southeastern. The navy recruiter said I could send home seventy-five dollars each pay period. That left a very meager three dollars every two weeks for spending money. (I stuck to the plan and paid off $900 in six months—twelve pay periods.)

When I joined the navy, I flew to boot camp in San Diego, California. After sixteen weeks I graduated. My next duty station was aviation electronics school in Memphis, Tennessee. The training included assembling a radio from three hundred tiny parts. It was common to receive one or more electric shocks during the process of putting the radio together. I got two huge jolts. Afterwards, I could not use my left wrist. I couldn't even pick up a pencil. I reluctantly went to the hospital at the Memphis Naval Air Station. After a thorough examination the navy doctor said the fractures above my wrist were not the problem. I had a severe arthritic condition in my hand. They speculated that the bones would have to be fused together by my twenty-ninth birthday to avoid excruciating pain. They recommended that I be honorably discharged.

Their decision puzzled me. My time in the navy had been a great experience. A family in a church in Frayser, Tennessee, near the naval air station, offered me a home away from home. And more good news—the company commander promoted me to squad leader. He and I were the same height so being tall was not a requirement for leadership in his squad. Life was good and I was looking forward to the four-year tour of duty. Looking at my x-rays, the doctors wondered how I would manage the many ship ladders with a damaged wrist. The discharge made sense and I prepared to leave, but I did not understand why this was happening.

Jim Brady was the only other sailor discharged at Memphis Naval Air Station on September 21 that year. The day we left we rode the train together to Kansas City.

He and I met at a local church earlier in the summer. I wondered how he got there since he did not have a car. Jim introduced me to hitchhiking. He, also, demonstrated how to share his faith with other sailors. One evening he was sitting on his bunk, reading his Bible. Two sailors sat down on the bunk opposite from him. Tears began to run down both of their faces. When he finished reading his Bible, he asked if he could help them. They both confessed their sins and asked him to pray for them. Jim explained what it meant to be born again. He led them in the sinner's prayer. The next Sunday they joined us in hitchhiking to church. I admired him greatly, paid attention to his stories, wanted to do what he did, but never did have sinful sailors shed tears while I had devotions.

Jim suffered greatly from asthma. He had been in the navy two years already but had not had a medical problem while he was stationed on a ship out of San Diego. He believed he was a missionary to the U.S. Navy so he had no desire to be discharged.

About the time I received the severe electrical shocks, he, too, went to the base medical center to receive treatment for asthma. They recommended he receive an honorable discharge. He objected strenuously but the navy doctors did not yield.

We were both surprised to be discharged. Being released on the same day was beyond coincidence. God was at work. I had thought God wanted me to enlist. The amazing acceptance from the church in Frayser seemed to confirm that I was where I belonged. The discharge would have confused me greatly if I had not been released on the same day as Jim Brady. Knowing His plan was unfolding was deeply reassuring.

I enrolled at Fort Hays Kansas State College. Looking over my discharge papers, the registrar encouraged me to apply to vocational rehabilitation for educational funds. They x-rayed me again and ran extensive tests to confirm the navy's diagnosis of severe arthritis in my wrist. Consequently, rehab gave me monthly financial aid to finish my undergraduate degree.

I learned to live with the misshapen bones and the arthritic pain. Healing was only an occasional thought. Then, one weekend my home church invited Chaplain Christman as a guest speaker.At the end of every evening service he prayed for the sick. He focused on different medical conditions each session. One night he invited anyone who suffered from arthritis to come to the front to receive prayer. That is when he prayed for me.

A few days after that, I had an appointment with an orthopedic surgeon in Topeka. For some reason, my knees were aching. I wanted to know if there was any helpful treatment or therapy. While I was there, I asked the doctor to x-ray my left wrist.

After his radiologist developed the x-rays, I asked, "How severe is the arthritis in my left wrist?"

"There is no arthritis."

"But the navy doctors were so sure!"

"Sir, I have the best radiologist in the state of Kansas. If he says there is no arthritis in your left wrist, there is none."

I walked out of the office, laughing.

"Yes, I know who to thank. God, thank you very, very much."

I still did not have full mobility in my left wrist, but I apparently would not need to have my wrist and arm bones fused. I rarely had pain. When my wrist ached, it seemed to come from it being weak, not arthritic.

Simple faith—will I know who to thank?

Mother reminded me of another miracle of healing.

"You are always looking for a dad. God knows that and He has been looking out for you your whole life. By the way, the chaplain's prayer is not your first miracle."

On the farm we did not have hot running water. To take a bath indoors, we heated water in a teakettle on the kitchen stove and then poured it into the tub.

We had just moved to the farm. I stepped into the tub to take a bath. The water was too cold. Elvera, one of Dad's older daughters, brought the teakettle in to add hot water. I stood up and stepped backwards, thinking she was going to pour the scalding water in front of me. She was already pouring and the boiling water went down my hips and legs.

Mother and Elvera did not panic. They immediately helped me out of the tub, spread butter on the burns, and pulled a pair of women's hose onto my legs and over the burns. They were praying fervently as they did this. The pain subsided almost immediately. Miraculously, after a few days of them applying butter, I had very little blistering and no scars.

After my six months in the navy ended, healing was still a puzzling topic for me. My counselor friend Dave served as a good sounding board.

"Dave, I am really grateful to be healed but I don't understand being completely healed one time and half healed the other."

"What do you mean by *half healed*?"

"The arthritis is gone but I still have severely limited motion in my left wrist. Why remove the arthritis and leave the bones with funny shapes?"

"What are your unanswered questions?"

"I want to trust God but I do not understand. Why does He do half the job sometimes? Other times, He doesn't show up at all. Why?"

"Start with the first time in your life God wasn't there."

I knew immediately when that happened.

"I was five. We were in Waxahachie, Texas. Dad said Rainbow Bread was hiring. He was going to turn in an application. Mother was upset and crying. I was sitting on a small stool, feeling invisible. Neither of them seemed to notice I was there. God was not there. At least I didn't see Him."

"So, you can't trust Him?"

"I know the right answer—I can trust Him. But, I feel like an abandoned orphan in those moments."

"Does God say He will be present in our worst moments?"

"I remember God promised to be with us always and to never leave us or forsake us" (Matthew 28:20, Hebrews 13:5).

"The question is do you believe that?"

"I know it is in the Bible but it doesn't always seem true in my life."

"I have a thought. Ask the Lord whether He was present when you were five and your folks were arguing."

"Lord, I do not know how to pray this prayer. If You were there the day Dad left, please show me a picture that includes You."

Immediately, I had a mental image like a video of that day. I was sitting on the small stool, feeling all alone. Dad was leaving and Mother was crying. The Lord was painting a picture of me at an easel on the other side of the room. I could see me, running to look at the painting. The Lord was ignoring my parents and only paying attention to me. I described this image to Dave.

When I finished, he had a question. "Does that help?"

"Well, if the Bible is true and He was present, it changes everything. The scriptures say He was there. They tell me I am not an orphan. I am part of God's family. That mental picture opens my heart. He was present so I was not alone. My parents were just thinking about themselves. That is why they ignored me in that moment. Yes, God being there changes everything."

"What about that half healing?"

"Actually, if He is present, I do not feel like an orphan even if I cannot understand what happened or did not happen with my wrist. If He is always present, I am not afraid or desperate. Knowing He is here now, I am grateful for what I receive instead of being angry about what I do not receive. I am quiet inside."

"So you need His presence more than what He can do for you?"

"I never thought of it that way before. Yes, if God is present, I do not worry about what I do not have."

Reflections

When God offered Solomon a gift, he chose a discerning heart. When Jacob wrestled with the angel, he did not let go until he received a blessing and a name change (Genesis 32). Moses' entreaty would be my request (Exodus 33:15-17, NIV):

> Then Moses said to him, "If your Presence does not go with us, do not send us up from here. How will anyone know that you are pleased with me and with your people unless you go with us? What else will distinguish me and your people from all the other people on the face of the earth?" And the Lord said to Moses, "I will do the very thing you have asked, because I am pleased with you and I know you by name."

When I am aware of His presence, I have increased insight. I am keenly aware of His favor. I worship Him with songs and with stories of His grace extended to me. I see people as He sees them. Out of gratitude I am eager to love well. I have divine appointments and they and I are refreshed. When I sense His presence, the enemy's attacks are inconvenient and painful but they don't define me. Hand in hand with Him, I am who He says I am and my destiny is what He says it is. In His presence there is fullness of joy.

Questions to Consider

1. What have you been taught about the presence of God? That He only makes Himself known to church leaders? That His presence is only evident on Sunday mornings or at the birth of your first child? What does the Bible say?

2. God walked in the Garden of Eden with Adam and Eve. In practical, down-to-earth terms what would it look like if He walked with you?

3. Do you know anyone who has an intimate relationship with God? Make an appointment to talk with him or her. Teach your children what you learn.

CHAPTER THIRTY-EIGHT

THE PICTURE OF GOD

ICHARD MCAFEE, A GUEST SPEAKER at our church, offered a workshop entitled, "What God Looks Like." He began the first session by asking each of us to close our eyes and describe our picture of God. The answers varied greatly.

"I see a judge behind a huge bench. He is waiting to tell me what I did wrong today."

"A grandfather! He likes me and he has a big smile on his face."

"Kind of like Santa Claus. He reads His big book each day, checking to see if we've been naughty or nice."

"The other shoe is about to fall and He is that giant shoe."

When Pastor McAfee asked me, I said, "What is my picture of God? All I see is a blinding light. I know He is powerful, intimidating, and a long ways off."

"Is there more?"

"I believe He is real but I cannot see His face. I have no idea whether He is smiling and happy or frowning and sad."

"How would you describe your dad?"

"My stepdad? He was a mystery to me. Most of the time I didn't know whether he was okay and calm or on the verge of beating me again. The constant tension kept me from knowing him."

"What did you say to him?"

"I told him I loved him because the Bible commanded me to but I rarely had any feelings of love for him."

He leaned forward and spoke quietly. "If this is a painful topic, we can talk privately tomorrow during the day."

I didn't hesitate. Anyone who genuinely cared got my attention immediately. "Sure, since you offered, tomorrow sounds great. I didn't know I was so easy to read."

He smiled warmly, patted me on the shoulder, and turned to the next person in line.

Our talk the next day was life changing. According to Pastor McAfee, most of us think God resembles our dad (or, in my case) our dads. We are generally unaware of that assumption. If we were, we might ask whether it is true.

He had written down what I said about my pictures of God and of Dad. "It sounds like there is a connection between the two pictures."

I tried to imagine God and Dad standing shoulder to shoulder. Did they look alike?

We took a break to pray and think. Then, we rejoined the group and shared our discoveries. The pastor asked me to share first.

"Both Dad and God seemed hard to get to know. My relationship with them was unpredictable. They both caught me off guard. Their surprises seemed to come at really awkward times."

"What do you mean?"

"Dad's whippings. I never knew whether he would overlook my mistakes—no questions, no lessons to be learned, and no criticism—or he would punish me. For instance, if I left the gate open and the horse got out, one time I received a whipping; the other, a calm statement in a matter-of-fact tone, "Catch the horse before he eats those green milo stalks. It will make his stomach bloat and it may kill him."

"How did God catch you off guard?"

"God's plans for character development struck me the same way. Why send the neighbors to pick me up at the last possible minute and give me a ride to school? I am guessing God wanted me to trust Him, but nearly missing the student council bus put me in a tailspin."

I choked with emotion. The hopeless feelings I felt years ago that morning on the highway threatened to engulf me again.

Thankfully, the pastor was not in a hurry.

"What else?"

"With both of them I felt powerless. Those vulnerable moments frightened me. I lived with a stomach ache every day."

"You said you told your stepfather you loved him but you did not feel love. Is your love for God the same or different?"

"I did not and still do not know how to enjoy either one of them. In fact, I don't know if they want to be enjoyed by me. I feel numb."

"Is it possible you have the wrong picture of God?"

"I listened to your talk, Pastor. I think you are asking if my view of Dad colored my picture of God."

"Okay, I want you to find your starting place. Did you start with your picture of your dad and then assume God looks like that as well?"

"I probably did."

"What would your picture be if you started with God? What if you began at the cross? That is an amazing picture of love and acceptance."

"I am grateful for Christ's death on the cross, but how do I ignore Dad whipping me?"

"Remember, we are not ignoring the abuse, but we aren't starting there either. Do we have a picture of God loving us? The cross proves that He does."

I felt hope like a fresh breeze right after a morning rain. It was my turn to ask. "Then what?"

McAfee continued.

"The Bible says His perfect love casts out fear. We still have pain and life is unfair but God loves us."

I started laughing.

"That is not only a different picture of God. It is a brand new picture of a loveable me. That is something else I have had a hard time seeing."

"Louie, let me tell you how much He enjoys us. He says when He thinks of us, He sings so joyfully, it sounds like a full choir." (See Zephaniah 3:17, *Living Bible*.)

That was such a happy thought. I opened my Bible and read it for myself. Pastor McAfee wasn't done. "May I ask you to look at one more scene?" When I nodded, he added this thought.

"Jesus really suffered in Gethsemane. He drank the cup that contained everybody's sins so He knows exactly how we feel and think. He knows the picture you have had of Him and He still loves you."

While I was absorbing that thought, he had a final question, one that completely disarmed me.

"Did God forgive you alone or did He include both dads? Does He sing songs of delight about only you or does He have at least a verse and a chorus about them?"

That was the day my pictures of both God and my dads changed.

Reflections

I lived many years with a wrong picture of God. The church often reinforced that. When I heard George Cook testify, I knew he had a different picture of God. Because of that, George's view of suffering and of people and of himself was very different. He talked about a God who was always present, bringing joy in the good times and the bad. I longed to see God the way George did, but I could not comprehend it.

The Bible offers an intimate look, picturing Him [a symbol of God] running joyfully towards the prodigal son, shedding tears over Jerusalem, looking out for His mother when He was on the cross, strumming His banjo and singing songs of delight about me and to me (that's my picture of Zephaniah 3:17), commending a widow's tiny offering, and laughing as He held children on his lap. Those snapshots and a hundred more draw me to Him and inspire me to be like Him.

Questions to Consider

1. Begin with the Bible. What would be your three favorite pictures of the Lord?

2. In your daily life what would be three snapshots of God in your life?

    • Whom has He sent to love you?

    • What has He done to bless you?

    • How has He surprised you?

    • Taught you?

    • Protected you?

    • Waited for you to respond?

    • Forgiven you?

3. If you see Him as He really is, you will have a powerful photo album to share with anyone who does not know Him. Find out how they see Him. Then share your pictures.

4.   What picture of God do your children have? How did the wrong pictures get in? Help them develop a the-truth-will-set-you-free, life-saving album (even if every picture of God the Father is a story and the album only has symbols which prompt the retelling of each story). In other words, the pictures don't have to be pictures..

CHAPTER THIRTY-NINE

IF YOU HAVE SEEN HER, YOU HAVE SEEN HIM

SOMETIMES, MOTHER AND I WERE just two kids. One day I raced into the house to use the indoor toilet. The door from the kitchen to the hallway would not open. I tugged on it and then I heard her giggling. She was holding the door shut. I grabbed the doorknob, put my foot on the doorframe, and gave a mighty jerk. The doorknob broke into two pieces, leaving a gaping hole in the door. She flew backwards and slid down the wall to a sitting position, holding her side of the doorknob. She was laughing and crying at the same time.

I went head over heels backwards, still holding my half of the doorknob. I ended up under the kitchen table.

Just as the doorknob came apart, Dad entered the kitchen.

"Mildred, what on earth is going on?"

Still shaking with laughter, she held up her side of the doorknob. As he helped her up, I raced out the door and began hoeing weeds in the garden.

Mother told me later she took the blame, begged for forgiveness, and promised to cook Dad's favorite meal, beef roast with potatoes, carrots, and onions.

Dad replaced the doorknob.

Sometimes, clowning around with Mother was dangerous. One evening, I hid just inside her bedroom. When she entered, I said, "Boo."

She screamed and began pounding me with her fists. The wall and a tall dresser trapped me. I could not get away.

"Mother, it's me, Louie!"

"I know. You scared me. Don't ever do it again."

If I am going to scare her, I'll need to hide behind something first.

From work to play to church I admired Mother. For instance, the church seemingly changed its rules about divorced people every year. In my mind, the way she responded to decisions made by the church added to her legacy.

After she married Fred and moved to the farm, pastors of our local church were either very sympathetic or were hardline about divorce and remarriage.

Pastor Williams concluded that my natural father refused to submit to counsel, broke his covenantal vows, denied the faith, and abandoned Mother and us boys. During his time as pastor, she was welcome to teach a Sunday school class, lead in the women's ministry, and work with the young adults, ages twelve to thirty-five.

Pastor York came two years later. According to him, since Dad filed for the divorce, it was not a sinful act for Mother to sign the divorce papers. In other words, it was okay to be single. However, according to the new pastor, when she remarried, she began living in a state of adultery. Consequently, she could not serve in the church in any way. He quickly removed her from all positions of leadership and service. The pastor apologized but said the Bible gave him no choice.

Mother remained at peace about the demotion.

"I am still the same person I was last week, Louie. I know how forgiven I am. Besides, this change will give me time to catch up on my sewing."

I was so angry I wanted to scream at the pastor. "Mother, I know this is a goofy question, but does God know what is going on down here?"

"Louie, please do not be offended. This is not the worst thing that has happened to me. God always showed up in the past and He will this time, too."

Many times Mother offered subtle correction. My freshman year in college I read Rosalind Rinker's *Prayer: Conversing with God*. The book taught us to pray sentence prayers—heartfelt but not more than one sentence long. It completely changed prayer in the small group I attended. When the goal was simple prayers, group members who had never prayed out loud joined in.

During spring break I was at home. I complained to Mother. "If we had had books like this when I was younger, it would have changed my life."

Mother had a thoughtful look. She pulled a book off the shelf in the living room. She had written on the flyleaf: "To Louie with love on his 17th birthday." It was a book by Rosalind Rinker, entitled *The Years That Count: A Book Which Allows Young People to Think for Themselves.*

I had very little to say the rest of the afternoon.

Later that evening she had a question for me. "Louie, is it possible your other prayer has been answered?"

"What prayer is that?"

"For years you have asked God to send you a dad. What if He already has done that?"

"Which man are you thinking of?"

Mother answered, "Jesus said, 'Anyone who has seen me has seen the Father' (John 14: 9, NIV). What if He has already sent *both men and women* as his personal representatives—living pictures of him? What about George Cook, Ward Williams, the chaplain who prayed for your healing, and the Catholic priest who answered your hard questions and taught you to dance? Oh, I left out Pastor Richard, Wayne Brooks, and the school newspaper editor who loaned you his car. I am sure there were others."

"That is really, really good, Mother." I sat in the blue La-Z-Boy to let that sink in. "You didn't name any women. If women were living pictures of God, wouldn't that include you?"

"I certainly hope so."

I had another question for her.

"I know Jesus represents the Father. You just read a verse that says we represent God, too. Then, it must be okay for us to believe that and say it as well."

"Look at John 14, Louie. Jesus is talking, first about Himself, 'I am in the Father... and the Father is in me. The words that I speak to you aren't mere words. I don't just make them up on my own. The Father who resides in me crafts each word' (John 14: 9-10, MSG).

"Then, He talks about our role. Verses 11-14 (MSG) explain how God wants us to be living pictures of Him, too. 'The person who trusts me will not only do what I'm doing but even greater things, because I, on my way to the Father, am giving you the same work to do that I've been doing.'

"Louie, I know there have been times when I have said exactly what He told me to say and done what He told me to do. As I look back over your life, God has sent at least a dozen others who have represented Him well. Your Father in heaven has been a good Dad."

"You have said about a hundred times you are a good mother but not a very good dad."

"I am still not a very good dad. But, I believe there have been times when I was a picture of the heart of your Father in heaven."

"So, I have been looking for one amazing man instead of realizing God was sending living pictures of the last dad."

"You lost me, Louie. What do you mean by the last dad?"

"We have talked over and over about the failures of my first and second dads. I have looked everywhere for the next dad. You are telling me the last dad I will ever need is already with me. We called out to Him and He came."

Mother asked why I had such a big smile.

"I underestimated you. I am beginning to see how much I learned from you about my best Dad. Mother, we have prayed The Lord's Prayer for years. 'Our Father, Thy kingdom come on earth as it is in heaven.' We have thought of him being in heaven. He taught us to pray that His kingdom would come *on earth*.

"On earth! Dad is here! He sent George Cook, the farmer, as a snapshot of him. Ward Williams, my New Testament prof, parented me for two semesters. But there have been many far-less-obvious messengers. "My favorites are the neighbors—Sharon Moss, telling me what farm kids do and don't do, and the Meis family, giving me a last-minute ride to catch the student council bus."

"Mother, do you remember when you helped us milk the cows every time we learned another Bible verse? Of course, you always wanted a practical example of that verse in real life."

Mother interrupted me. "Thank God we moved to town and there are no more cows to milk!"

"You would be milking tonight if you had not sold the cows. I have a scripture and an example. James 1:17, 'Every good and perfect gift is from above, coming down from the Father ...' Every good gift comes from him—the train conductor's kindness, the college job at Burger Queen, the upperclassman loaning his car—even the principal, reprimanding me for disrespect in physics."

She continued the thought. "He used their hands and their voices but the gifts were from His heart."

"Mother, I did not realize how funny my heavenly Father is. He sent you to teach me to laugh and learn!"

Mother wore the happiest smile I have ever seen. "So, I am not a very good dad but the best Dad ever is here."

"The best Dad and the last dad I will ever need."

Reflections

For twenty years I wondered why God emphasized fatherhood but did not answer my heart cry for a dad. I know now that the answer was so important He sent handpicked representatives to reflect His fatherly heart. Most of them came in disguise as other kid's dads, pastors, teachers, neighbors, and coaches. With a certain playfulness, He also sent women and Catholics and bosses and librarians and traffic cops. Remember, when He sends someone, it is personal.

Each day invite the Holy Spirit to intercede for you because He knows this *last Dad's* thoughts, His will, and His purposes. If you do that, your *last Dad* will work in all things for the good. His desire is: "that His joy may be in you and your joy may be full" (John 15:11).

Questions to Consider

1. Do you know God as your Father "on earth as He is in heaven"? Do you know anyone who does?

2. If you are a single mom, I bless you. You are not a dad but God has offered to fill that role for your children. He will often use your hands, your hugs, your words, your tears, and your humor to provide a living and loving picture of Him. Tell them about the *last Dad* they will ever need. (He may or may not send a dad to marry you, to love them, and to represent Him in your home.)

3. If you have a question or a story of discovery or triumph, please e-mail me. You have read my story. What is yours?

ABOUT THE AUTHOR

I AM THE AUTHOR, LOUIE KAUPP, and my life is a collection of stories. First, the tale of redemption, God loving me to life, teaching me to trust Him totally and inspiring me to love well out of a deep gratitude. Next, the account of three dads: one who ran away, another who relied on a bull whip, and the last dad a boy would ever need, the one who invited submission and in response, promised all things would work together for the good. The family history—marriage to Beverly (7-17-1964), three awesome sons (Greg, David, & Jonathan), their wonderful families, and a multitude of best friends forever—is a wonderful part of the tapestry. Preparation and service are significant layers of story—Southeastern Bible College, Ft. Hays Kansas State College (B.A., English), and Kansas State University (M.A., English). Where I worked—teaching at Russell and Manhattan, Kansas High Schools, Kansas State University, Ft. Riley, Kansas, Covenant School in San Antonio, the University of Texas—San Antonio, and Region 20, San Antonio. Pastoring Covenant Churches in Manhattan and San Antonio; serving on the staff at Eagle's Nest Christian Fellowship and Summit Christian Center (San Antonio); and volunteering at Maranatha Bible Church and Community Bible Church in San Antonio. Where we lived, the context for story—from life in a hospital and then, on the farm—Ransom and Ness City, Kansas, to wonderful years in Manhattan, Kansas, and finally, 34 years in my favorite city—San Antonio. Most of all, the adventure unfolded, living in His presence and enjoying Him as the Dad my heart longed for.

To order additional copies or request the author for a speaking engagement, please send an email to thelastdad@gmail.com